Global Issues Series

General Editor: **Jim Whitman**

This exciting new series encompasses three principal themes: the interaction of human and natural systems; cooperation and conflict; and the enactment of values. The series as a whole places an emphasis on the examination of complex systems and causal relations in political decision-making; problems of knowledge; authority, control and accountability in issues of scale; and the reconciliation of conflicting values and competing claims. Throughout the series the concentration is on an integration of existing disciplines towards the clarification of political possibility as well as impending crises.

Titles include:

Kelley Lee
HEALTH IMPACTS OF GLOBALIZATION (*editor*)
Towards Global Governance

GLOBALIZATION AND HEALTH
An Introduction

Nicholas Low and Brendan Gleeson (*editors*)
MAKING URBAN TRANSPORT SUSTAINABLE

Catherine Lu
JUST AND UNJUST INTERVENTIONS IN WORLD POLITICS
Public and Private

Graham S. Pearson
THE UNSCOM SAGA
Chemical and Biological Weapons Non-Proliferation

THE SEARCH FOR IRAQ'S WEAPONS OF MASS DESTRUCTION
Inspection, Verification and Non-Proliferation

Andrew T. Price-Smith (*editor*)
PLAGUES AND POLITICS
Infectious Disease and International Policy

Michael Pugh (*editor*)
REGENERATION OF WAR-TORN SOCIETIES

Bhaskar Vira and Roger Jeffery (*editors*)
ANALYTICAL ISSUES IN PARTICIPATORY NATURAL RESOURCE MANAGEMENT

Simon M. Whitby
BIOLOGICAL WARFARE AGAINST CROPS

Global Issues Series
Series Standing Order ISBN 0–333–79483–4
(*outside North America only*)

You can receive future titles in this series as they are published by placing a standing order. Please contact your bookseller or, in case of difficulty, write to us at the address below with your name and address, the title of the series and the ISBN quoted above.

Customer Services Department, Macmillan Distribution Ltd, Houndmills, Basingstoke, Hampshire RG21 6XS, England

Just and Unjust Interventions in World Politics

Public and Private

Catherine Lu

Assistant Professor, Department of Political Science,
McGill University, Canada

First published 2006 by
PALGRAVE MACMILLAN
Houndmills, Basingstoke, Hampshire RG21 6XS and
175 Fifth Avenue, New York, N.Y. 10010
Companies and representatives throughout the world

PALGRAVE MACMILLAN is the global academic imprint of the Palgrave Macmillan division of St. Martin's Press, LLC and of Palgrave Macmillan Ltd. Macmillan® is a registered trademark in the United States, United Kingdom and other countries. Palgrave is a registered trademark in the European Union and other countries.

ISBN-13: 978–1–4039–8947–5 hardback
ISBN-10: 1–4039–8947–8 hardback

This book is printed on paper suitable for recycling and made from fully managed and sustained forest sources.

A catalogue record for this book is available from the British Library.

A catalog record for this book is available from the Library of Congress.

10   9   8   7   6   5   4   3   2   1
15   14   13   12   11   10   09   08   07   06

Printed and bound in Great Britain by
Antony Rowe Ltd, Chippenham and Eastbourne

For my family

Contents

Acknowledgements

In producing this book I have incurred many debts – personal, intellectual and institutional – which I would now like to acknowledge.

Although much changed to engage the normative challenges posed by interventionary practices in world politics since the tragedy of 9/11, this book began life as a doctoral dissertation in the Department of Political Science at the University of Toronto. I am most grateful to David Welch, my thesis co-supervisor, for his consistently prompt and constructive engagement with my work, as well as his enduring concern, encouragement and sense of humour. I am equally deeply grateful for the advice, support and friendship of Melissa Williams, who gave me valuable feedback while serving on my dissertation committee and, most importantly, urged me to persevere in the post-9/11 revision process.

I would also like to thank Joe Carens, co-supervisor of the thesis, as well as Ed Andrew and Ronnie Beiner for their careful and critical engagement with the thesis version. In addition, various parts or versions of this book have benefited from constructive comments by Jean Cohen, Daniel Gordon, Fran Harbour, Annabelle Lever, Linda Miller, Rosemary Nagy, Terry Nardin, Alan Patten, Hans Schattle, Daniel Weinstock and a couple of anonymous reviewers. For many stimulating and friendly conversations over the years on themes related to this book, I would like to thank Beth and Peter Digeser, Toni Erskine, Antonio Franceschet, Josh Goldstein, Maureen Hiebert, Nancy Kokaz, Simon Kow, Gisèle Szczyglak, Kok-Chor Tan, Laurel Weldon and Reinhard Wolf. I would also like to thank my teachers at the University of British Columbia, especially Ian Slater and Sam LaSelva, who inspired my interest in political philosophy, and Robert Jackson, who introduced me to issues of international ethics. For his relentless professional support and encouragement of my work, I would like to acknowledge a special debt of gratitude to Bob Goodin.

Since 2000, I have enjoyed excellent support from my colleagues in the Department of Political Science at McGill University. I would like to thank especially my department chair, Chris Manfredi, without whom this manuscript might not have found its way to a publisher. In addition, I am particularly grateful for the friendship, advice and encouragement of Arash Abizadeh, Michael Hilke, Juliet Johnson, Brian

Lewis, Hudson Meadwell, Sue Morton, Phil Oxhorn, Alan Patten, Jim Ron, Dietlind Stolle and Christina Tarnopolsky. My work also benefited from the support of the department's dedicated staff – Helen Wilicka, Emilia Scognamiglio, Effie Poulis, Pina Giobbi, Angie Coppola and the late Susan Bartlett. For his computer wizardry in the spring of 2005, I thank Marc Desrochers. For his assistance with proofreading this manuscript, I thank Ryan Griffiths. For the steady, efficient and enterprising research assistance she provided practically during her entire under-graduate career at McGill, I am especially grateful to Suzanne Marcuzzi.

Thanks to a 2004–2005 faculty fellowship from the Edmond J. Safra Foundation Center for Ethics at Harvard University, I was able to complete this book in an intellectually stimulating and relatively carefree environment. I would like to thank Arthur Applbaum and Fred Schauer for leading the faculty fellows seminars, as well as Michael Blake, Jennie Hawkins, Debbie Hellman, Simon Keller, Ken Mack, Mathias Risse and Angelo Volandes for their intellectual companionship during my time at the Center. I am also grateful to the Center's energetic support staff, especially Jean McVeigh, who spoiled me with many kindnesses.

My year away from McGill was made possible with the generous support of the McGill Faculty of Arts. In addition, this book has benefited from grants and fellowships provided by the Social Sciences and Humanities Research Council of Canada, as well as the University of Toronto, and the Ontario Graduate Scholarship Fund.

Chapter 5 of this book is a slightly altered version of 'The One and Many Faces of Cosmopolitanism,' *The Journal of Political Philosophy*, 8, 2 (2000) 244–267. Significant parts of Chapters 6 and 7 of this book are drawn from 'Whose Principles? Whose Institutions? Legitimacy Challenges for Humanitarian Intervention,' in *Humanitarian Intervention, Nomos XLVII*, T. Nardin and M. Williams eds (New York: New York University Press, 2005). I would like to thank the editors, and Blackwell and New York University Press, for their permission to reprint these works here.

I am deeply grateful to Jim Whitman, the editor of the Global Issues series, for his immediate and enthusiastic support for this project. I would also like to thank Jennifer Nelson, Alison Howson and the production staff at Palgrave; their wonderful professionalism has ensured the prompt publication of this work.

For all the personal support they have given me, I would like to thank Don and Sarah Munton, who were there from the beginning. And most of all, I am grateful for Lorenz Lüthi, whose love, discipline and encouragement made all the difference in the end.

1
Introduction

Where the word of a king is, there is power;
and who may say to him, What doest thou?

Jacques-Bénigne Bossuet,
Politique tirée des propres de l'Ecriture Sainte[1]

I In the name of humanity?

The end of the Cold War did not herald the end of human conflict,
cruelty and catastrophe. On the contrary, millions of people have
continued to suffer the fate of flies in indifferent, thoughtless or reck-
less human hands. Scenes of depravity and misery in a long list of
places have generated pleas for the international community to uphold
'the collective conscience of humanity' and to act 'in defence of our
common humanity.'[2] Contemporary cases of politically induced
humanitarian disaster have reinvigorated debate about the ethics of
'humanitarian intervention,' a term commonly used to refer to military
action, employed without the consent of the target sovereign state, to
prevent or halt large-scale violence and human suffering perpetrated or
permitted by its government.

The post-Cold War and post-9/11 worlds have witnessed extreme
vacillations on this theme. In the 1990s, international attention turned
more readily towards the plight of victims caught in intrastate humanitarian crises and conflicts, but when international responses yielded
morally mixed outcomes, practitioners and observers moved from
'unfounded enthusiasm' for intervention to 'unwarranted disillusion-
ment' with it.[3] After a botched 'humanitarian intervention' in Somalia
in 1993, the United Nations and its most powerful member states could

not muster enough political or moral will in the spring of 1994 to halt a genocide in Rwanda that was more efficient than the Holocaust. The moral questioning in the international community that was sparked by that avoidable tragedy was cut short by the events of September 11, 2001 (9/11), when the world's remaining superpower suffered a series of atrocious attacks, not by a rival state, but by a small organized group of foreigners. The US administration's response to 9/11 was to wage a 'war on terror' by engaging in military interventions, first in Afghanistan against the Taliban government that was seen to be aiding militants hostile to the United States, and then more recently in Iraq, against Saddam Hussein's domestically brutal, but internationally vulnerable, regime. The US President George W. Bush's justification for waging wars against both Afghanistan and Iraq included a humanitarian dimension. According to the Bush administration, both the regimes of the Taliban and of Saddam Hussein needed to be overthrown not only because they endangered US national security, and international peace and security, but also because they were known to have violated the human rights of their own citizens.

In his address to the United Nations one year after 9/11, for example, President Bush outlined Iraq's human rights violations, citing a report by the United Nations' own Commission on Human Rights:

> Tens of thousands of political opponents and ordinary citizens have been subjected to arbitrary arrest and imprisonment, summary execution and torture by beating and burning, electric shock, starvation, mutilation and rape. Wives are tortured in front of their husbands, children in the presence of their parents – and all of these horrors concealed from the world by the apparatus of a totalitarian state.[4]

Six months later, at the beginning of hostilities, Bush addressed Americans and had the following message for any Iraqis who could hear the translated broadcast: 'In a free Iraq there will be no more wars of aggression against your neighbors, no more poison factories, no more executions of dissidents, no more torture chambers and rape rooms. The tyrant will soon be gone. The day of your liberation is near.'[5] The tyrant fell rather quickly, but over two years later, the struggle for 'human rights' and 'human dignity' in Iraq continues with the active engagement of over 100,000 US troops.[6] At the same time, events in the Darfur region of Sudan reveal another site of government-induced inhumanity, but like in Rwanda, the response of the UN and Western powers has been thick on resolutions and thin on concrete interventionary actions.[7]

These cases reveal different but equally worrying deficiencies in international responses to domestically brutal, tyrannical or neglectful regimes that produce humanitarian catastrophes. From a normative point of view, they pose deep legitimacy challenges to international law and order, and the twin normative pillars of international society – state sovereignty and nonintervention. In the era of decolonization, these norms were considered vital for securing equal respect and self-determination for previously subjugated peoples and states; recognition of the right of sovereign equality and its corollary, the duty of nonintervention, came to define the basic ground rules for international cooperation between states. As a consequence, international law and society have traditionally condemned intervention, defined as 'dictatorial or coercive interference, by an outside party or parties, in the sphere of jurisdiction of a sovereign state, or more broadly of an independent political community.'[8]

The genocide in Rwanda and other similar mass atrocities committed within sovereign borders and often with the complicity, if not direct involvement, of ruling governments, however, call into question the supreme moral value and significance attached to sovereign rights in international society. In the face of such cases, those who are concerned to promote global respect for the rights and duties of humanity have argued that the norms of sovereignty and nonintervention are too strong or restrictive, and have the perverted consequence of protecting abusive and neglectful sovereigns from international intervention and accountability. In the face of US unilateralism, expressed most loudly in the 2003 invasion of Iraq, however, proponents of human rights and humanitarianism were united with defenders of international law and society in condemning the United States for paying insufficient respect to the foundational legal and moral norms of international society.

Debates about the moral rightness of intervention and nonintervention in these situations reveal a complex set of ethical disputes and questions. What ought to be the status of duties of humanity and human rights in the normative foundation of international order? What are the moral foundations of the state and the conditions for legitimate sovereign authority? What ought to be the relationship between rights of sovereignty and duties of humanity in international law and foreign policy? Can the use of force ever be an appropriate instrument for pursuing humanitarian interests? What kinds of legal and institutional reforms ought to be pursued in the development of an international adjudicative mechanism to govern uses of force by states for humanitarian purposes? What legitimacy criteria should such an adjudicative mechanism employ? Clarifying the nature and bases of ethical disputes surrounding these questions will help policymakers think more clearly and consistently about the relationship between 'our common humanity,' state sovereignty, and the ethics of 'humanitarian intervention.' Furthermore, understanding the ethical challenges to various forms of 'humanitarian intervention' may lead policymakers to think about the conditions for effectual and authoritative international law and institutions, as well as the importance of devising, establishing and implementing other proactive principles, policies and practices that would more effectively serve to establish a global order that is morally responsive to the claims of our common humanity.

II Bridging the divides

Normative debates about the legitimacy of 'humanitarian intervention' often focus on the moral problems associated with the use of military force by states. If we leave aside this issue, however, what makes intervention or the violation of a state's sovereignty so morally problematic in international relations? Cornelia Navari has observed that implicit 'in the very idea of intervention is an outsider's entrance into a political space.'[9] Yet it is not so much the state as political space that makes intervention morally problematic; it is, rather, the idea of the state as *private* space. The concept of intervention encompasses any action by an outside party in the internal affairs or jurisdiction of a distinct unit; it thus assumes some distinction between private and public domains. In the Westphalian model of interstate relations, the posited sovereignty of states functions like privacy to give states a right to be free from interference by outside parties – especially other states, as well as noncitizens, nongovernmental organizations, and even the international community – in their own internal affairs. Intervention as a moral problem in the world of states thus entails an image of 'sovereignty as privacy.' Just as in domestic discourse, 'the basic element in a violation of privacy is intrusion,'[10] in international discourse, the basic element in a violation of sovereignty is intervention. The duty of nonintervention has thus traditionally been viewed, in classical international law, as a natural corollary to the principle of state sovereignty.

In the domestic realm, intrusion by the state and the society into the private affairs of individuals and certain social groups, such as the family, has also been a subject of great moral controversy. The growing concern in western countries with domestic violence in the last half century, for example, has brought the issue of state intervention in the family to the forefront of social policy agendas. Debates recur over a tension between the desire to curb domestic abuse and the worry governments have about passing tougher family-violence laws if they are seen to intrude too deeply into family lives. This inquiry into the legitimacy of intervention will involve comparing claims to sovereignty made by states in the international realm, with similar normative claims to privacy traditionally accorded to families in the domestic realm.

The comparison between state sovereignty and family privacy entails the application of a structure of concepts, including privacy, that has so far largely eluded normative scholarship in International Relations. This book proposes to understand and assess contemporary normative debates about intervention in world politics through a central theoretical construct: the public/private distinction. In structuring how we conceive of the boundaries that shape individual, collective and institutional identity, agency and responsibility, the public/private construct in international relations is intrinsic to how we conceive of other high-lighted distinctions in the discipline, between the national and the international, citizen and noncitizen, the particular and the universal. By studying the public/private distinction we are embarking on an intellectual journey into the very heart of the 'dividing discipline.'[11]

Competing normative assessments about the legitimacy of 'humanitarian intervention' rely on unstated and largely unexplored understandings of the public/private distinction in world politics. Central to disciplining these ethical debates, the public/private distinction provides us with a conceptual key with which to explore the moral visions of realism, communitarianism and cosmopolitanism. While the distinction structures these perspectives' views of all issues of international ethics and justice, I will explore its impact only on their normative assessments of international intervention for humanitarian purposes.

This inquiry's use of a domestic analogy between the state and the family faces deep resistance from conventional International Relations theory, which assumes a fundamental divide between political theories about interstate relations and theories about individual relations within the bounds of a single political community. Martin Wight has distinguished the fields of political theory and international theory, noting that if 'political theory is the tradition of speculation about the state, then international theory may be supposed to be a tradition of speculation about the society of states, or the family of nations, or the international community.'[12] At first glance this characterization of the distinction seems rather innocuous. However, Wight subsequently makes clearer the deeper qualitative divide he envisages between international and political theory, predicated ultimately on profound differences between domestic and international politics:

> the language of political theory and law is... the language appropriate to man's control of his social life. Political theory and law are maps of experience or systems of action within the realm of normal relationships and calculable results. They are the theory of the good life. International theory is the theory of survival.... [T]he stuff of international theory... is constantly bursting the bounds of the language in which we try to handle it. For it all involves the ultimate experience of life and death, national existence and national extinction.[13]

Wight criticizes the tradition of political theory, not for being inattentive to international issues, but for being ultimately incapable of addressing them. This inability stems from what he perceives to be the radical differences separating international from domestic life; whereas the international arena is marked by a divided humanity, lack of central and ultimate authority, and a constant preoccupation with national survival, the domestic arena is typically characterized by national unity, centrality of authority and the effective pursuit of social goals beyond immediate survival, such as welfare and justice.

Of course, the label of incompetence attached to political theory in the study of International Relations has served as a compelling excuse for the 'moral inferiority of international politics.'[14] The discipline of International Relations has tended to discourage the normative study of international issues, as well as analyses that draw comparisons between domestic (national) and international politics.[15] Scepticism about the normative dimension of International Relations, however, has been especially pernicious, for its effect has been to render problematic moral study in general. This is evident in discussions about the morality of 'humanitarian intervention.' For example, one 'formidable argument' against legitimizing 'humanitarian intervention' is that in 'the real world,... moral arguments tend to become used as [political] instruments of battle in a decentralized system of self-help.'[16] This seems to imply, however, that in a centralized system of authority, moral arguments are seldom used as instruments for justifying self-serving policies or conduct. If we view intrastate or domestic politics realistically, we must recognize the self-serving nature of many moral arguments, yet we do not conclude from this that we should give up the idea of moral argument in domestic politics. Similarly R.J. Vincent has noted that those 'who argue against the legitimacy of humanitarian intervention are inclined to observe that it is a doctrine used by the great against the small, that it smacks of imperialism, [and] that it disguises ignoble motives.'[17] One is inclined to ask those who find these objections cogent if there exists any general norm or principle which cannot be similarly corrupted. Such arguments seem to cast doubt on the use of moral and ethical rules and principles in general to order human relations. Yet one cannot maintain a radical scepticism about moral arguments in International Relations, without holding an equally sceptical view of moral discourse in domestic politics as well.

While the dichotomous characterization of ethics and politics has made it difficult to theorize about International Relations in ethical terms, recent decades have witnessed a revival of normative international theory, that aspect of the study of International Relations explicitly concerned with moral goods, norms, values, foundations and reasoning in an international context.[18] A normative study of the kind I am proposing rejects the assertion that international issues lie beyond the pale of normative theorization. I want to claim that political philosophy's concern with the moral life does not serve as a credible reason for confining its purview to issues that arise within the locus of a single political community.[19] On the contrary, in the contemporary world, the task of political philosophy – to illuminate the 'good' or 'moral' life – is incomplete if it can only meet issues that arise at the global level with silence. This book thus contributes to the growing efforts in the fields of Political Theory and International Relations to expose the normative structures of global and international politics and society to the kind of critical scrutiny that political theorists have traditionally dedicated to domestic politics and society.

III The plan of the book

The book will begin with an exploration of the rich literature in social and political thought on the public/private distinction, which functions to structure the agency, interests and obligations of diverse actors in any given society. In the following chapter, I will consider the applicability of a public/private construct in the realm of international relations, and highlight two distinct approaches – atomistic and organic – to understanding the publicness and privateness of the state. This analysis leads to one main theme of this book, which is to construct a morally coherent and defensible account of the distinction that will shape the public and private lives of states in international society. After highlighting ways to understand and misunderstand 'public' and 'private,' I move to examine normative arguments about intervention from three ethical perspectives – realist, communitarian and cosmopolitan.

Chapter 3 is devoted to an examination of the realist perspective, which has dominated the study, and some would say practice, of International Relations for much of the twentieth century. The distinct ethical issues which realism brings to normative debates about intervention focus on the problem of the tyranny of the private in international relations. Due to the dominance of private or self-interested motivation and judgement in international relations, realists argue that there is little space for morality, understood as a public or shared system of normative rules. Realist assessments of intervention, humanitarian or otherwise, thus tend to be largely negative; they argue that intervention is, at best, imprudent if it requires compromising a state's national interest, and, at worst, a mask for the self-interested pursuits of great powers. Realism's moral scepticism stems from its impoverished atomistic views of private and public. Ironically, although the private dominates a realist vision of world politics, contemporary realism is incapable of sustaining any normative conception of state privacy, upon which a coherent normative argument for or against intervention would depend. In a very basic sense, such a perspective is incapable of supporting any normative position in favour of or against 'humanitarian intervention.' The real ethical debate, then, is between communitarians and cosmopolitans over how international and global societies ought to conceive of the international/domestic distinction, which affects how the sovereignty claims of states and the humanitarian claims of individuals are to be reconciled.

In Chapter 4, I turn my attention to communitarian perspectives that have enjoyed prominence in the normative structure of classical international law and society. Communitarians, statist and nonstatist, are concerned to validate the moral worth of state or communal sovereignty as privacy, and to uphold the nonintervention norm between communities in international society and law. Far from realism's portrayal of states' privateness as a barrier to international morality, then, communitarianism seeks to defend a conception of state privacy as a key component of international morality. Using liberal feminist theoretical critiques of privacy, especially 'family privacy,' my examination reveals the inconsistency, inadequacy and incompleteness of communitarian accounts of the public and private lives of states, absent certain fundamental moral considerations that cannot be internally generated by a communitarian approach.

Those moral considerations can be traced to a cosmopolitan moral orientation. Chapter 5 begins an exploration of cosmopolitanism by addressing first some common realist and communitarian objections to cosmopolitanism as a moral perspective, specifically its utopianism, excessive rationalism and imperialist proclivities. In response, I consider a nonidealist, nonalienating and nonabsolutist account of a cosmopolitan ethical perspective which also eschews the opposite vices of misanthropy, determinism, and passivity. Such an account entails a recognition of the public and private faces of humanity in its commonality and diversity. Human beings are united by a common human condition marked by vulnerability to suffering. In this sense, humanity is one. Yet human individuals are also unique centres of consciousness, purpose and agency. In this sense, humanity is many. Any defensible moral theory must do justice to humanity as one and many.

In Chapter 6, I defend a liberal cosmopolitan account of the public/private distinction in world politics that places duties of humanity at the foundation of both domestic and international orders. Cosmopolitan humanitarianism's dedication to preventing and alleviating human suffering is inspired by an acknowledgement of the natural equality of human vulnerability. Such an account is able to recognize the normative interrelatedness of international and domestic realms, and conceives of state sovereignty primarily in terms of the authority and responsibility of political agents to promote or secure conditions for the exercise of accountable power and authority that affirm rather than subvert human (moral and social) agency, dignity and responsibility. Whereas the communitarian account of 'sovereignty as privacy' emphasizes the exclusive power of sovereigns to order their domestic realms and entails their right to noninterference in this respect, the alternative cosmopolitan account of 'sovereignty as responsibility' highlights the conditional nature of state sovereign authority, and its embeddedness in a global normative structure that is morally responsive to the claims of common humanity.

Although a cosmopolitan ethical perspective provides clear justification for the abrogation of state sovereignty for humanitarian purposes, Chapter 7 deals with the ethical challenges faced by agents of global civil society, and agents of the society of states, when they attempt to respond to politically induced humanitarian disasters in current world political, social and economic conditions. With regard to practices of cosmopolitan humanitarianism by human rights and humanitarian relief organizations, I explore and defend how a liberal cosmopolitan conception of the international society/global civil society distinction shapes the contours of their agency and autonomy vis-à-vis the society of states. With regard to the use of force by states, I address problems of law and community at the international level that undermine the legitimacy of processes of adjudicating uses of force for humanitarian purposes, given current world political conditions and structures.

The cruel irony may be that an increase in the number of legitimate 'humanitarian interventions' may not indicate progress towards a more accountable world order founded on a respect for our common humanity. Rather, it might actually signify moral regress and a decreasingly legitimate global order. In the Conclusion to the book, I ponder on the limits of focusing on the ethics of 'humanitarian intervention,' or on duties of cosmopolitan humanitarianism rather than on duties of cosmopolitan justice.

2
Public and Private: Towards Conceptual Clarification

> ... the liberalism of fear as a strictly political theory is not
> necessarily linked to any one religious or scientific doctrine... It
> must reject only those political doctrines that do not recognize any
> difference between the spheres of the personal and the public.
>
> Judith N. Shklar, *Liberalism and the Moral Life*[1]

I 'Public' and 'private' in international relations

When Ukraine's presidential elections in November 2004 seemed
tainted by massive fraud, the European Union and the United States
called for a review, implicitly favouring the then opposition leader,
Viktor Yushchenko, against the Kremlin's preferred man in Kiev, Viktor
Yanukovich. In response, Russian President Vladimir Putin condemned
EU and US criticisms of the elections as 'inadmissible,' while a
Russian official in the United States deplored the 'unprecedented interference' in Ukraine's domestic affairs.[2] Everyone knew that the United
States and Russia in this case disagreed over the question of who should
lead Ukraine, but the exchange reveals a more general dispute between
them about whether and how external governments and organizations
can ever legitimately play an interventionary or interfering role in the
domestic politics or affairs of another state.

The very intelligibility of the concept of intervention relies on a structure that distinguishes between an internal and an external context,
insiders and outsiders, private and public. The concept of intervention
paradigmatically entails the situation of an outsider acting within an
insider's preserved domain, or an intrusion from a public into a private
realm. The legitimacy of intervention depends in part on the normative
nature of the boundaries separating these categories, affecting issues

such as whether we consider domestic electoral processes and outcomes, or the treatment of a state's citizens, to be an exclusive concern of that society or state, or a legitimate concern of other states, international society, or the wider global civil society as well. At the conceptual level, an inquiry into the ethics of intervention needs to focus on the construction of these boundaries, from which the normative meaning of intervention and its controversies ultimately derive. Indeed, the legitimacy of intervention in a state's domestic jurisdiction depends on how the normative framework of international society distinguishes between and relates diverse moral obligations, such as those states may have towards their own citizens, and those they may have towards the citizens of other states. A normative study of intervention thus must interrogate the structure as well as substance of moral obligations at domestic, international and global levels of governance.

What concepts can we employ to illuminate the normative structure of international society? Ideas like 'the national interest,' 'state sovereignty' and 'human rights' are prominent players in normative political debates at the international level, but it is the construction of the 'international/domestic distinction' that mediates their roles in shaping the agency, interests and obligations of states and other actors. Disputes about the legitimacy of interventionary actions reveal the contested nature of this distinction, as proponents and critics of intervention disagree over the characterization of controversial state actions as 'international' or 'domestic' affairs, even before they engage in any substantive debate about the actions themselves. Debates about the legitimacy of interventionary actions, whether they are military or economic, political or social, involve a dispute, then, not only over the substance of those actions, but also over their location in a world that is largely structured by territorially exclusive and politically independent states claiming ultimate political and legal, if not moral, authority over their own citizens and society.[3] Despite its centrality in disciplining ethical debates about intervention, however, the nature of the international/domestic construct has been more often assumed than examined or defended in such debate.

How might we better understand the functions of the international/domestic construct in international normative discourse? I suggest that the concepts of 'public,' 'private' and the 'public/private distinction' can be used to clarify competing conceptions of the international/domestic construct that informs international and global normative order, upon which evaluations of the legitimacy of intervention depend. Different conceptions of 'public' and 'private,' their distinction as well as their relationship, lead to different understandings of intervention as a moral problem in world politics. Using these concepts we can rephrase the normative issues raised by the issue of intervention in the following manner: Is the treatment of individual human beings a private concern of the state in which they are citizens, or is it a legitimate public concern for the wider society of states, and of global civil society? What moral obligations do states have towards their own publics, and do states have any moral obligations that extend beyond their own publics, for example, to other citizens, other states, the international society of states or the wider global community? Do states have any public (international or global) moral obligations? If so, what is their relationship with a state's private (national) obligations?

Answering these questions requires us to examine the construction of the public/private distinction at the international level, which informs what state leaders consider they may legitimately say and do internally and externally, what responses to their domestic and international actions they expect from other states or the global community, and how they assess the legitimacy of the actions of other states or groups.[4] There is little dispute that states have some public or external accountability at the international level for their actions towards other states. For example, international society's prohibition of state-to-state aggression justifies the use of force by other states and the international community to counter aggression. Since under the legalist paradigm, aggression constitutes 'the only crime that states can commit against other states,' it alone warrants punishment by other states and the international community.[5]

The external or international accountability of states for the treatment of their own citizens, however, is greatly contested in international society. *Can* states or sovereigns commit crimes, not against other states, but against humanity, or more specifically, against their own citizens? And *should* they be held accountable for them at the international level? The operation of international courts – such as the International Court of Justice, the Inter-American Court of Human Rights, the European Court of Human Rights and the African Court of Human Rights – indicates that states admit some degree of international accountability for violations of international humanitarian and human rights law.[6] The introduction of the International Criminal Court (ICC) also makes it possible for the international community to hold social, political and military leaders *as individuals* accountable not only for external acts of aggression and war crimes, but also for internal acts of genocide and crimes against humanity.[7] The possibility of holding states or individual leaders accountable for such actions depends on how the moral rights and obligations of individuals, groups and states are reconciled at the international level. In an international society where the treatment of citizens is considered to be a solely private concern of each state, a state would not expect any external responses or criticisms by outsiders on this subject, and it would look on any negative reactions as undue or illegitimate interference in its (legitimately) internal affairs. When Russian leaders demand that external organizations stop criticizing their conduct in Chechnya, or when Chinese leaders insist that their policies towards Taiwan are a matter of internal affairs, they invoke a certain construction of the international/domestic or public/ private distinction that places their actions and policies in these realms beyond the legitimate purview of international concern and intervention.[8]

How scholars and practitioners think about almost any normative issue in world politics, from global economic justice to 'humanitarian intervention,' involves some conception of a public/private construct that functions to structure agency, interests and obligations at the international level. While some conception of this construct is implicit in normative arguments about the legitimacy of intervention, these debates in world politics have yet to benefit from the rich and diverse intellectual study of the distinction in western political and social thought.

The few discussions of the public/private distinction that have appeared in the field of International Relations have been initiated by scholars with predominantly feminist concerns. They have pointed to the gendered construction of the distinction in international relations that has similar negative effects on women as the public/private distinction within western societies. Hilary Charlesworth observes that 'international law and its institutions have been designed in a gendered way, mediated by public/private dichotomies.'[9] Her work focuses on the public/private distinction in international law and the effects of its construction on women's lives, especially their oppression and marginalization. Similarly, Kristen Walker argues that the public/private distinction is gendered at the domestic and the international levels, and that the 'distinction, if it is to be retained, must be deprived of its current gendered nature.'[10] Thus Walker is similarly concerned with the impact of the public/private distinction in international relations on women: 'Before women can emerge as distinct subjects of international law, this dichotomy needs to be broken down at all levels, so that women are no longer relegated to the domestic jurisdiction of states under international law.'[11] Celina Romany also criticizes the public/ private distinction's role in the global subjection of women, focusing her analysis on 'why gender issues are deemed private within international society' and especially human rights law.[12]

While I am sympathetic to these arguments, it seems to me that more basic conceptual problems exist in the prevailing construction of the public/private distinction in international relations, which have even more pervasive impacts than these feminist analyses suggest. Indeed, with some basic exceptions, the public/private distinction in international relations currently relegates not only women, but practically all human beings, to 'the domestic jurisdiction of states under international law.'[13] Although we owe some of the most insightful critiques of the public/private distinction to feminist political theory, the construct has deeper, greater and more general normative significance in International Relations than a gender analysis has so far allowed.

While my discussion seeks primarily to make a contribution in the field of international ethics, this exploration of the public/private construct also speaks to a controversy in feminist theorizing about the distinction.[14] Feminists of all philosophical persuasions agree on the indefensibility of traditional, patriarchal conceptions of the public/ private distinction.[15] Yet while feminist theorists have made cogent critiques of the construct, they disagree over how to reconceive it, and even over whether such a distinction should have any use at all. In attempting to formulate a morally coherent and defensible account of the distinction for international and global relations, I intend to defend its normative utility against those who deny its relevance.

'Public,' 'private' and 'the public/private distinction' are fairly familiar, if contested, concepts in modern western political philosophy, and especially prominent in liberal theory. The origins of the distinction can be traced to Roman law, which used it to distinguish between issues that pertained to the condition of the Roman commonwealth and those that related to the interests of individuals.[16] From its inception the distinction has marked the division between other-regarding and self-regarding spheres, interests and activities. Clearly, the need for such a construct arises in the context of a society of interacting agents. Solitary individuals, in the absence of social interaction, would hardly have need of a public/private distinction. The function of the distinction as a descriptive organizing construct allows us to distinguish between various social relations, such as the following: society/individual, civil society/family, state/family, state/civil society, state/market, and we may add international society/domestic state, and international society/global civil society.

Senses of 'publicness' and 'privateness' generated by the distinction, according to Stanley Benn and Gerald Gaus, are complex-structured concepts, with a multiplicity of dimensions that serve to delineate norms relating to access, agency and interest in any given society.[17] Within states, the public/private distinction serves to structure these dimensions between individuals, within civil society, and the state; in international relations, the distinction functions similarly to organize relations between citizens, states, international society and global civil society. Different ways of distinguishing and relating 'public' and 'private' categories at the international level inform different normative visions of international society's 'institutions, practices, activities and aspirations.'[18] The construction of the distinction affects our ideas about international relations as an area of practice and study, including who or what counts as actors and what is significant about them, what powers, rights or claims they have in relation to each other, and what characterizes the context in which they relate. For example, different understandings of the distinction lead to disparate accounts of the contrast between international and domestic politics, and between citizens and noncitizens. Furthermore, the construction of the distinction reveals how international society conceives of the appropriate scope of international concern and intervention, and of individual states' rights to self-regulation.

The neglect of the vocabulary of 'public' and 'private' in international relations theory may seem surprising, given the salience of boundaries in most normative controversies at the international level. The use of this group of concepts to interrogate the normative structure of international society, however, faces two kinds of distinct challenges that might explain its relative obscurity in international normative discourse. One line of argument questions whether it is possible to make the public/private construct relevant to the international domain. The other type of argument raises the issue of whether it is desirable to do so.

First, the relative absence of the distinction in international discourse may be attributed to the dominance of a particular realist perspective in the last half century. Realists are inclined to argue that since there is technically no international or world government, there is no 'public' or state-like agent or power at the global level, and therefore the life of states in the international realm is characterized wholly by self-help. From a methodological perspective, contemporary realists are thus sceptical of attempts to explain or understand international politics by importing domestic concepts and analogies. From a normative perspective, realists might wonder about the applicability of a concept such as 'the public interest' to the international realm; indeed, they mainly tend to view 'national interest' as the sole guiding justification for foreign policy.

I will examine realist assumptions about the public/private construct in the next chapter, but it is worth noting that the main irony of the realist position is that it rejects the relevance of the distinction at the same time as it relies on a certain conception of it, in the form of an international/domestic dichotomy, which ultimately cannot be sustained by a realist conceptual framework. This problem becomes starkly apparent in realist attempts to use the concept of the 'national interest' to evaluate the ethics of 'humanitarian intervention.' Diverse interpretations of national interest lead to sometimes radically divergent evaluations of the legitimacy of intervention, revealing the problem of an incoherent understanding of the international/national distinction in contemporary realist theory.

Those who emphasize the cultural diversity of the world might also challenge the possibility of using the public/private construct to make sense of the normative foundations of international society. The cultural pluralism of the world, these critics might argue, yields radically different and irreconcilable ways of negotiating public and private between cultures. Given the lack of a universal cultural framework that can fix one conception of the distinction on all societies, is it possible to talk about *a* public/private distinction at the international level, or is an anarchy of such distinctions more likely?

Different societies evidently may hold distinct conceptions of the public/private construct in the ordering of their internal social relations. I would argue, however, that a common political culture among states does exist at the international level, which relies on a distinct public/private construct, informing the shape and meaning of the principles of state sovereignty and nonintervention that are universally embedded in the normative structure of international society through such instruments as the UN Charter. However a state configures the public/private relationship internally, all states rely on a certain conception of this construct at the international level to order their moral standing, agency, interests and obligations within international society. This is not to say that one conception of the public/private construct is wholly accepted by all states or the larger international community; indeed, we are living in a moment when the prevailing understanding of the distinction is undergoing severe contests from within the world of states, as well as from nongovernmental agents.

Another cultural critique leads to the second line of argument which questions whether the public/private construct is a desirable addition to normative political discourse at the international level. In this vein, some critics might observe that the distinction is based on a group of concepts that are parochial to western civilization. 'Public' and 'private' may appeal to shared moral understandings in western and especially liberal societies, but they are not cultural universals. These concepts will not find resonance within many nonwestern societies; their use may therefore obscure rather than clarify the normative world order. In answer to this objection, we might take heed of Martin Krygier's warnings to avoid 'conceptual imperialism, a common disease among philosophers, and equally to avoid conceptual parochialism, which, like malaria, often afflicts anthropologists who have spent time in the field.'[19] Using the language of public and private to examine the normative structure of international society does not entail an unreflective endorsement of western or liberal constructions of the distinction. Indeed, contestation about the distinction abounds *within* western and liberal societies, in practice and in theory.

It must be acknowledged, however, that the current normative map of global and international orders has its origins in western historical developments. The Westphalian moment, which established the principle of state sovereignty and the duty of nonintervention in the normative foundation of international society, began as a parochial European order, which has expanded to encompass the globe only in the twentieth century.[20] Given this history western political and philosophical concepts are likely to be prominent, even if contested, in the normative structure of international society. The public/private construct provides us with a powerful conceptual tool with which to make sense of this structure, without necessitating an allegiance to any one conception of it. The long history of these concepts also allows us to make critical comparisons between their evolution at domestic and international levels.

Another critique against the utility of the public/private construct might focus on the unsettled and mutable qualities of the distinction that drive the deep contestations over its meaning, significance and potential for transformation in western domestic political discourse. According to Jeff Weintraub, the distinction 'is not unitary, but protean. It comprises, not a single paired opposition, but a complex family of them, neither mutually reducible nor wholly unrelated.'[21] This comment suggests that there is not a single use of the public/private distinction but a complex of meanings that generate public/private *distinctions*. Unfortunately, although these distinctions are widely employed domestically – in ordinary language, journalistic reporting, domestic political debates and scholarly discourse – inattention to their variations often results in theoretical confusion and error. Critics may be right to worry that importing the distinction will only confuse the moral landscape of international relations.

The utility of the distinction, I believe, lies in its ability to help us to schematize a diversity of agents, interests and obligations at the international level. Studying the distinction enables theorists to grasp and explore a complex normative structure that disciplines contemporary debates in international ethics, including those relating to the issue of 'humanitarian intervention.' The distinction's continuing controversy in political and social theory attests to its vitality and richness; it is important enough to be contested. In fact, International Relations theory has its own version of this battle in the form of disputes about the international/domestic distinction, which are becoming more salient in an age of increasing sociability between states themselves as well as between nongovernmental civil society agents. It is time to bring these strands of contestation together, so that normative international theory can benefit from as well as contribute to the study of the public/private construct in contemporary political and social theory.

II The 'public' in international and global societies

How ought we to think about 'publicness' in international society? Who or what constitutes 'the public' at the international level? What is 'public' about them? Is there such a thing as a 'public interest' at the international or global level? If so, how should we conceive it? As we will see in the course of our examination, competing ethical perspectives offer different answers to these questions about the 'public' in international and global societies.

Historically, western political theory has designated the state as the quintessentially public actor, leading to one characterization of the public/private distinction as political/nonpolitical. In a descriptive sense, the political/nonpolitical distinction can refer to a difference between state and nonstate, or governmental and nongovernmental, actors, spheres and relations. This descriptive use of the distinction to mark a difference between the state and nonstate actors has been adopted unproblematically at the international level. International law, for example, classifies states as public entities *par excellence*, just as they comprise the public realm in relation to individuals and domestic civil society. In international legal terms, the public/private distinction so conceived has been translated into a distinction between public and private international law; the former relates to law that governs the political relations between states, while the latter relates to foreign transactions of nonstate entities, such as individuals and corporations.[22]

What does it mean for the state to be a public actor at the international level? One way to understand the 'publicness' of the state in international society is in terms of its visibility in the international domain. Indeed, the public/private construct functions domestically as well to mark a division between that which is open, visible or accessible and that which is closed, hidden or inaccessible. That which 'appears in public can be seen and heard by everybody.'[23] In contrast, when something is private, we mean that it is hidden from the view or scrutiny of outsiders. In this sense, the private is connected with privacy, and the public with publicity.

In international relations and law, states enjoy the greatest visibility as the designated public actors in world politics; indeed, states are intrinsic to the characterization of the domain beyond states as an inter*national* realm, and have defined and dominated International Relations as a discipline and field of inquiry.[24] This visibility affords states an international presence, status and agency, as well as some forms of accountability at the international level. Since the era of decolonization, despite a wide range of disparities in economic, political and social conditions, all states are seen as equally sovereign in the eyes of international law. This formal equality and independence mean theoretically that each state is master of its own destiny, even those 'quasi-states' that lack internal resources or capabilities to establish *de facto* sovereignty. Indeed, as Robert Jackson has noted, *de jure* sovereignty 'has given Third World states global institutional standing, influence, and support'[25] that they might not otherwise have been able to command. The formal equal independence of states recognized under international law may thus act as a corrective for the deep inequalities that persist in international social life, giving weaker states membership, visibility and voice in the political, economic and social structures of international society.

If it is states alone, and more specifically, their political representatives, that constitute members of the international 'public,' it is also their relations and interests that constitute proper subjects of international political concern, debate and intervention. Since individuals and nongovernmental groups are not members of the international 'public' so construed, their relations and interests have only indirect standing in international society, primarily through their affiliation with a national government or state. Nongovernmental agents and interests may gain visibility only through states, just as planets have no internal light, but must rely on a star for their illumination.

Yet the relevant collectivity whose voices, interests and concerns would constitute 'the public' at the international level is far from settled. Competing normative visions differ over who or what may constitute 'the public' in the domain of world politics. Statist communitarians might perceive the relevant community to consist of the politically organized collectivity of states that comprise international society. Meanwhile, cosmopolitan theorists articulate an alternative understanding of the relevant collectivity in advancing claims derived from the largely unorganized social collectivity of individuals and groups that comprise humanity, or the even larger and disparate collage of living things that comprise the globe's ecology.[26] We should remember that disputes about the relevant collectivity, and what is public about it, have shaped the evolution of 'the public' at the domestic level as well. Our understanding of the domestic common has historically suffered from partial views about who and what matters in the collective. In domestic and international domains, unequal distributions of social, economic and political status and power within and between societies all conspire to create partial publics and partial states.

The dispute over who or what constitutes the relevant public in international society engages the normative dimension of a state's publicness. In its historical evolution, the modern state acquired the status of a public actor because of its 'claim to be responsible for the general interests and affairs of a politically organized collectivity ... as opposed to 'private' – that is, merely particular – interests.'[27] Hendrik Spruyt offers an interesting account of the evolution of the state from private to public status in medieval Europe, which involved a qualitative change in the identity of the state leader, the king, from a private to public actor.[28] The purview of the political after this transformation derives from the function of the state as the bearer of responsibility for the general public interest, and the collective or common good, most prominently security and justice. It is this ethical mandate that legitimizes the use of coercion by the state, and distinguishes it from 'robber bands.'[29] In theory then, the state as a public actor represents a fusion of the political and the ethical, with a mandate to serve the public interest.

Yet how are we to conceive of 'the public interest' in the international or global domain? Realists, as we have noted, might be sceptical of the very idea of an international public interest; in the absence of a global Leviathan, the public interest in the international arena can only be the national interest of our own territorially bound political community. Even perspectives that admit the utility of thinking about an international 'public interest,' however, still disagree over how to conceive it.

Stanley Benn and Gerald Gaus identify two divergent approaches to modelling the relationship between individuals and society at the domestic level that lead to two different conceptualizations of the public interest.[30] They call these models the individualist and the organic models. I will refer to them as atomistic and organic models.[31]

An atomistic orientation sees individuals, or the basic units of society, as private self-directed units with internally generated interests and goals. The self is ontologically independent and distinct from the other. The image of social reality under an atomistic view is that of self-directing actors interacting rationally, that is, based on their self-interest, with the patterns of their interaction curbed only by the restrictions imposed by an administrative state which stands apart from and above civil society. The ontological priority of the individual translates into the ethical priority of the individual's interests and claims. Atomistic moral visions must take into account and accommodate the self-directed nature of individuals in society. An atomistic view of the public/private construct, for example, is implied by a Benthamite conception of the public interest as the aggregation of private interests: the whole is composed of the sum of the many particulars, and is reducible to them.[32]

In contrast to the atomistic model which takes a self-directing individual as its basic and *a priori* starting point, an organic model sees individuals in society as members of a greater whole from which individuals derive their interests, goals and direction. The self and the other are interdependent and mutually constituted. An organic image of social reality is that of a collective body consisting of 'mutually connected and dependent parts constituted to share a common life.'[33] The ontological priority of the social group translates into its ethical priority. An organic moral vision thus privileges the collective or common good of the social group as a whole. It sees the public interest as a common good derived from a whole that is something more and qualitatively different from the sum of all the parts; the whole is not reducible to its parts. Rousseau's general will, for example, is distinct from and antithetical to the sum of particular or private wills of citizens.[34]

It should be noted that this contrast between atomistic and organic conceptualizations of individuals, society and their relationship is quite abstract, which means that these models may be compatible with many political programmes. At the same time, however, they inform *how* diverse political programmes conceive of the public interest in domestic society, which leads to different types of justificatory arguments for public policy.

Different conceptions of the public interest, when directed to the international realm, affect our assessment of the possibility and nature of international ethics and morality. When E.H. Carr argued, for example, that international morality was necessarily impoverished because in the international system, 'the principle that the good of the whole takes precedence over the good of the part, which is a postulate of any fully integrated community, is not generally accepted,'[35] he is clearly using a more organic conception of the international 'public interest' as his reference point. His argument is a simplification of sorts, but it shows the importance of the public/private construct, which relates domestic public interest to international public interest, in any conception of international normative order.

Carr's comment also leads us to suspect the publicness of the state in international society, especially in the actual performance of existing states. By designating states as public entities we may acknowledge the ideal of serving the public interest or the common good, however conceived, to which political agents should continually aspire. Yet the question of whether any particular government fulfills the state's mandate to advance the public interest is not answered by the mere designation of the state as a public actor. Indeed, whether the state is a monarchy or a democracy, its leaders and its people may fail to meet their responsibility of serving the public interest in the domestic or international realm, through error, malice or lack of virtue. If we confuse the descriptive categorization of the state as a public entity with the normative assessment that any and every state manifests the public interest, we are in danger of obscuring issues that arise when states or regimes fall short of these ideals, such as how the political realm may lessen the likelihood of such failure, or be held accountable in such an eventuality.

III   The private lives of states

States are public actors in a few different senses that have implications for their standing, agency and obligations in international society. Their interactions with other states are public in the sense of being visible and open to international scrutiny, debate and sometimes intervention. States are also public in a normative sense of representing, safeguarding and promoting the public interest domestically and internationally, although how we conceive of the public interest at both levels is hotly contested by competing normative visions of politics. The adoption of the public status of the state at the international level is thus not as unproblematic as has been assumed by the formal rules of international law and sociability. Furthermore, even if a state can claim, through participatory democratic institutions, to comprise a public all-inclusive sphere at the domestic level, no existing state can claim to be 'public' in this sense at the global level. In relation to its own citizens and society, the state may comprise a public realm, but in relation to other states and entities in international society, the state seems at times to constitute a private, partial and parochial sphere.

The unquestioned designation of states as public actors in world politics can lead us to overlook their private lives. One way to understand the privateness of the state in international society is to focus on aspects of states that are considered to be invisible, or inaccessible to international scrutiny and regulation. If the public and the political refer to the common visible world and the common good, the private and the nonpolitical, in contrast, consist substantively of that which is particular to members and beyond the legitimate purview of the collective. The realm of the household or domesticity, for example, typically epitomizes the private sphere, considered to be essentially nonpolitical or concerned primarily with its own particular welfare and survival. At the same time that the Westphalian international order privileges the visibility of states at the international level, it also allows certain aspects of states, specifically their internal affairs, to enjoy invisibility at the international level. In international society, the privacy of the state is institutionalized through the construction of state sovereignty, which functions like privacy to shield certain issues, activities and units from external scrutiny, regulation and intervention. The public, in this context, is anything that intrudes.

For example, if a government considers an issue such as human rights to be a domestic matter, it will regard external criticism by other governments or nongovernmental organizations of its human rights record as illegitimate interference in its internal or private affairs. Wenhui Zhong makes this point in relation to the Chinese government's position on human rights: 'According to the official Chinese position, international debates on the human rights situation in China can...easily become debates on sovereignty. Therefore, criticising human rights abuses in China is often regarded as interference in China's internal affairs.'[36] Designating an issue as a 'private' or 'sovereign' concern in this way gives it an automatic immunity from external or public intervention. The designation of an issue as a private or sovereign concern cuts off substantive discussion with outsiders about the issue; this explains why debate at the international level about the nature and function of sovereignty as privacy appears to take precedence over any international debate about the nature and substance of human rights.

The invisibility of the private creates an arena for freedom that is distinct from the freedom afforded by the visibility of the public sphere. Indeed, the atomistic and organic conceptions of the public/private construct yield different understandings of the nature and location of freedom. Under an organic view, participation in a common life is inherent in the individual subject. Freedom for individuals thus lies in this ability to partake in this collective deliberation and decision-making that characterize republican notions of citizenship in a political community. Freedom under this view is located in the public realm of membership and belonging. Similarly, Hannah Arendt has argued that 'freedom is exclusively located in the political realm',[37] in the life of the *polis*, which she contrasts to life in the household, a thoroughly private and nonpolitical realm of inequality, of slavery and mastery, of silence and of the provision of the most basic human needs. The private realm may be necessary, but it is the public realm that is free.

In contrast, under an atomistic view, because self-direction is inherent in the individual subject, its freedom lies in being able to think, feel, identify, create and express its own projects without external interference or coercion by others, especially the state. Freedom is located in a private sphere that is off-limits to outsiders and external control or regulation. Hobbes articulates this notion of freedom when he defines liberty as the absence of external impediments, which depends on 'the silence of the Law.'[38] When we designate a space, unit or activity as 'private' we mean that it is free from intrusion. Similarly, when we say that something is a private matter, we are indicating to other people that they do not have a right to interfere in the matter. Western liberal capitalist societies typically understand families and markets to be private, characterizing them as spheres that enjoy a large degree of freedom from state intervention. As Judith Wagner DeCew has noted at the domestic level, the public/private distinction is used 'to reflect differences between the appropriate scope of government, as opposed to self-regulation by individuals.'[39] When we conceive of the public/private distinction as an intervention/freedom distinction, locating freedom in the private sphere, the image of the public that comes to the fore is one of a coercive 'apparatus of rule which stands above the society and governs it through the enactment and administration of laws,'[40] rather than the organic view of the public as a site of active citizenship and collective self-determination.

Despite the contradictions between atomistic and organic conceptions of publicness and privateness, Benn and Gaus call both models 'liberal.' Indeed, I noted earlier that the public/private distinction is a foundational construct of liberal philosophy and societies. As Judith Shklar noted, 'The important point for liberalism is not so much where the line [between public and private] is drawn, as that it be drawn, and that it must under no circumstances be ignored or forgotten.'[41] Liberalism's preoccupation with the moral significance of freedom explains the commitment of self-avowed liberal societies to finding 'an equilibrium of the public and private spheres of life.'[42]

The centrality of the public/private distinction in disciplining normative debates in International Relations reveals the salience of liberalism's promises, problems and controversies in the moral foundations of international society. For just as the 'political agenda of liberal societies is permeated by issues of the bounds of the public and the private,'[43] these issues, expressed in the form of contestation over the nature and bounds of the global, the international and the domestic, also pervade the political agenda of global society. How we conceive of the public/private distinction in international relations clearly has direct bearing on the shape and nature of freedom that individuals and states may legitimately enjoy, as the distinction functions to separate realms of coercion and regulation from realms of free and voluntary association.

Yet as Jeff Weintraub has pointed out, it is strange to attach the liberal label to the organic model that draws from theorists whose works are considered to be critical of liberalism.[44] I think Benn and Gaus might have meant that both models of publicness and privateness are concerned broadly with the issue of human freedom, which of course is the main motivation behind liberal attempts to find a public/private equilibrium. The contestation between atomistic and organic approaches to constructing the public/private distinction affects our interpretations of the meaning and significance of individual and social freedom. The issue of human freedom, however, is bigger than liberalism, and the need to reconcile public and private is not just a liberal problem. Indeed in contemporary international society, it seems that most states and societies, liberal and nonliberal, are concerned with preserving various aspects of their own freedom in international society.

My analysis suggests that states enjoy both public and private freedom derived from the terms of their membership in the society of states. Furthermore, in the Westphalian international political and legal order, intervention and freedom are polarized opposites; international society and law prize the freedom of states as a moral good while casting intervention as a general moral vice. Recent humanitarian claims at the international level, however, challenge the privacy of states as a moral good.

The moral value of individual and family privacy in domestic society has also been a subject of debate. Feminist theorists have argued that the construction of domesticity as a private or invisible sphere in western political theory and practice has historically served to justify the exclusion of women from direct and equal participation in civil and political society.[45] These spheres traditionally have recognized only men, whose visibility allowed them to claim 'equality and agency in the modern world, as independent actors in civil society and as citizens in the political community.'[46] The public/private distinction thus establishes patterns of recognition and nonrecognition that create insiders and outsiders, defined by their inclusion or exclusion from spheres of social interaction. Whereas visibility entails membership and inclusion, invisibility, by contrast, signifies exclusion, if not alienation. The discipline of International Relations has typically considered the majority of human beings in the world irrelevant to international life, as they were relegated to the private domestic jurisdiction of states. In the worldview spawned by Westphalia, states and their representatives are the insiders, the rest of humanity the outsiders. The freedom of states thus does not necessarily translate into freedom for individuals and groups within states, just as traditional conceptions of family privacy have not always translated into desirable forms of privacy for individuals, and especially women, within families. The resonance of feminist critiques of privacy in domestic relations with critiques of sovereignty as privacy in international relations leads us to re-examine the moral basis for states' public and private lives in international society.

IV Caveats

This discussion so far may allow one to agree with Jeff Weintraub that the public/private construct 'can neither be conveniently simplified nor usefully avoided,' in international as well as domestic political theory.[47] In the following chapters, I will explore how some prominent ethical perspectives understand the public/private construct at the international level, and the attendant implications for their understanding of intervention as a moral problem in world politics. Before embarking on this exploration of the ethics of intervention and the public/private construct in world politics, it may be helpful to highlight some caveats.

Distinction and dichotomy

To distinguish between 'public' and 'private' is to mark a difference between them. How are we to understand this difference in empirical and normative terms? Most obviously, when we distinguish between public and private agents, spheres, interests, activities or obligations, we are rejecting their conflation or complete identification. In positing a distinction between 'public' and 'private,' however, we must be careful not to assume a natural or unproblematic dichotomy between them. Yet the dominant trend in contemporary International Relations theory has been to assume a stark contrast between international and national spheres, interests and obligations.

Excessive dichotomization of the international/domestic distinction, evident in Martin Wight's work, for example, has led to a mistaken understanding of the problems of politics in domestic and international settings. Indeed, Wight's aim in positing such a radical divide between international and domestic realms seems to be to accentuate the unsettled, conflictual and dangerous nature of international politics. Yet the gulf he envisions disappears when we discard excessively idealistic assumptions about the nature of domestic politics, and acknowledge that even stable polities face enduring internal divisions, debates and conflicts. In reality, then, the arena of domestic politics is hardly the settled realm of certainty and 'calculable results' envisioned by Wight.[48] The claim that 'man's control of his social life' has been achieved by the institution of the modern state ignores the enduring contests over its empirical and normative dominance. For example, as Hedley Bull has noted, the 'territorial integrity of states, new and old, is now more threatened by separatist violence within their frontiers than by violence from outside.'[49] The unsettled, dynamic, and hence problematic nature of ordering social relations pertains to the domestic realm, as well as to the international domain.

Empirically, dichotomization of 'private' and 'public' leads to a denial of the complexity of units, relations and activities covered by these categories. The uniformity of the 'private' or 'domestic' realm implied by a simple dichotomous view of the distinction hides the internal complexity of most states, characterized by ethnic, religious, economic, social and normative, if not political, plurality. These nongeographical and nonstate foci of identification comprise sources of difference and affinity between people, creating patterns of community that evade the international/domestic divide. A dichotomous conception of the distinction also seems too simple when we think about the complexity of the 'public' or international stage, which admits many kinds of actors, including not only sovereign states, but also a host of regional and international organizations such as the Organization for African Unity, the United Nations, and the International Monetary Fund, as well as a plethora of nongovernmental entities ranging from multinational corporations, global religious institutions and international drug cartels, to humanitarian organizations such as the International Committee of the Red Cross, environmental groups such as the World Wildlife Fund, and individuals with an international presence such as Nelson Mandela.

Part of the complexity sacrificed by dichotomization consists of the denial that actors typically have both public and private faces. For example, an organization such as Médecins Sans Frontières may be a private or nongovernmental organization, but with a self-defined mandate that is highly public or universalist in a normative sense. Many organizations in domestic as well as world politics, that are private in the sense of being nongovernmental entities, may also be dedicated to the advancement of the common good. Both public and private actors may have responsibilities to contribute to the global collective good, albeit in distinct ways. A dichotomous conception of the public/private divide thus fails to acknowledge the complex realities of domestic, international and global life, including an intricate web, and sometimes tangle, of sources of moral legitimacy, authority and accountability feeding normative distinctions and debates that exist at both domestic and international levels. Dichotomization of the public/private construct thus not only misdescribes the nature of domestic and international politics, it also offers an inadequate account of the moral landscapes of national, international and global relations. Furthermore, dichotomization tends to pose the normative relationship between public and private in competitive terms, contrasting their moral value.

Indeed, it is common to depict the moral value of 'public' and 'private' as a zero-sum game. Norberto Bobbio, for example, notes that 'when a positive evaluative meaning is attributed to one, the second acquires a negative evaluative meaning and vice versa.'[50] This zero-sum view of the moral relationship between public and private pits them in an opposing and dichotomous ethical relationship. The more positive the moral evaluation we ascribe to the public, under this view, the more negative our moral assessments of the private must be. The ethical contrast between public and private is most apparent in the characterization of private interest as exclusively self-regarding and of the public interest as exclusively other-regarding. In a modern liberal capitalist framework, for example, the market is distinctly nonpolitical or private when we conceive of it as 'a legitimate field for competitive and self-interested individualism'[51] or 'instrumental calculation of individual advantage.'[52] In direct contrast, the state is quintessentially public in its dedication to a public interest or common good that is understood to be antithetical to individual or particular advantage. The public/private construct, so conceived, constitutes a political/ethical divide which is like the division between night and day; the public and political comprises a common world of action in concert to serve the collective good, and the nonpolitical denotes a private world that caters to individual or particular necessities and advantage.

Yet the opposite is also true; in exalting the public, we may obscure the moral potential of the private.[53] Whether we endorse a view of the primacy of the public over the private, or vice versa, such competitive constructions of the distinction miss the possibility of the ethical mutuality of public and private, international and domestic, or the extent to which the moral quality or potential of one may depend on that of the other. Rejecting dichotomous views of the distinction challenges us to reconceive the relationship between public and private, leading us to a view of their mutual interconnectedness. The public/private distinction, so conceived, is less a 'grand dichotomy' than a grand relationship that, properly conceived, allows us to recognize and reconcile the public and the private faces of individuals, collectivities and humanity.

Description and prescription

While excessive dichotomization of the public/private construct obscures the empirical and normative complexity of the world, inattention to the logical distinction between descriptive and prescriptive uses of the distinction yields theoretical confusion. As Ruth Gavison clearly admonishes, the 'terms "private" and "public" ... typically have both descriptive and normative meanings which, if not carefully distinguished, can lead to confusion or equivocation.'[54] We can detect a blending of normative description and argument in popular usages of the public/private construct. Consider statements such as 'This letter is private' or 'This problem is an internal affair.' As Benn and Gaus point out about the first example, declaring that a letter in one's possession is private implies a normative argument that it ought not to be read by others without permission: ' "Smith's letter is private (so don't read it)" invokes norms of privacy regarding letters and also prescribes a consequent forbearance.'[55] Similarly, 'China's treatment of journalists or student demonstrators is an internal or domestic matter (so don't interfere)' invokes norms of sovereignty regarding the treatment of a professional class or of dissident citizens, and also prescribes a consequent forbearance on the part of outsiders, especially other governments and state-centric international institutions.

Whereas the norms of privacy regarding letters may be located in a particular culture or society, the norms of sovereignty regarding the treatment of citizens are located in international society as much as in domestic society. Indeed, the prescription not to interfere with a state's domestic matters, however that is understood, is aimed directly at other states, the international community, and global civil society, and only indirectly at a state's internal audience. Furthermore, the rhetorical force of employing the terms 'private' and 'internal' or 'domestic' clearly lies not in their descriptive function, but in their normative and prescriptive implications.

Acknowledging the difference between normative description and argument allows us to describe something as 'private' or 'public' ('domestic' or 'international'), without committing us automatically to certain normative conclusions. For example, a person can commit an action in a private setting, hidden from the view of others, without being able to assert automatically that the action ought to remain private, or beyond the purview of social concern or public authorities. Child abuse typically occurs in private settings, hidden from the view of friends and outsiders, but in many contemporary societies, this fact does not automatically lead us to accept the normative prescription that public authorities ought not to play any interventionary role to halt such abuses. Given the varied ways in which we employ the terms 'public' and 'private,' we need to beware of uses that combine normative description and prescription.

R.J. Vincent has noted that much confusion arises in normative debates about intervention from blending 'the use of the word intervention as a description of an event in international relations and its use as a normative expression by international lawyers.'[56] To avoid such conflation, definitions of concepts such as 'public' and 'private,' 'intervention,' 'privacy' and 'sovereignty' should aim for neutrality in terms of moral value. As Anita Allen has put it in relation to defining privacy, 'privacy is a descriptive, neutral concept denoting conditions that are neither always [morally] desirable and praiseworthy, nor always undesirable and unpraiseworthy.'[57] Similarly, in domestic discourse, the term 'medical intervention' refers to actions taken by medical personnel, but the term itself is generally morally neutral, so that one can talk about appropriate and inappropriate medical interventions. Similarly we can understand state sovereignty as denoting conditions of territorial integrity and political decisional agency of a recognized government (that typically claims to represent a particular group of people within its territory), but exclude from the definition of sovereignty specific evaluative prescriptions and conclusions. Normative arguments for or against the protection of individual privacy or state sovereignty, then, cannot end with the mere designation of spheres as 'private' or 'public,' of actors as 'sovereign' or of activities as 'interventionary.'

Intrinsic and Extrinsic Valuation

Conceptions of the public/private distinction as a normative construct rely in part on how we understand the nature of the actor or activities to which the construct applies. To argue that some state action ought to be free from external interference, for example, one must defend some conception of state sovereignty as privacy, which presupposes a moral theory of statehood, just as the idea of individual privacy presupposes some moral theory of personhood. Competing moral theories of statehood differ in the kinds of moral value they attribute to the state or political community. For example, does the institution of the sovereign state have some intrinsic moral worth? Or, is the state primarily an instrumental construct, and does its sovereignty have moral value only as a norm that protects certain moral interests and goals? And how do answers to these questions help us to assess the legitimacy of interventionary practices?

In International Relations the state has historically assumed an unassailable moral right to be 'the master of what goes on inside its territory.'[58] Classical International Relations theory has tended to hold the state and a certain conception of its sovereignty as so inextricably linked that no entity that did not possess this kind of sovereignty could be considered a state; the 'state' and 'sovereignty' were largely synonymous.[59] Sovereignty understood as 'a kind of unconditional and absolute jurisdiction'[60] has thus been essential to the concept of statehood. Consequently, the ethical primacy of such sovereignty has been a normative given in the moral landscape of international politics until very recently. Such a view, however, makes intervention inherently morally problematic, since 'intervention, defined as an act aimed at influencing the domestic affairs of a state,' directly contravenes state sovereignty.[61] In an international society of states where such sovereignty is elevated to the status of an inviolable feature of statehood, it would be difficult to justify its violation.

The desire to preserve an absolutist conception of state sovereignty has thus been tied to preserving the sovereign state's intrinsic, as opposed to instrumental or derivative moral value. Endowing the sovereign state with intrinsically positive moral worth accounts for the convoluted battles in the International Relations literature over the definition of intervention, the basic logic of which was to bypass direct questioning of sovereignty's value by denying that justifiable forms of intervention constituted intervention; such a definitional strategy created the awkward need to assert that 'intervention by right is not intervention.'[62] Adopting this value-laden account of sovereignty tends to close off the possibility of justifying intervention for any reason, as it pre-empts the ability to question sovereignty's moral value.

In contrast, those who argue against sovereignty's inviolability typically characterize the state as an instrumental construct, and the right of state autonomy as 'derivative of more basic principles of justice.'[63] Adopting a functionalist or instrumental view of sovereignty seems to clear the path towards the possibility of assessing sovereignty's normative worth. Anita Allen addresses the question of intrinsic versus instrumental value in her account of individual privacy.[64] If we take an instrumentalist view, however, we need to clarify whose and what types of moral interests and goals state sovereignty is designed to serve, and the relationship between these and other moral interests and goals. In cases where protection of the sovereignty norm would undermine these or other more significant moral goods, its violation may be justified. Understanding sovereignty as an instrumental norm allows us, then, not to deny that intervention contravenes sovereignty, but to justify that violation. We can then argue about whether a certain action in the context of a specific situation constitutes justified or unjustified intervention, instead of arguing about whether it is or is not intervention.

In fact, as Katie McShane has so cogently argued, the determination that something has intrinsic value, by itself, cannot sustain the argument that it is therefore inviolable or trumps all other values: 'intrinsic value does *not* mean absolute value. There's nothing about the concept of intrinsic value . . . that says intrinsic values are always more important than extrinsic values, or that they can never be outweighed by other considerations, or that possessing intrinsic value makes a thing inviolable.'[65] This is especially true when we understand intrinsic value claims as arguments about '*how* it make sense for us to care about the thing' in question, rather than how *much* to care about them.[66] This means that one can hold that the state or, more broadly, political community has intrinsic value, but still argue that intervention is justified in certain circumstances for certain morally-weighty reasons. Or, one may determine that the state only has extrinsic or instrumental value, but still be able to argue that, under certain conditions, its rights to sovereignty or nonintervention ought not to be violated.[67] Debates about the intrinsic versus instrumental or derivative value of the state thus will not settle the question of the legitimacy of intervention, although they may affect how interventions are justified.

V   Conclusion

Understanding intervention as a moral problem in domestic, international and global relations requires an examination of the public/private construct that disciplines the public and the private lives of various kinds of units, including individuals, states and civil society actors at multiple levels of interaction. In the next two chapters, I will explore realist and communitarian constructions of the public and the private in international relations. It will become clear that both perspectives want to endorse states' claims to privacy vis-à-vis international society. Yet although both are concerned to preserve state privacy as a moral good, they rely on models of the public/private distinction that fail to generate a morally compelling account of sovereignty as privacy. Consequently, both offer morally flawed assessments of the legitimacy of interventionary actions in world politics. The rest of this work will then be devoted to an examination of a cosmopolitan conception of the public/private construct at the global level, and its implications for our understanding of state privacy in international society, and the legitimacy of intervention in general, and various forms of 'humanitarian intervention' in particular, in contemporary world politics.

3
Realism and the Tyranny of the Private

> In an unorganized realm each unit's incentive is to put itself in a position to be able to take care of itself since no one else can be counted on to do so. The international imperative is 'take care of yourself'!
>
> Kenneth Waltz, *Theory of International Politics*[1]

I Introduction

The realist vision of world politics has enjoyed great intellectual prominence in the discipline of International Relations. How does this perspective see the structure of the international domain and its players? What is its understanding of the public/private construct that underlies the international system? What contributions can it make to a normative inquiry into the legitimacy of intervention, especially 'humanitarian intervention'?

Before tackling these questions it is important to note that realism is internally varied, with its proponents as well as its critics engaged in a perpetual debate over the substance, meaning and cogency of its fundamental precepts. Modern realism was born amidst the rubble of two World Wars, and like an orphaned child of war who grows to maturity in relation to an unrecoverable past, it is a perspective that has had to invent its own history and original founders.[2] The search by contemporary realists for their roots – in Thucydides, Machiavelli, Hobbes and Rousseau – has led to diverse interpretations of the precise nature of realism's vision of world politics.[3] Interestingly, these efforts have perhaps been more revealing of the views of modern realists than of the past thinkers on whose works they draw their insights. In this discussion I will focus my critique on the neorealist perspective and, in particular,

Kenneth Waltz's enduring work, *A Theory of International Politics*, that has dominated American contemporary realist scholarship. I will also employ Hobbes as a foil to neorealism in order to point the way towards a more compelling normative vision of realism.

Many neorealists such as Waltz are likely to object to the characterization of their views as constituting a normative vision of world politics, for they tend not to see the enterprise of theorizing about international politics as a normative endeavour. These realists tend to be moral sceptics who claim to premise their analyses and prescriptions on how things *are* in the world, rather than on how one might think or wish they *ought* to be. Machiavelli articulated this view in his famous tract, *The Prince*:

> my intention being to write something of use to those who understand, it appears to me more proper to go to the real truth of the matter than to its imagination; and many have imagined republics and principalities which have never been seen or known to exist in reality; for how we live is so far removed from how we ought to live, that he who abandons what is done for what ought to be done, will rather learn to bring about his own ruin than his preservation.[4]

Against the idealism of political philosophers who presuppose the significance of human moral agency and vision, 'realism is founded on a pessimism regarding moral progress and human possibilities.'[5] To these realists, whatever visions of justice or the good life one imagines may govern International Relations in theory, they can only remain unfulfilled strivings in an international arena governed by certain immutable laws of political necessity founded on the elemental goal of national self-preservation in an anarchic international system.

Given that international politics can only ever be a repetitive and incessant struggle for power between states striving to maximize their own national interests,[6] a significant strand of realism questions the very relevance of moral motivation, reasoning and inquiry in the international domain. Realists, however, are not mere observers of the international scene; they not only describe how states conduct themselves in international affairs, they also engage in debates about how states ought to act. As Sheldon Wolin has observed, even Machiavelli's vision of politics entails a combination of imagination and representation.[7] A realist prescription, such as the common one that a state must always act in its national interest if it is to survive, constitutes a normative argument or imperative that advances a narrowly conceived national interest as the sole motivation of state conduct, and political necessity as its ultimate justification or apology.

The dominance of realist political discourse in the study of International Relations is evident in the persistent use of the concept of national interest by scholars and practitioners to determine foreign policy, especially in the United States. As David Welch has figuratively observed, 'It is difficult to find two consecutive pages of prominent journals such as *Foreign Affairs, Foreign Policy*, and – of course – *The National Interest* where the term does not appear.'[8] Meanwhile, statesmen and pundits continue to pay homage to realist rhetoric.

During the 1999 NATO intervention in Kosovo, former statesman Henry Kissinger asserted that a viable American and NATO foreign policy must be anchored 'in a clear definition of the national interest.'[9] The US President George W. Bush justified the military invasion of Iraq in terms of securing US national interest, declaring that the United States 'has the sovereign authority to use force in assuring its own national security.'[10] In the autumn before the war, 33 prominent International Relations scholars, many of them realists, declared in an advertisement on the New York *Times* op-ed page that 'War with Iraq is *not* in America's national interest.'[11] As violent conflict in Iraq continues, former advisor to Bill Clinton, Sidney Blumenthal, has taken the Bush administration to task for allowing the 'dream world of ideology' to trump 'the national interest.'[12] These divergent uses of the concept of national interest show that even if one accepts the realist insistence on using the national interest as an inescapable guide for foreign policy, it is not clear how realism disciplines and evaluates proper and improper appeals to the concept.

While realists might use the concept of national interest to set limits on the interventionary actions of states, some might argue that it sets the wrong ethical limits. Thus Roméo Dallaire, the former commander of the UN mission in Rwanda during the 1994 genocide, has criticized Western governments for their failure to intervene in the Darfur region of Sudan. He laments, 'Although the early stages of the Darfur situation received more news coverage than the Rwanda genocide did, at some level the Western governments are still approaching it with the same lack of priority. In the end, it receives the same intuitive reaction: "What's in it for us? Is it in our 'national interest?' " '[13] The issue of 'humanitarian intervention' creates special discomfort for the realist perspective precisely because it challenges the narrow interpretation of national interest that many realists have assumed as a fixed and unchanging given. In opening debate about how to conceive of the national interest, the problem of 'humanitarian intervention' also challenges other core realist tenets, such as the ethical primacy of state interests over wider moral interests and claims, as well as the assumption of a positive connection between interstate peace and 'human security.'[14] Understanding and assessing a realist view of 'humanitarian intervention' entails an evaluation of the theoretical and practical cogency of realist interpretations of national interest, political necessity and morality in international relations. This involves an examination of how realism conceives of the nature of the state, as well as its distinction from and relationship with others in the international realm. In other words, one must examine how a realist perspective conceives of the public/private construct at the international level.

II Private states, atomistic world

Realists typically characterize the arena of international politics as a Hobbesian state of nature, where states, with no political superior above them and no common morality between them, act according to the principle of self-help and pursue their own interests, the most fundamental of which is survival. For Hobbes, the state of nature in which individuals without a common superior engage in a zero-sum struggle for survival arises as a logical conclusion of his assertion that self-interest, defined by each individual as the satisfaction of his or her own particular appetites and the avoidance of his or her particular aversions, is the spring of all human behaviour. Hobbes's great work, *Leviathan*, begins with an account of the human physical body as the source of all human experience and thoughts.[15] The physical separateness of human beings as individuals is significant in Hobbes's philosophy because it is there that he locates the original source of all human motivations and behaviours, appetites and aversions. Given Hobbes's account of human motivations, efforts to achieve human solidarity, or to motivate individuals to act in concert for a common purpose, are fraught with complications, for 'men have no pleasure, (but on the contrary a great deal of griefe) in keeping company, where there is no power able to over-awe them all.'[16] Humans are essentially private beings, thus they do not naturally seek society, but have to be enticed or terrorized into society, through positive and negative incentives that affect their self-interest, the most fundamental being their own physical survival.

Modern realists have transferred this account of individuals and human motivation to the dominant actors in the international realm, encouraged perhaps by Hobbes's characterization of states as artificial persons.[17] Kenneth Waltz thus sees the self-interest of states as a key element of realism:

> The ruler's, and later the state's, interest provides the spring of action; the necessities of policy arise from the unregulated competition of states; calculation based on these necessities can discover the policies that will best serve a state's interests; success is the ultimate test of policy, and success is defined as preserving and strengthening the state.[18]

Waltz does not merely assert that self-interest is one element of state motivation, it is the spring of all state behaviour. States have at bottom only private, or exclusively particular, identities, interests and aims. A contemporary realist conception of the national interest is thus quite narrow: neorealism's dominance in international relations can be seen in 'the prevalent tendency to interpret all state behavior as narrowly self-interested.'[19] According to a neorealist perspective, then, although states may comprise the public realm in domestic relations, in international relations, states are fundamentally private actors, atomistic and self-regarding, without any shared identities and interests greater than themselves. Furthermore, neorealists often conceive the national interest to be dichotomously opposed to the interests of others, a typical outcome of an atomistic conception of the public/private construct.

Waltz employs analogies with microeconomic theory to depict the international context and its players. 'International-political systems, like economic markets,' he writes, 'are formed by the coacting of self-regarding units.'[20] Just as a classical liberal market-model of society conceives of 'individuals pursuing their self-interest more or less efficiently and rationally,'[21] a neorealist image of international society sees the same kind of social reality between states. The market image of the international system assumes the preferences of actors as given, as social constructivists have pointed out.[22] For our purposes, however, it is not just the fact that the liberal market model assumes actors' preferences that is problematic; more substantively, the problem is that it privileges a specific account of actors' preferences, as being driven by private or exclusive aspects of actors' identities, interests and ends: 'The market arises out of the activities of separate units – persons and firms – whose aims and efforts are directed not toward creating an order but rather toward fulfilling their own internally defined interests by whatever means they can muster. The individual unit acts for itself.'[23] The assumption of a radical separation between the self and the other is clear: units have only particular and exclusive 'internally defined interests,' and lack any externally defined or internalized common or shared interests or norms. This market model of systems and units when transferred to the realm of politics confirms Waltz's image of the international domain as one tyrannized by atomistic private interests and judgement.

Paradoxically, although neorealists identify national survival as a universal interest, in that it accounts for all state behaviour, it is not universal in a public or common sense, in that the interest each state has in its own preservation is not shared by other states. In the following passage, Waltz confirms that a neorealist perspective views states as quintessentially private rather than public actors in world politics, and asserts that this atomism means that states have no shared or public interest in preserving each other:

> Nationally, private force used against a government threatens the political system. Force used by a state – a public body – is, from the international perspective, the private use of force; but there is no government to overthrow and no governmental apparatus to capture. Short of a drive toward world hegemony, the private use of force does not threaten the system of international politics, only some of its members.[24]

What is universal, then, is private interest and judgement. It is this belief in the absolute privateness of the state, resulting in the complete lack of any foundation for a common life between states in the international realm that underpins the neorealist construction of the public context in which states relate.

Waltz and other structural neorealists attempt to argue that the fault lies not in the nature of states, but in their stars, as it were; states are not innately selfish, but their self-centredness is imposed by their external environment, which is defined by the absence of common identities, interests, power, authority and norms. In this vein Waltz asserts that internationally, 'decisions are made at the bottom level, *there being scarcely any other.*'[25] Given this absence, international politics can only be the by-product of clashes between mutually exclusive private actors and interests. Even where opportunities for mutual gain might lead to the development of common interests and cooperation between states, Waltz claims that the structure of anarchy fragments whatever commonality may exist, compelling states 'to ask not "Will both of us gain?"

but "Who will gain more?" '[26] Waltz's realism clearly cannot comprehend an organic conception of the public international realm as an organized society, 'consisting of mutually connected and dependent parts consti- tuted to share a common life.'[27] As Leo McCarthy has noted, such realism even 'denies the existence of an international society, where "society" is understood to imply states co-existing in mutually recog- nised interdependence, according to common and binding rules and with a significant degree of shared moral and cultural understanding.'[28]

It is important to remember, however, that a realist image of the international realm stems from its atomistic understanding of the nature of states, just as Hobbes's state of nature finds its origin in his atomistic conception of the individual human being. States are fated to co-exist in mutual insecurity in an unintended system, according to universally private, as in particular and exclusive, interests and judge- ment, because of their essentially atomistic nature, which produces their anarchic environment.[29] It is this exclusively atomistic interpreta- tion of the ontology of states that accounts for the realist tendency to assume a restrictive conception of national interest. In the realist alphabet, 'A' is for 'atomism,' rather than 'anarchy.'

Realism's atomistic conception of the state affects its interpretation of sovereignty, a state's primary external attribute. Waltz is careful to caution that sovereignty does not give states the practical ability to do as they please. Rather, the attribute of sovereignty means that a state

> decides for itself how it will cope with its internal and external problems, including whether or not to seek assistance from others and in doing so to limit its freedom by making commitments to them. States develop their own strategies, chart their own courses, make their own decisions about how to meet whatever needs they experience and whatever desires they develop.[30]

As self-directing actors in international society, states possess decisional agency. Waltz clearly views such sovereignty as an integral aspect of a state's identity and interest. National survival means not only territorial integrity but also political independence.

Although realists do not tend to evaluate state sovereignty in normative terms, Waltz clearly favours a system of sovereign states over a world government, the tyranny of the private over the potentially devastating tyranny of the public.[31] Indeed, while he mostly laments anarchy as a necessary feature of interstate relations, he also celebrates its virtues, which seem to lie in the freedom it affords states in international society. Although from a realist point of view, security is the central preoccupation of states, Waltz observes that states, 'like people, are insecure in proportion to the extent of their freedom. If freedom is wanted, insecurity must be accepted.' One virtue of anarchy is the freedom it affords all from the will of others, for in anarchy 'people or states are free to leave one another alone.'[32] With this argument, Waltz seems to be making a normative claim that an anarchic world order is more desirable from a moral point of view than a more integrated one that might impose burdens on states and inhibit the state's privacy understood in terms of national decisional autonomy.

Realism's atomistic interpretation of sovereignty is akin to Catharine MacKinnon's critical characterization of privacy as 'that which is inaccessible to, unaccountable to, unconstructed by, anything beyond itself. By definition, it is not part of or conditioned by anything systematic outside it.'[33] Yet realism's atomistic conception of the social context in which states relate to each other makes the maintenance of state sovereignty as a normative right to decisional autonomy highly problematic. For given the problem of the tyranny of private judgement and the consequent absence of meaningful moral discourse at the international level, it would seem theoretically impossible for realists to construct any normative understanding of state sovereignty as privacy. Thus, although the absence of any common public interest between states means that 'there can be no intervention which is expressive of the common purposes of international society,'[34] realists also cannot make any meaningful normative arguments against intervention, humanitarian or otherwise.

As Hobbes realized, the idea of a *moral* entitlement to anything cannot have validity in the state of nature: 'It is consequent also to the same condition, that there be no Propriety, no Dominion, no *Mine* and *Thine* distinct; but onely that to be every mans that he can get; and for so long, as he can keep it.'[35] Leo McCarthy thus concludes, 'No sort of interventionary activity is [morally] problematic from a Hobbesian viewpoint, because there can be no binding principles in states' relations with each other.'[36] In this vein, Hans Morgenthau similarly argued that 'it is futile to search for an abstract principle which would allow us to distinguish in a concrete case between legitimate and illegitimate intervention.'[37] Ironically then, although realists assert that private judgement prevails in the international domain, there is no possibility to safeguard state privacy in a normative sense of denoting either decisional autonomy or an inviolable sphere of territory or action from which a state may justifiably exclude others. States may be wholly private actors at the international level, but precisely because of this, they cannot make any meaningful moral claim to sovereignty as privacy.

Hobbes recognized this in his assertion that in the state of nature, 'every man has a Right to every thing; even to one anothers body.'[38] By 'right,' Hobbes means only the natural ability people have to secure anything that helps them to maintain their own lives. He does not see rights as moral claims, but as liberties (conceived in a nonmoral sense as the mere ability to do something due to the absence of external impediments) that 'each man hath, to use his own power, as he will himselfe, for the preservation of his own Nature; that is to say, of his own Life; and consequently, of doing any thing, which in his own Judgement, and Reason, hee shall conceive to be the aptest means thereunto.'[39] To Hobbes, without society, people have this natural 'right,' but it is precisely because they all nearly possess this natural 'right' or ability that people have no security over their possessions, including their own lives. Similarly, by having such a 'right' to everything, no state has security over anything, not its own government, population, territory or other resources. In the absence of international society, states may not be owned by a world Leviathan, but states also may not be secure in owning themselves. Logically, then, if states exist in a Hobbesian state of nature, it is not possible to maintain a meaningful distinction between public and private spheres, or international and domestic realms, as most realists have assumed. Hobbes solves the problem of sovereignty only internally, but he does not offer states any guarantee of external sovereignty. The internal sovereignty of states is thus perpetually contingent on a state's power or ability to maintain its independence from other states that have no obligation at the international level to recognize its internal sovereignty.

This logical consequence of an atomistic conception of international society has been lost on some contemporary realists. Part of Kissinger's critique of American involvement in the Kosovo conflict, for example, relied on the concept of sovereignty as a normative right. In a disapproving tone he writes that the Kosovo agreement reached 'under the threat of NATO bombardment...involves nearly unprecedented international intercession. Yugoslavia, a sovereign state, is being asked to cede control and in time sovereignty of a province containing its national shrines to foreign military force.'[40] Kissinger may be right in his critique of the agreement, but in a world resembling a Hobbesian state of nature, no normative argument for the protection of Yugoslav sovereignty can have much validity.

This limitation of neorealism highlights the social or public nature of rights as moral claims, even of such rights as privacy and sovereignty, for the very idea of a moral, as opposed to natural, right to privacy or sovereignty can be established only 'within the embrace of community norms.'[41] As Robert Post has noted about privacy in a domestic context, 'privacy is for us a living reality only because we enjoy a certain kind of communal existence.'[42] Neorealists, by denying the social foundations necessary for a normative conception of sovereignty, cannot make a coherent moral defence of sovereignty as privacy. Without it, intervention as a moral problem ceases to exist. Deprived of the power of words, only the sword is available to realists to protect states and people from external intrusion. Practically, then, only the most powerful actors in the system, the great powers, can enjoy any security in the maintenance of their privacy in terms of decisional autonomy. The logic of a neorealist view of international morality thus does not provide any standpoint from which to mount a moral critique of the actions of powerful states, even when they intervene in the internal affairs of weaker states, for humanitarian or any other purposes. In such a world, justice quickly becomes the interest of the stronger party.[43] In this vein, Richard Ned Lebow has noted that while contemporary realists and neorealists opposed the 2003 war in Iraq, and therefore cannot be held responsible for contemporary US foreign policy, 'the discourse they sustain is surprisingly influential and illustrates the dangers of divorcing political analysis from ethical discourse.'[44]

The paradox is that in the absence of society in the form of shared norms, there can be no normative right to privacy; in the absence of international society, there can be no normative right to sovereignty, upon which a coherent normative account of intervention depends. This paradox points to the mutual interconnectedness of private and public, domestic and international, rather than their dichotomous separation as neorealists imagine. Ironically, in positing the radical dichotomization of private and public, modern realism can provide no coherent argument in favour of their distinction. Thus, intervention as a moral problem, in so far as it implies the existence of such an argument, eludes contemporary realist understanding.

III The social construction of necessity

One prominent strand of realism holds that the absence or irrelevance of stringent common norms at the international level is a regrettable but inevitable feature of international life. This is because the ontological atomism of the state translates not only into the political fragmentation of international society, but also into a moral atomism between states. Indeed, the dominance of private judgement in Hobbes's state of nature seems to render problematic the very idea of a public interest or morality. Hobbes argued that given a state of nature where individuals were moved only by self-interest in the form of particular appetites and aversions, and were without a common superior, morality as a public or shared system of normative rules could not be established:

> these words of Good, Evill, and Contemptible, are ever used with relation to the person that useth them: There being nothing simply and absolutely so; nor any common Rule of Good and Evill, to be taken from the nature of the objects themselves; but from the Person of the man (where there is no Common-wealth).[45]

The problem for any conception of international justice and morality is the problem of the tyranny of the private. While the idea of morality is possible in the context of domestic society, according to modern realists, only due to the presence of a coercive power, conventional morality is unintelligible in an anarchical international realm, for '[to] this warre of every man against every man, this also is consequent; that nothing can be Unjust. The notions of Right and Wrong, Justice and Injustice have there no place.'[46] Steven Forde thus observes that while many realists want to maintain a distinction between international and domestic morality, the 'most thoroughgoing realist maintains that ... morality is a fraud or an illusion in all areas of human life.'[47] Thus realists cannot argue for a qualitative difference between public and private morality, but at best only a quantitative difference in terms of how much right behaviour can be enforced under each condition. One should note here neorealism's impoverished conception of morality, which equates coerced compliance with moral action. To neorealists this is the only kind of 'morality' possible, a morality of fact rather than intention, because the atomistic depiction of states deprives them of the capacity for moral agency. On this interpretation, the dominance of private judgement means that no notion of public interest or morality is conceivable at the international level.

This moral absence in relations between states leads such sceptical realists to depict the international realm as a domain of amoral necessity. As Benjamin Frankel has observed: 'There is no debate among realists ... that, at a minimum, states are worried about their security and that they act vigilantly to enhance that security in an environment which offers them *no choice* but to do so.'[48] It was in this vein that Hans Morgenthau argued, for example, that although 'lying is immoral' in individual relations, 'when you are dealing in the context of foreign policy, lying is *inevitable*.'[49] The dominance of necessity, fated by international conditions, absolves states of moral responsibilities,[50] just as it dissolves ordinary moral duties of individuals in society. For example, one may not think that the 3 million children who die annually from diarrhoeal infection, caused by poor sanitation and the lack of clean drinking water,[51] deserve in any sense their impoverished and perilous conditions; rather one thinks of their plight as bad luck, a piece of misfortune. One might also think that it was sheer luck to be born in, or to have emigrated to, richer climes. Thus, we tolerate the moral inferiority of international to domestic conditions out of a view of its necessity rather than a belief in its justice.

The idea that justice and morality can be bounded, or excluded from certain realms of public and private life due to necessity, has a long history. The ancient Greeks, as Bernard Williams has shown, believed that chance and necessity governed certain types of social relations, precluding considerations of justice. Thus, being a slave was the paradigm, not of injustice but of bad luck. It is not that the Greeks denied the misery of slaves, or thought that it was just for some to be slaves. They simply viewed necessity and luck to '*take the place of* considerations of justice.'[52] Yet I am reminded of *The Mission*, a film in which a papal delegate, Altimirano, must come to terms with his own role in the slaughter of Guarani Indians and European Jesuits at a mission in Paraguay that occurs in the context of eighteenth-century religious and political battles between Spain and Portugal.[53] A subordinate attempts to appease him, saying that the destruction was inevitable and necessary, for 'the world is thus.' The film closes with Altimirano's response: 'No, thus have we made the world.' Characterizing the international domain as a realm of necessity obscures the highly normative and intersubjective nature of its construction, just as viewing slavery as an institution of necessity hides its injustice. The idea of necessity assumes an unchanging permanence to existing norms and interests, and thus does not help us to explain or understand changes, in practice and in theory, that have occurred in our understandings of the national interest, state sovereignty and humanity, nor does it prompt us to explore how and why our interpretations may change in the future.[54]

While neorealists such as Waltz acknowledge only mutually exclusive sources of national interest, social constructivists point to the public sources of states' identities, interests and conduct. What realists miss in denying the public face of states is the public or social construction of their private interests. As Martha Finnemore has put it in a perceptive study of national interests in international society, 'Interests are not "out there" waiting to be discovered; they are constructed through social interaction.'[55] The work of social constructivists in the study of International Relations opens the door to a more expansive view of states' identities, interests and motivations by recognizing the embeddedness of states in an international web of social norms. If we accept the constructivist insight that state interests 'are shaped by internationally shared norms and values that structure and give meaning to international political life,'[56] then we only ignore the tools, process and purposes of that construction to the detriment of our understanding of states and international society.

At one level Waltz seems to acknowledge the socially constructed nature of states' interests; he sides with Rousseau in asserting that the 'context of action must always be considered.'[57] Indeed, he argues that it is precisely because states exist in a certain social context, that is in the presence of other similarly motivated actors and in the absence of an overarching coercive power, that their strategies for survival are dependent on the strategies of others. What social constructivists challenge is the necessity of Waltz's particular construction of the international context, a necessity driven primarily by fixed and partial images of private and public, of states and their interaction.

International politics will certainly remain impoverished if states and other actors at the global level come to the public realm with only narrowly construed private interests, seeking only to satisfy exclusively singular interests by any means necessary. Indeed it was precisely the economic model of politics that Hannah Arendt viewed as a threat to the ancient Greek idea of public life, a quintessentially common political life that distinguished Greeks from barbarians, and participation in which marked the attainment of a truly human existence.[58] The logic of the economic domain that Waltz employs as an analogy for the international realm accords with Arendt's category of 'society,' which was a 'curiously hybrid realm where private interests assume public significance.'[59] Arendt deplored the rise of the social or economic view of humanity, and the privatized vision of politics that dominated the public realm in its wake. Her condemnation can be aptly applied to the neorealist depiction of an international realm dominated by private interest and judgement:

> [in such an instance] men have *become* entirely private, that is, they have been *deprived* of seeing and hearing others, of being seen and being heard by them. They are all *imprisoned* in the subjectivity of

their own singular experience, which does not cease to be singular if the same experience is multiplied innumerable times. The end of the common world has come when it is seen only under one aspect and *is permitted* to present itself in only one perspective.[60]

Whereas realists view the public realm as a battleground for essentially private interests, Arendt envisions the public realm as a space devoted to the common good, a realm of public concerns that are qualitatively different from those that arise in the private realm. Whereas Arendt 'tried hardest to renew our access to politics as a positive gratification, a "public happiness," '[61] Waltz and realists in general conceive of politics as an inherently and inescapably burdensome struggle to maintain survival at a minimum, and private gratification and happiness at a maximum. In some ways, however, Arendt and Waltz have strikingly similar views of the public/private distinction. For both hold a dichotomous view of the construct, and both exalt images of the public, while morally debasing the private. Adhering to this ethical contrast between public and private means that both miss the transformative potential generated by the mutual interconnection of private and public.

Hanna Pitkin seeks to validate Arendt's conception of public life, arguing that it is only with a public life in an Arendtian sense that we have 'the possibility of a shared, collective, deliberate, active intervention in our fate, in what would otherwise be the by-product of private decisions.' As opposed to the unintended and seemingly undemanding system produced by Waltz's image of international politics, this vision of public life affords us the opportunity and challenge 'jointly, as a community, [to] exercise the human capacity "to think what we are doing." '[62] Attempts to achieve a public life in this sense at the international level may be especially difficult, yet the efforts to survive in a Waltzian dog-eat-dog world would certainly be no less taxing.

Waltz and most contemporary realists deny the possibility of any sense of public interest developing between states, mainly because they deny the transformative potential afforded by a mutually interconnected view of the public/private relationship. Recognizing this transformative potential does not rely on a denial of self-interest as a human motivation. Rather, it relies on an image of the mutual implication of private and public as opposed to their radical dichotomization and contrast. States may initially enter into the public international realm with self-defined needs and interests. Through interaction, or a dynamic interplay of private and public, however, states' interests and motivations may change even as they contribute to changing the nature of the public normative context in which they find expression. As Pitkin has so eloquently put it in relation to individuals in society,

> Drawn into public life by personal need, fear, ambition or interest, we are there forced to acknowledge the power of others and appeal to their standards, even as we try to get them to acknowledge our power and standards. We are forced to find or create a common language of purposes and aspirations, not merely to clothe our private outlook in public disguise, but to become aware ourselves of its public meaning.... In the process, we learn to think about the standards themselves, about our stake in the existence of standards, of justice, of our community, even of our opponents and enemies in the community; so that afterwards we are changed.[63]

Of course, this transformative vision of public life only admits the possibility of developing an international 'public interest' and morality, rather than determining its inevitability or even the desirability of its actual development. The denial of the very possibility stems from a blindness to the agency of states to effect transformations of private interests through public interaction. It is ultimately this morally stunted view of states' privateness, rather than the 'fact' of anarchy, that fates neorealism to perpetuate a morally limited world. With a more expansive view of states, one that includes the public sources of their identities and interests, agency and motivation, we give rise to the possibility of a radically different vision of international politics for humankind.

It is important to note that in asserting that the private nature of states makes untenable, rather than merely difficult, the creation of public or common identities, interests, norms and ends, Waltz departs significantly from Hobbes, whose political philosophy offers a rigorous system of public morality, albeit one that is ultimately derived from the self-interests of atomistic individuals. Although Hobbes likened the realm of international politics to a state of nature, wherein 'Kings, and Persons of Soveraigne authority, because of their Independency, are in continuall jealousies, and in the state and posture of Gladiators ... which is a posture of War,'[64] Hobbes also affirmed the possibility and efficacy of leagues of commonwealths founded on the interests of states (in peace and justice), just as commonwealths themselves are founded on the particular interests of individuals:

> For a League being a connexion of men by Covenants, if there be no power given to any one Man or Assembly, (as in the condition of

meer Nature) to compell them to performance, is so long onely valid, as there ariseth no just cause of distrust: and therefore Leagues between Common-wealths, over whom there is no humane Power established, to keep them all in awe, are not onely lawfull [because they are allowed by the commonwealth], but also profitable for the time they last.[65]

The realist challenge that international politics is dominated by self-interested states may thus not be as catastrophic for international morality as it may seem. Indeed for Hobbes, self-interest in individual survival is precisely what leads to the creation of the Leviathan, or a moral order, between individuals. If the establishment of a world Leviathan, or a global moral order, is not as likely between states, it is not because of the necessities imposed by anarchy, but precisely because it is unnecessary to establish such an order, since 'that misery, which accompanies the Liberty of particular men'[66] is mitigated in a condition of interstate anarchy. Despite his atomistic conception of individuals, Hobbes's political philosophy allows us to envision the establishment of a commonwealth and public authority. Waltz's political vision, blind to the mutual interconnections between public and private, misses their transformative potential; hence, for Waltz, atomistic states are fated to live in a morally barren world.

IV   National interest and the public interest

To recover a more viable interpretation of realism as a normative perspective, a realist might return to Hobbes, who based his system of public morality at the domestic level on individuals' interest in self-preservation. A Hobbesian realist might construct rules of international morality based on the mutual advantage of states, with national survival as the most basic interest that must be served by any legitimate system of normative rules between states. International standards of right and wrong, just and unjust, would be grounded in the self-interests of states, the main actors in world politics. The motivation to be just has to appeal to the national interest, and the international public interest cannot require states to act at the expense of their national private interest.

One normative position that flows from this characterization of international morality is that the moral duty of each state to look to its own survival constitutes a limiting factor on what the public interest can demand of states in the way of sacrifice. No state can have a moral obligation to act in accordance with a conception of the public interest that would require it to forfeit its own survival, or the survival of its people. Safeguarding the national interest in survival leads to a morality of prudence that eschews confrontational actions that might threaten a state's self-preservation. Given the controversial nature of interventions in the internal affairs of other states, a morality of prudence is likely to counsel state leaders against embarking on such dangerous enterprises. Yet as David Welch has pointed out, 'the survival of the state is almost never at stake in international politics.'[67] Where the survival of a state is not jeopardized, it is difficult to see how realist prudence so construed would constitute a determinate principle to guide state policies regarding intervention. For example, even despite ill-conceived, not to mention illegitimate, interventions, such as the one in Vietnam, the United States has not perished as a state.

Realists might use the idea of the national interest to place limits on what may be risked in terms of military losses. Thus in 1999, Kissinger drew the line at using American ground forces in Kosovo.[68] Yet losing some soldiers in a military enterprise cannot be equated with the death of the intervening state. This is not to argue that one should be morally indifferent to risking the lives of one's soldiers, but it seems misleading to equate the national interest with the safety of one's military forces, for if that were the case, it would be difficult to justify the use of military force for any purpose, including the maintenance of international peace and security. The rhetoric of the national interest thus obscures important normative debates about how national military forces may be legitimately and effectively employed in response to humanitarian crises and conflicts in other countries.[69]

One can also understand Waltz's normative evaluation of an anarchical international system as entailing a conception of international morality based on a narrowly conceived national interest. Waltz's account of the virtues of anarchy constitutes a normative endorsement of the pursuit by states of their narrowly conceived national interests, since he argues that such conduct leads to an outcome that is favourable to states' interests in self-preservation, in particular, their independence. Similarly, George Kennan has argued that if states act only out of narrowly self-interested concerns, they are unlikely to engage in grand imperialistic projects or interventions that threaten the independence of other political communities.[70] Yet the idea that a system of states acting on a narrow interpretation of national interest may yield a morally defensible or desirable international order would seem to share affinities with the harmony of interests thesis, forwarded by nineteenth-century liberal idealists, that realists have sought to critique.[71]

E.H. Carr's indictment of the harmony of interests thesis is considered a classic realist critique of idealism. His arguments, however, could be interpreted as a moral critique of a realist, rather than idealist, view of politics. He rightly found fault with the illusion that 'nations in serving themselves serve humanity,'[72] which involved the assumption of an unproblematic harmony of the general with particular interests. He recognized clearly that the common public interest might entail a sacrifice of some particular or private ambitions, and that denial of this reality was 'fatal to any effective conception of international morality.'[73] Rather than endorsing a self-interest-driven politics, he sought to expose its moral failings, for by attacking the harmony of interests thesis, he was removing the cloak that gave realist self-interest-driven politics an illusion of respectability. Seen in this light, his ethical critique is first aimed at those who pursued narrow national interests at the expense of, or with indifference to, the general interest, and second, at those who naively identified 'the good of the whole international community with the good of that part of it in which we are particularly interested.'[74] If it were idealism that Carr was attacking, it was a rather strange brand, for the 'idealists' he attacked were not those who acted altruistically to serve humanity, forfeiting their self-interests, but those who served themselves while claiming to serve all of humankind.

Carr, unlike Waltz, does not claim that the idea of a public, general or common interest at the international level is inconceivable. His arguments actually raise the question of what might constitute the general interest at the international level, which he thought states and 'liberal idealists' wrongly neglected to the detriment of international morality. Although Waltz claims that no such general interest can exist in an anarchical system, his normative arguments in favour of anarchy actually reveal a certain conception of the international public interest as consisting of two elements: states' interests in preserving their political and territorial independence, and in maintaining international peace or stability. It is clear from the preceding discussion that Waltzian realism can provide no coherent argument to support a normative right of states to their continued independence. What positive contributions can anarchy, or an atomistic international system, make to the public interest understood as the preservation of international peace and stability?

In his earlier work, Waltz found in international anarchy the permissive cause of war,[75] but in *Theory of International Politics*, he also notes its potential to contribute positively to the maintenance of world peace. The condition of international anarchy, it seems, does not necessarily facilitate the scourge of humankind, but may be its saviour. Under the condition of anarchy, he argues, the 'constant possibility that force will be used limits manipulations, moderates demands, and serves as an incentive for the settlement of disputes. One who knows that pressing too hard may lead to war has strong reason to consider whether possible gains are worth the risks entailed.'[76] Of course, in a world with a considerably unequal distribution of military capabilities, the constant reliance on the threat or use of force to discipline relations between states obviously favours the more powerful, having an immoderate effect on their demands, while effectively silencing the (right and just) claims of weaker states. To Waltz, however, since states can have no claims of justice or right against other states, this defect of anarchy is negligible, and the 'virtues' of anarchy in contributing to *some* national freedom and international stability stand.

Waltz does acknowledge the inequalities in power between states, but again makes it a public virtue for its contribution to international peace and stability. In his discussion of 'the virtues of inequality,'[77] he thus retracts his previous enthusiasm for the virtues of anarchy, for here he concedes that too much anarchy, or equal freedom, in the form of a large number of states all fairly equal in power and thus equally capable of making credible threats to use force would actually lead to instability. This is why Waltz, in the end, only endorses asymmetrical anarchy, in the form of a bipolar international system. In doing so, however, his argument loses the entire normative appeal that he exploited in discussing the virtues of anarchy, which lies in its implication of *equal* freedom.

Waltz's arguments in praise of anarchy's contribution to the international public interest, understood as peace between states, are clearly flawed, yet it is difficult to reject the realist preoccupation with international peace and security as an integral component of that interest. Realists typically characterize war between states as the greatest evil. Always mindful of the potentially devastating costs of war on human life and society, realists would rather that states keep to themselves than embark on external actions, however noble the reasons, that might jeopardize the security of all states and citizens.[78] Even if we accept this realist account of the international interest as peace between states, however, it is unclear how that is related to the security and welfare of human beings. Contemporary realism tends to assume a positive connection between interstate and human security. Yet Rudolf Rummel has found that 150 million people have been killed by their own governments, compared to 35 million killed in *all* civil and international wars of the twentieth century.[79] Geoffrey Best may be right that 'even a bloody government can be better than no government,'[80] but for millions of perished men and women, this has not been the case. The realist assertion that an international order of atomistic states, concerned solely with their own self-interests, makes a positive contribution to the public interest in human security is difficult to sustain. Without a positive connection between interstate and human security, a realist conceptualization of the international public interest as peace between states seems morally inadequate.

For Hobbes, the preservation of the state and the maintenance of individual lives are inextricably linked. The state exists for the protection of individuals' physical integrity; a state that no longer serves this interest for an individual is owed no obligations by that individual. Even Kissinger seems to appreciate an interpretation of the public interest based on human rather than statist terms; for example, he supported the Dayton agreement to end the Bosnian war, endorsing the justification of 'easing human suffering.'[81] Yet realism's state-centric view of international relations tends to discount the voices, interests and claims of nonstate entities, be they individuals or groups. This means that whatever disasters people must suffer in one state, and no matter the degree of responsibility for that disaster by the ruling body or government or other internal factors, a realist perspective can give little weight in principle to humanitarian considerations in the calculation of how other states should construct their foreign policies towards that state and its government. Indeed, it is hard to see how a realism concerned to legitimize states' preoccupations with a narrowly interpreted national interest can endorse a goal such as alleviating the suffering of citizens in other countries.

It is true that some have framed arguments in favour of 'humanitarian interventions' in terms that appeal to the national interest. For example, humanitarian interests and national security interests blended together in the Bush administration's justifications for invading Iraq in 2003. Earlier, Robert Kaplan argued that the United States should intervene in Kosovo for a variety of self-interested reasons, including to avoid a larger, more catastrophic war in the region later, to protect the Middle East oil supply, to maintain a close connection with European allies and to improve the skills, experience and solidarity of NATO and American military forces.[82] Yet if the concept of the national interest is so elastic as to be able to explain and justify a wide spectrum of state conduct and policy prescriptions – from why states should intervene to why they should not, from why they fight to why they cooperate – it is hardly a useful, sufficient, or meaningful concept for explaining or justifying any state conduct. Thus when Morgenthau asserts that all countries 'will continue to be guided in their decisions to intervene and their choice of means of intervention by what they regard as their respective national interests,'[83] the indisputability of his statement is outweighed by its triviality, for he merely begs the question of how states ought to conceive of their national interests. In this vein, Welch has argued that the concept of the national interest is pernicious and superfluous.[84] The idea of the national interest may be useful for its rhetorical appeal, and may serve to promote a substantive conception of international morality, but it cannot generate a morally compelling account of the public interest in international relations on its own; it can serve as a pretty frame, but not as a morally substantive picture of international ethics.

V Conclusion

A realist ethical perspective, as articulated by contemporary realists, generates a series of contradictions. Although neorealists assume a stark dichotomy between private (national) interest and public (international) interest in international relations, they can offer no viable way to distinguish between them. Although the privateness of the state dominates a realist vision of world politics, contemporary realism is incapable of sustaining any normative conception of state sovereignty as privacy, upon which a consistent normative argument for or against intervention would depend. Although realist objections to intervention, humanitarian or otherwise, stem from the fear of legitimizing imperialistic interventions by powerful states, realists can offer no coherent principled argument to oppose them. Given these inconsistencies, it is difficult to find a coherent and compelling realist account of intervention as a moral problem in world politics.

Although cynical and sceptical realism does not admit the possibility or relevance at all of moral principles or ethics in international politics, and therefore does not help us to formulate an ethically coherent conception of national interest, realism as an ethical perspective is best redeemed when it provides 'a cautionary view about the role that normative considerations should be allowed to play in practical reasoning about international affairs.'[85] The role of what Charles Beitz has termed 'heuristic realism' is indeed crucial in determining the moral soundness of various interventionary activities, especially the use of force by states.

A realist interpretation of the national interest, however, is clearly misguided, confusing and morally insubstantial. Despite this, what can explain the enduring *normative* appeal of the idea of the national interest? A realist might think that it confirms a realist image of individuals, including state leaders, as atomistically self-interested actors. Because of this, 'Tens of thousands of words and a shelf of books... about our moral interest... do not add up to one sentence of national interest.'[86] Yet this realist explanation of the power of the concept may ultimately be misguided, for the normative appeal of the national interest may lie beyond the scope of a realist perspective. As Welch has observed, the idea of the national interest has historically been wedded to notions of the public interest of a bounded political community; it denotes 'a common good, something that benefits a collectivity as a whole even though it might not benefit any particular member.'[87] The power of the national interest as an idea stems from its status as a *moral* interest, rather than as an amoral interest. The conception of the national interest as a moral interest and its implications for the ethics of intervention are more fully explicated by a study of a different ethical perspective, 'communitarianism.'

4
Sovereignty as Privacy

Only domestic tyrants are safe, for it is not our purpose in international society (nor, Mill argues, is it possible) to establish liberal or democratic communities, but only independent ones.

Michael Walzer, *Just and Unjust Wars: A Moral Argument with Historical Illustrations*[1]

The domestic life of domestic tyrants is one of the things which it is the most imperative on the law to interfere with.

John Stuart Mill, *Principles of Political Economy and Chapters on Socialism*[2]

I Introduction

While the tyranny of the private state constitutes *the* fundamental problem of international ethics from a realist perspective, communitarianism is concerned to establish moral grounds for state sovereignty as privacy vis-à-vis international society. Statist communitarians, or proponents of an 'international society' perspective, generally seek to endorse an international order resting on the principles of state sovereignty and nonintervention in a state's domestic affairs. Such communitarianism has enjoyed prominence in classical international law and the conventional rules of international sociability between states. Nonstatist communitarians also want to defend the internal and external autonomy of communities, but typically make a distinction between states and nations, and expand their concern beyond internationally recognized states to include the self-determination claims of sub-state national groups. Common to both statist and nonstatist communitarians is the concern to advance a distinction between the internal and the external life of a state or, more broadly, national or political community.

This distinction undergirds a central freedom that states may claim in international society – their freedom from external intrusion into their domestic affairs. Because international society and law accord positive moral value to this kind of freedom, 'intervention' is a term 'fraught with connotations of illegality and immorality.'[3] Hedley Bull has asserted that intervention or 'dictatorial or coercive interference, by an outside party or parties, in the sphere of jurisdiction of a sovereign state, or more broadly of an independent political community... is generally believed to be legally and morally wrong: sovereign states or independent political communities are thought to have the right to have their spheres of jurisdiction respected, and dictatorial interference abridges that right.'[4] The public/private construct in International Relations serves to demarcate a distinction between the public and the private lives of states, a central purpose of which is to afford states and their citizens an arena of freedom from external interference.

The norm of sovereignty thus functions like the norm of privacy to shield the internal or self-regarding domain of the relevant unit from nonconsensual external intrusion. Michael Walzer's interpretation of communal integrity and freedom is also suggestive of an analogy between sovereignty and privacy norms. In his discussion of the Melian dialogue, for example, Walzer characterizes the Melian argument against the imperialistic Athenian generals as a moral claim for the 'right to be let alone.'[5] This choice of words echoes the depiction of privacy by US Supreme Court Justices Warren and Brandeis in 1890 as 'the right to be left alone.'[6] Anita Allen has characterized privacy as denoting limited accessibility or inaccessibility, as well as freedom from coercive outside interference.[7] The notion of sovereignty shares with the idea of privacy these characteristics of restricted accessibility, and freedom from unsolicited external intervention. How does a communitarian perspective understand the normative basis or justification for state privacy in international society? That is, what is state privacy good for? Any justification of state privacy ultimately must rest on a normative theory of statehood, just as any notion of individual privacy relies on a moral theory of personhood. Communitarian assessments of intervention as a moral problem in world politics thus turn on their visions of the nature and value of community.

II   The state as a private home

While the depiction of sovereignty as privacy implies an analogy between the state and the individual, one can think of another collective unit – the family – that has enjoyed a similar moral claim to privacy. International Relations theorists have tended to leave unexamined a more compelling and pervasive domestic analogy, between the family and the state. Indeed, familial terms and symbols abound in the domain of the political, national and international. It is common in some parts of the world for people to refer to their native country as the 'motherland' or 'fatherland'; the founders of republics as 'fathers'; and fellow citizens, revolutionaries and/or ethnic compatriots as 'brothers' and 'sisters.' Historically, colonialists have likened indigenous peoples to children who needed the paternal guidance of colonial masters to direct their entry into civilization or the 'family of nations.' Likening political communities to family homes draws on elusive concepts that seem to convey a bundle of unspecified but intuitively understood meanings. What exactly does the use of the language of home and family life convey about the idea of political community?

One function of the metaphor is to capture the exclusive nature of political communities. If 'being in a private place is a central part of what it means to be "at home,"'[8] it is also a central, if neglected, feature of the sovereign state. Contemporary western societies typically envision the home as 'a secure space where a person is not answerable to outsiders..., captured in the characterisation of the home as a "castle".' A home of one's own is 'valued as a place in which the members of a family can live in private, away from the scrutiny of others, and exercise control over outsiders' involvement in domestic affairs.'[9] International Relations scholars might recognize in this depiction of a private family home the prevailing image of the sovereign state. As collective units, the state and the family share a similar conceptual history as 'private spheres,' with rights to privacy understood in terms of communal integrity and freedom from external interference.[10] Arguments about intervention in international relations thus share normative affinities with debates in western liberal societies about public intervention in the family.

While comparing the family and the state in this way seems obvious, the comparison is also perplexing, because in domestic politics and theory, and especially in liberal theory, the state is known as the quintessentially public actor or realm, while the family is cast as the paradigmatically private sphere. The image of the state as a public actor has been adopted seemingly unproblematically in the international realm.

The family/state analogy exposes a different face of the state. As Hilary Charlesworth has noted, the state conceived as a private sphere appears in a distinction drawn in the realm of public international law, found in Article 2(7) of the UN Charter, which distinguishes between matters of international (public) concern and issues belonging to a national or domestic (and private) jurisdiction: 'Nothing contained in the present Charter shall authorize the United Nations to intervene in matters which are essentially within the domestic jurisdiction of any state or shall require the Members to submit such matters to settlement under the present Charter.'[11] While the state, in relation to its own citizens and society, may comprise the public realm, an emblem of the universal, in relation to other states and international society, it constitutes a private realm, a repository of all that is particular to its members.

The family/state analogy has enjoyed prominence in the historical development of the concept of the state and its sovereignty. Writing in the sixteenth century, Jean Bodin asserted, 'the well-ordered family is a true image of the commonwealth, and domestic comparable with sovereign authority.'[12] Both families and states involve an authority structure which imposes distinct rights and obligations on its members that nonmembers do not share. The historical and philosophical development of the state and sovereign authority in the West owes much to the models provided by the family and parental authority. Exploring this historical connection between conceptions of the political authority of sovereigns and mainly paternal authority in the household can provide insight into communitarian interpretations of statehood and sovereign authority.

Perhaps the most well-known articulation of paternal political thought can be found in Robert Filmer's *Patriarcha*, written tellingly at a time and in a society where the patriarchal image of political authority was coming under increasing attack. Filmer's work represents an entire tradition of political thought that derived political obligation from a conception of familial obligation.[13] Identifying political power with paternal power, Filmer argued that 'all the duties of a King are summed up in an universal fatherly care of his people.'[14] As Gordon Schochet has noted in his study of patriarchal political thought in seventeenth-century England, 'the simple requirement to "Honour thy father and thy mother" was expanded to include loyalty and obedience to the king and all magistrates, as well as to masters, teachers, and ministers.'[15] Kings were the metaphorical fathers of their subjects; the nature of public political power and authority, and that of private paternal power and authority were inextricably linked.

Filmer believed that all human relationships were subject to the law of God, which ultimately and alone provided the original basis for the legitimacy of both monarchical and paternal rule. Thus Filmer assumed that fathers and kings were bound by the law of God and nature to seek the preservation of their families or kingdoms. Clearly, Filmer's moral image of God informed his idealized conceptions of earthly political and personal rule. In arguing 'for the superiority of Princes above laws,' he placed any hopes for remedies against the abuse of royal authority in the realm of the divine. Similarly, he put the subject of how a patriarch managed relations within his own household beyond the scope of political regulation: 'The Father of a family governs by no other law than by his own will, not by the laws or wills of his sons or servants. There is no nation that allows children any action or remedy for being unjustly governed.'[16] Bodin also conceived of paternal authority in absolutist terms: not only should each household have only 'one head, one master, one seigneur,' but parents should also have 'that power of life and death over their children which belongs to them under the law of God and of nature.'[17] Neither Filmer nor Bodin conceived of families or states to be private in a morally atomistic sense, since both were ultimately bound by the law of God. Yet their theories of paternal rule clearly entailed a public authority structure that refrained from interfering within the private domain of the patriarchal household. Similarly, Bodin's theory of sovereign rule also entailed international forbearance from interfering in the private domain of a sovereign prince.

Contemporary western liberal democratic societies continue to consider the realm of the family as a paradigmatically private sphere:

> Family life has been singled out in the modern world as that realm in which the particular concerns, interests and needs of individuals are dominant and from which political and other public matters are largely excluded. The family has often been conceived as a private refuge from the exacting demands of civil society and the *res publica*.[18]

The family constitutes a 'haven in a heartless world,'[19] a primary source of personal and collective identity and fulfillment, and home is 'the only setting where intimacy can flourish, providing meaning, coherence, and stability in personal life.'[20] The moral evaluation of the family and home as deserving of the status of a 'private sphere' relies on an ideal image of the domestic realm as a source of protection for individuals from the often harsh and cold dealings of the outside world. Familial relationships, under this view, contrast with those found in the world of commerce and politics; while the bond between family members develops out of love, mutual affection and natural empathy, relationships between individuals in society are marked at best by the cold virtue of justice, mutual disinterest and cooperation, and at worst by domination and exploitation, mutual distrust and conflict. Bodin's advocacy of an absolutist conception of parental power and authority within the household clearly relies on an idealization of family and home life, for he held 'that the natural affection of parents for their children is incompatible with cruelty and abuse of power.'[21] The home, ideally conceived, merits noninterference because it is the harbour for social relationships that are qualitatively different from those that can be attained in the wider public context. Because familial relations are typically guided by positive mutual care and concern, their qualitative superiority renders public regulation and interference in the family home unnecessary and undesirable.

Communal membership and belonging

Somewhat ironically, these positive images and functions attributed to the familial community also inform communitarian interpretations of national and political communities. As Krishan Kumar has observed, one's country, 'when conceived as the homeland, is explicitly modeled on an idealized version of the private realm of the household or family.'[22] Hilary Pilkington observes that the persistence of the ideal of 'homeland' in contemporary political discourse suggests that 'an important element of the modern world outlook is the linking of individual identity to a territorially bounded collective identity via a perceived biological connectedness.'[23] The concept of the 'nation-state' has historically evoked an image of the state as a private home that houses a nation resembling a traditional family. The language of family and home in depictions of political community serves to convey a sense of connectedness between members that nonmembers do not share. Identifying the source of that connection in a set of objective features is characteristic of primordial notions of national identity. Such conceptions, however, tend to naturalize the nation, obscuring its deeply contested and political nature.

A primordial nationalist discourse in Russia, for example, assumes an automatic connection between members of the Russian nation or people, yet the reality and the significance of this connection, and hence of a primordial notion of Russian national identity, have been severely challenged following the demise of the Soviet Union. For ethnic Russians who lived in some of the former Soviet republics other than Russia, returning to their 'national homeland' has been 'an experience fraught with confrontation and contestation rather than a smooth journey "home." '[24] Indeed, many Russians who became forced migrants due to the political prevalence of primordial notions of national identity and citizenship in some Soviet successor states returned to Russia feeling more like foreigners entering a hostile land than compatriots going home.[25] Not only did they identify more with the republics that denied their claims to membership and belonging, but they also felt a disconnection with the local Russians in Russia. As Pilkington found, ethnically Russian migrants 'claimed that they were labelled as outsiders by locals [in Russia] who referred to them as: "newcomers" or "strangers"..., "immigrants"..., "refugees" or, according to the republic from which they came, "Kazakhs," "Kirghiz," and so on.' The senses of national identity put forward by Russian-speaking returnees and locals in Russia thus challenge a primordial conception of the nation as 'a homogeneous cultural unit formed on a common territory and linked by blood ties.'[26]

Yael Tamir has concluded more generally that 'all attempts to single out a particular set of objective features – be it a common history, collective destiny, language, religion, territory, climate, race, ethnicity – as necessary and sufficient for the definition of a nation have ended in failure.'[27] Similarly, as contemporary debates about the family show, the definition of the family – including the issue of who can claim to be a member, as well as the types of social groupings that can call themselves families – has always been political and contested. Historically in many societies, public laws and social mores prevented children born out of wedlock from the right of family membership, not to mention its privileges, despite their biological tie. The contemporary world of blended families, and same-sex couples and parents challenges the use of biology or nature as a sufficient or necessary criterion for defining the family. An enlightened communitarian perspective thus, rightly, moves the concept of community, familial and national, from the realm of objectivity to intersubjectivity.

Yet while communitarians want to avoid primordial notions of national or political community, they are at the same time reluctant to embrace constructivist accounts. The latter, in inspiring a view of nations and states as 'imagined communities,'[28] might imply the existence of pre-social individuals who imagine and construct the community, rather than the existence of an ontologically prior social context that shapes its members' imaginations of community. Indeed, contemporary communitarianism developed as a response to a prevailing strand of liberalism that exalted an atomistic account of individual identity and agency at the expense of notions of collective identity, solidarity and belonging. Communitarians seek to challenge the thin instrumental notion of political community generated by an atomistic account of individuals as unencumbered selves, capable of being divorced from all social roles and attachments.[29] Although communitarians want to avoid conceiving of families, nations or states as 'natural' communities (which they clearly are not), in also wanting to reject their depiction as 'imagined' communities (which too easily makes them derivative of individual imaginations, and possibly *imaginary*), communitarians seek to put forward a view of social groups as intersubjectively felt communities, collective imaginings with weight. A community may not be as tangible as an individual biological organism, yet it is not as intangible as a mental fiction; rather, a human community, through its cultural beliefs and practices and shared historical memory, has an enduring presence, personality and life of its own that is not easily reducible to its individual members.

A communitarian conception of a family or a nation is thus marked by the organic quality of the relationship between its members; that is, the members of an authentic family or nation must adopt a view of themselves as parts of a greater whole.[30] Alasdair MacIntyre has described this orientation as distinctive of a morality of patriotism: 'For precisely the same reasons that a family whose members all came to regard membership in that family as governed only by reciprocal self-interest would no longer be a family in the traditional sense, so a nation whose members took up a similar attitude would no longer be a nation.'[31] The public, according to this organic strain of communitarianism, cannot be just an arbitrary aggregation of individuals, but must be composed of individuals who identify themselves as members loyal to a collective project called the 'nation' or the 'political community.' This shared sense of identification and belonging is intrinsic to a communitarian conception of community, so that the authenticity of a collective without this shared consciousness becomes suspect. Although Yael Tamir finds the notion of national authenticity highly problematic, she too asserts that a nation is defined by 'connectedness, the belief that we all belong to a group whose existence we consider valuable.'[32]

Communitarians tend to attribute intrinsic moral worth to having a community of one's own, the preservation of which justifies special obligations between members, and requires respect for communal integrity and autonomy by nonmembers.[33] These claims require an image of communities with clear boundaries, something which, in communitarian philosophy, is provided by the concept of connectedness. Yet while connectedness might very well provide the basis for an inter-subjective collective reality, it is not likely to be capable of supporting an image of community that could be the basis of a collective moral right to nonintervention. For as the Russian example shows, the feeling of connectedness in reality is likely to be subjected to continual contestation, problematizing the very boundary between insiders and outsiders that defines the distinctiveness of nations and upon which claims to collective self-determination and nonintervention depend.

The highly problematic nature of the concepts of connectedness, home and belonging in individual lives and collective imaginations also raises questions about what it means to have a community *of one's own*. Attaching value to self-determining communities does allow us to reject on moral grounds imperialistic and paternalistic political and social arrangements between communities, and to affirm normative rights of the relevant communities to self-determination and noninter-vention. Concerns about imperialism, paternalism and communal self-determination are not just communitarian concerns, but also inform much of liberal thinking. Theorists such as Yael Tamir and Michael Walzer have attempted to fuse communitarian and liberal theoretical approaches by arguing that membership in a community one can call one's own is ultimately an expression of individual agency, autonomy and self-fulfillment. Yet there is a difference between the idea of membership in a community one can call one's own, and membership in a community one has *chosen*. Individuals belong to many communities that undeniably *are* their own, but are not self-chosen. As Judith Shklar has noted, 'Very often we have no choice at all whether we belong to a group or not. . . . Now you have a choice to be either loyal or disloyal to these groups, but you do not have the choice of being neither.'[34] One's family, racial or ethnic group, may be indisputably one's own, but membership and belonging in these communities may not entail voluntaristic individual agency. Nor does membership in them necessarily contribute to individual self-fulfillment. A person who is a member of an abusive family or relationship, or a nation respons-ible for mass atrocities, for example, may undeniably belong to the family or nation, yet that belonging can be a source of pain and low self-esteem rather than self-fulfillment.[35]

Tamir's concern for individual agency leads her to attach moral value only to self-chosen communities. Thus she argues that 'the right to national self-determination should be seen as an individual right, contingent on a willed decision of individuals to affiliate themselves with a particular national group and to give public expression to this affiliation.' This voluntarist individualist account of communal membership and belonging, however, is not easy to reconcile with the fact that most social groups, especially national and political communities, are *inter*subjective constructions; an individual's membership in such communities requires not only her self-declared individual choice but also external recognition of that choice by the collective or its members. Furthermore, if communal affiliation and identity are solely self-chosen by individuals, there may be many more conceptions of community in individual imaginations than that currently exist in the world, or are dreamt of in a communitarian vision of nationhood and nationality. The limitations of that vision are evident in Tamir's critique of exclusionary citizenship laws in some Soviet successor states. She argues, 'Estonia and Latvia must face the fact that the injustices inflicted on them have turned them into binational states, and there is no way of turning the clock back.'[36] The idea of 'binational states,' however, does not capture the 'cultural hybridity of Russian-speaking forced migrants,'[37] which indicates a blended rather than dual national identity. While communitarians tend to emphasize that communities such as nations are not reducible to their individual members, one who takes seriously individuals' capacity for self-direction would be attuned to the reality that individuals' identities and sense of connectedness with others are not likely to be reducible to any one community, such as a nation. As Shklar has argued, individual 'rights create a culture that is a threat to the clubby life of traditional groups. It allows us to move about as we please, socially, intellectually, geographically and personally. And one cannot have it both ways.'[38] The complex intersubjective reality of nations and collectives means that the categories of members and nonmembers, which are essential to notions of *collective* self-determination and nonintervention, are more problematic in moral and practical ways than a communitarian view might suggest.

Since communitarians tend to simplify and idealize communal membership and belonging at individual and collective levels, they argue that the balance of the public and the private lives of political communities in international society must include the common recognition of their normative right to self-determination and nonintervention in their internal affairs. An ideal communitarian image of world order consists of a plurality of communities that recognizes reciprocal claims among themselves to self-determination and nonintervention in their domestic arrangements. States, rather than cultural nations, are currently the subject of these rights and duties not only in the public arena of formal international law, but also in the informal public domain of international relations. This latter public realm can be understood as 'a sphere of fluid and polymorphous sociability.'[39] As Jeff Weintraub explains, the function of the public as sociability 'is not so much to express or generate solidarity as, ideally, to "make diversity agreeable" – or, at least, manageable.'[40]

International society attempts to manage great political, social and economic diversity not only through universal law, but also through more localized codes and conventions that define the virtue of international civility. Although these codes vary, the prevailing terms of international sociability include the provision that a state's internal affairs are largely shielded from scrutiny and intervention by other states.[41] For example, the Canadian government does not expect the US government to make any official observations or statements about how it deals with Quebec sovereigntist demands for secession. The prevailing wisdom in international society is that 'Good fences make good neighbors.'[42] Sovereignty as privacy in domestic and international legal and social institutional arrangements functions to project, on the one hand, a vision of states as autonomous and distinct collective agents and, on the other, a vision of the international public realm as one of tolerant communal diversity. Michael Walzer thus endorses 'sovereign statehood' as 'a way of protecting distinct historical cultures, sometimes national, sometimes ethnic/religious in character,' and rejects a centralized global order because 'I don't see how it could accommodate anything like the range of cultural and religious difference that we see around us today.... For some cultures and most orthodox religions can only survive if they are permitted degrees of separation that are incompatible with globalism. And so the survival of these groups would be at risk; under the rules of the global state, they would not be able to sustain and pass on their way of life.'[43] Recognition at the international level of the value of community, and the norms of communal autonomy and nonintervention, may be important to curbing the appetite of a hegemonic or global state to re-make the world in its own image.

The dark side of privacy

In recent decades the designation of the realm of domesticity as a private sphere has been deeply contested, most prominently by feminists, who point to the double-edged nature of family privacy, which 'can signify deprivation as well as advantage.'[44] While the norm of privacy ideally functions to protect family relations from conformist public pressures and totalitarian public policies, the designation has also had the effect of rendering the domestic realm nonpolitical, unworthy of public attention and regulation. One issue that has made the privacy of the family morally problematic, and brought public intervention in the family to the fore of social policy agendas in western countries, is domestic violence. The conventionally organic images of the family and home life make it difficult to conceive of family homes as dangerous situations themselves from which individuals may need protection. Families may be places where people develop and maintain their most intense bonds of intimacy and community with others, yet research shows that 'more than anywhere else in society, the family is the site of murder, child abuse and assault.'[45]

Feminist scholars have criticized the construction of families as private spheres, for its effect has been to hide some of the most depraved acts of inhumanity and injustice from public view: 'by classifying institutions like the family as "private"...the public/private distinction often serves to shield abuse and domination within these relationships from political scrutiny or legal redress.'[46] According families legal and social rights to privacy has historically translated into an inability to subject internal family relations to public moral standards and accountability. Judith DeCew notes, for example, that the old rape shield laws in the United States deprived women of the legal ability to charge their husbands with rape, since marriage was assumed to confer consensual sex automatically between husband and wife.[47] Feminists who recognized the disproportionately adverse impact of this invisibility on women have thus been united in rejecting conceptions of family privacy that support the exclusion of family issues, especially those relating to women's oppression, from the political agenda.[48]

Efforts to make domestic violence a public and political issue rather than a private problem of particular families have met with resistance mainly because of what one scholar, Elizabeth Pleck, has called 'the Family Ideal,' encompassing 'ideas about family privacy, conjugal and parental rights, and family stability.'[49] Indeed, not long ago in western social history, domestic abuse was largely considered 'a private family matter to be worked out within the family.'[50] If one doubts the strength of the 'family ideal,' it is sobering to remember that in the western world, organizations for animal protection, such as the Society for the Prevention of Cruelty to Animals (SPCA), were formed before counterparts dealing with child protection. Pleck is most likely right to argue that this was not so much an indication that society cared less about children than animals, but that child rescue faced special normative barriers because it 'involved interference in the fundamental unit of the family,'[51] conceived as a private sphere with rights to autonomy and immunity from external interference.

Just as those who study domestic violence find the 'family ideal' a consistent barrier to social reform, international attempts to deal with intrastate violence typically come face to face with the 'state ideal,' involving a set of ideas about state privacy, sovereign rights and national integrity. Comparing the history of western experiences in reform against domestic violence and recent international efforts to deal with intrastate violence, it becomes clear that both have faced similar normative barriers due to the conception of families and states as private spheres. Indeed, as Craig Calhoun has observed, 'suggesting that international recognition [of new states] should be linked to democratic institutions or . . . condemning domestic human rights abuses are as problematic within [a certain conception of the] division of public and private as attempts to intervene in families on behalf of the rights of children or spouses have been.'[52]

While the norms of sovereignty and nonintervention may protect political communities from imperialist ambitions, they also explain the entrenched reluctance of states and international organizations to intervene in issues considered to belong to the domestic jurisdiction of states. This reluctance parallels the past reluctance of domestic law, the police and court systems in western societies to intervene in what were perceived to be 'private' family disputes. In the late 1800s courts in Canada ruled, with relation to spousal assault, that it was better 'to draw the curtain, shut out the public gaze and leave the partners to forgive and forget.'[53] Just as the doctrine of nonintervention served to hide inhumanity, cruelty and injustice within families from public scrutiny and redress, the same doctrine underpinning the Cold War international order barred states and other international actors from intervening, forcibly or nonforcibly, to alleviate human suffering even on a massive scale, especially when such suffering was confined within state boundaries and resulted from the exercise of sovereign power. In international law and society, sovereign leaders possessed something like the ring of Gyges; when turned outward in the glare of international politics, their actions were public and visible, but when turned inward in their domestic jurisdictions, their conduct became private and hence, invisible.[54] State leaders could thus enjoy the reputation of being vanguards of the public interest or the common good in international society while, in their internal relations, being 'indecent without shame, cruel without shuddering, and murderous without apprehension of fear of exposure or punishment.'[55]

During the Cold War era, both the United Nations and its members interpreted the right of sovereignty and the duty of nonintervention in a way that protected domestically irresponsible sovereigns from formal international censure. Although some Cold War era military interventions yielded positive humanitarian consequences for populations in crisis, humanitarian concern was not a legally recognized ground for abrogating sovereignty in international relations.[56] States that intervened against a government responsible for mass atrocities chose to justify their interventions on nonhumanitarian grounds.[57] The legitimation criteria for the use of force between states therefore excluded the validity of humanitarian reasons, especially in contexts where there was no direct threat to international peace and security. The dominant interpretation of international law thus maintained the invisibility of the suffering of victims of intrastate violence.[58] Domestic tyrants could feel at home in the world of public states and private humanity.

As Oliver Ramsbotham and Tom Woodhouse have observed, humanitarian issues and concerns were unmentionable in the relations between states:

> A general conclusion on state reaction to massive human rights violations during the cold war era would have to be that the normal response was to do nothing. Not only were instances of forcible intervention rare, but even formal protest and the initiation of collective measures through recognized human rights procedures were seldom, and even then, only reluctantly invoked.[59]

It is, of course, not only those who commit active brutality who use the rhetoric of sovereignty as privacy to claim an unassailable moral right to be free from intervention. More disturbingly perhaps, potential intervenors – those who have the capacity to intervene effectively to halt grave acts of inhumanity – also use the rhetoric of sovereignty and nonintervention to avoid moral responsibility. The use of 'sovereignty as privacy' to shield abusive sovereign conduct, with some significant exceptions that will be discussed in Chapter 6, carried over into the post-Cold War world. Roméo Dallaire, the Canadian commander of the United Nations Assistance Mission for Rwanda (UNAMIR) during the 1994 genocide, notes that not only was his request for more troops denied, he was not even able to halt transmissions from the local radio station, Radio Télévision Libre des Mille Collines (RTLM), that were inciting genocide. As he explains, the United Nations lacked the equipment to halt the broadcasts, but the United States did possess deployable jamming aircraft:

> The issue was studied by the Pentagon, which in due course recommended against conducting the operation because of the cost – $8,500 an hour for a jamming aircraft over the country – and the legal dilemma. Bandwidth within a nation is owned by the nation, and *jamming a national radio station would violate international convention on national sovereignty.* The Pentagon judged that the lives of the estimated 8,000–10,000 Rwandans being killed each day in the genocide were not worth the cost of the fuel or the violation of Rwandan airwaves.[60]

Whatever the actual motivations were behind this decision, it is clear that the legal problem of violating sovereignty was used as an independent normative argument against the proposed action.

When sovereignty as privacy is construed as an absolute right, intrastate violence tends to be viewed by outsiders largely as an internal problem. Not only must those suffering from various kinds of intrastate crises and conflicts – from state collapse and communal war to tyrannical government and genocide – suffer alone, they must bear the responsibility for addressing their own suffering in the context of an international society of distinct and autonomous political communities that have no moral obligation to help them. A communitarian vision of organic self-determining communities may thus collapse into a realist vision of atomistic self-helping ones.

Construed in absolutist terms, sovereignty as privacy leads to a vilification of all forms of intervention. As R.J. Vincent has observed, 'If the members of international society are taken to be sovereign states acknowledging each other's rights to rule in their own domains, then it follows that intervention – the attempt to subject another state to one's will – is illegitimate as an infraction of sovereignty: if sovereignty, then nonintervention.'[61] In this formulation, a descriptive account of intervention as an infraction of sovereignty is inextricably linked to a normative assessment of intervention as an illegitimate act. An absolutist interpretation of sovereignty as privacy is encouraged by standard descriptive accounts of what sovereignty *is*. Bull, for example, assumes that states by definition have an entitlement to nonintervention, since a state's internal sovereignty '*means* supremacy over all other authorities within that territory and population.'[62] Positing a logical link between the definitions of sovereignty and nonintervention, however, obscures normative debates about the value of sovereignty as privacy, and the ethics of intervention. The consequence of depicting sovereignty as privacy in absolutist terms has been the historical inattention of international society and law to contexts of intrastate violence, which remained private tragedies, much like domestic familial violence within western societies until recent decades.

III Community, humanity and intervention

Michael Walzer's enduring work, *Just and Unjust Wars*, details a normative theory of intervention that opens moral space for international intervention in contexts of intrastate violence. His more recent works on the legitimacy of military intervention in contexts of humanitarian crises show that he has found it 'easier and easier to override the presumption' of nonintervention that he vigorously defended in his earlier work.[63] I will address more fully the subject of military intervention in Chapter 6. For now, I want to explore how Walzer's liberal communitarianism led him in *Just and Unjust Wars* to some misguided arguments about the legitimacy of intervention in certain types of cases.

The sovereign individual and the sovereign community

In his discussion of 'emergency ethics,' Walzer argues that acting immorally, such as deliberately killing the innocent, is not 'permissible (or necessary) when anything less than the ongoingness of the community is at stake, or when the danger that we face is anything less than communal death.' Although he does not like the metaphor of a contract, he endorses a Burkean conception of political community as a contract between 'those who are living, those who are dead, and those who are yet to be born.' Walzer's conception of community entails generational continuity and an 'ongoingness' of 'a way of life,' of 'people like us.'[64] He is consistently careful not to equate the value of community and communal integrity and self-determination to the value of states and state integrity and autonomy. He thus departs from 'international society' theorists in asserting that the 'real subject of [his] argument is not the state at all but the political community that (usually) underlies it.' The legitimacy of any state depends on 'the 'fit' of government and community, that is, the degree to which the government actually represents the political life of its people.'[65] While international society theorists have generally privileged the state in their account of international order and morality, Walzer privileges the historical communities of men and women whose claims can sometimes trump the claims of the state, especially when that state can no longer be seen as an authentic expression of the political community that underlies it. Still, he endorses states to the extent that they can ensure the security and welfare of national, religious and political communities.[66]

Walzer relaxes the legalist paradigm of nonintervention, asserting that states can in certain circumstances justifiably intervene in the internal affairs of other states. The moral basis for such intervention, in cases of secession and counterintervention, and in response to acts that shock the conscience of humankind, however, lies in the ideal of the self-determining community itself.[67] Even interventions to halt gross human rights violations are justified because such interventions do not threaten communal integrity or autonomy, since 'when a government turns savagely upon its own people, we must doubt the very existence of a political community to which the idea of self-determination might apply.' Intervention is thus justified because it is not really intervention, since there is no authentic political community whose autonomy can be violated, where gross human rights violations, such as 'enslavement or massacre of political opponents, national minorities, and religious sects,' are committed.[68]

Walzer employs an 'individual/community analogy' to develop his account of a political community's right to self-determination. Drawing on John Stuart Mill's arguments, Walzer asserts that 'the members . . . of a single political community, are entitled collectively to determine their own affairs.'[69] This right of communities to self-determination 'derives its moral and political force from the rights of contemporary men and women to live as members of a historical community and to express their inherited culture through political forms worked out among themselves.'[70] The right of individuals as members of a political community to exercise collective self-rule logically entails a rule of nonintervention by nonmembers.

Although the ideas of communal self-determination and nonintervention seem pre-eminently organic and communitarian, it is the idea of the sovereign individual, derived from a liberal conception of individuals as self-directing beings, that provides the model for Walzer's conception of the sovereign community.[71] Just as the recognition of individual privacy affords individuals a sphere in which they may exercise their agency without external scrutiny or intervention, the recognition of state sovereignty, according to Walzer, establishes 'an arena within which freedom can be fought for and (sometimes) won. It is this arena and the activities that go on within it that we want to protect, and we protect them, much as we protect individual integrity, by marking out boundaries that cannot be crossed, rights that cannot be violated. As with individuals, so with sovereign states: there are things that we cannot do to them, even for their own ostensible good.'[72] Walzer's conception of state sovereignty as privacy draws on a liberal interpretation of privacy as conferring on individuals an inviolable sphere for self-regarding activity. Adapting this conception of individual privacy to the state supports an interpretation of the sovereign state as an inviolable arena for collective self-determination, entailing such rights as political autonomy and territorial integrity. Although this construction of privacy relies on the normative appeal of a liberal view of individual freedom as self-direction, its application to the collective level ultimately serves an organic interpretation of freedom as collective self-rule, and carries the potential to subvert individual claims to self-direction and privacy.

This irony is not particular to Walzer's work, but is generally evident in communitarian philosophy. In Rousseau's work, for example, it is precisely his organic vision of domestic politics that accounts for his largely atomistic account of international politics.[73] Michael Sandel and Alasdair MacIntyre critique the liberal view of morality for its individualism: as an end-in-itself the liberal self is 'installed as sovereign, cast as the author of the only moral meanings there are.'[74] Yet communitarians tend to grant this authorship and sovereignty to the bounded political community, positing that 'it is an essential characteristic of the morality which each of us acquires that it is learned from, in and through the way of life of some particular community.'[75] Thus individual moral development is contingent on membership and participation in a collective life. The view of bounded political communities as ultimate sources of morality and sole guardians of the public good ironically translates into a devaluation of individual claims to autonomy.[76]

Indeed, although Walzer's justification for state sovereignty as privacy, and hence the rule of nonintervention between states, relies heavily on a liberal conception of individual privacy, he argues that the communal right to privacy applies to liberal and illiberal regimes alike: '*domestic tyrants* are safe, for it is not our purpose in international society (nor, Mill argues, is it possible) to establish liberal or democratic communities, but only independent ones.' It is the individual/community analogy that provides the basis for this assertion: 'The members of a political community must seek their own freedom, just as the individual must cultivate his own virtue. They cannot be set free, as he cannot be made virtuous, by any external force.' Walzer seems to value individual rights to autonomy, and to adopt an instrumental view of political community in arguing that it is *individual* rights that 'are violated when communal integrity is denied, even if the denial is benevolent in intention.'[77] Yet respect for communal integrity and autonomy does not always translate into a respect for individual integrity and freedom. It is not clear how communal privacy can consistently claim any moral force if it fails to respect the model of individual privacy upon which it is based, and from which it draws its normative appeal. By using a state/individual analogy, Walzer opens his theory to the problem of linking communal and individual integrity and self-determination, the solution to which might require an acknowledgement of the instrumental rather than intrinsic value of community. His arguments in support of a rule of nonintervention are morally sustainable and consistent only if the exercise of communal agency is consistent with respect for individual integrity and self-determination.[78]

The moral functions of nonintervention: Autonomy, neutrality and plurality

Justifiable interventions, according to Walzer, should 'be as much like nonintervention as possible,' so as to conform to the principal rule of international morality, which is '*always* [to] *act so as to recognize and uphold communal autonomy.*'[79] Walzer's endorsement of the nonintervention principle between states is guided by a concern to support communal autonomy, neutrality in zones of conflict, and international social pluralism. Justifying intervention and nonintervention on the basis of preserving communal autonomy leads Walzer to the thorny subject of evaluating the authenticity of communal identities and boundaries. As Walzer concedes, 'it isn't always clear when a community is in fact self-determining, when it qualifies, so to speak, for nonintervention.' The case of secession is difficult because 'evidence must be provided that a community actually exists whose members are committed to independence and ready and able to determine the conditions of their own existence.'[80] The problems with identifying inauthentic political communities or a lack of 'fit' between a political community and its government also partly explain why Walzer legitimizes 'humanitarian intervention' only in the most egregious cases of mass atrocity.[81] It would seem more direct, however, to argue that intervention is justified, not because practices such as enslavement or massacre reveal the lack of an authentic political community, which is notoriously difficult to determine, but because such practices are morally intolerable affronts to common human interests in individual integrity, agency and dignity.

Walzer seems to imply this line of argument in his assertion that a government 'engaged in massive violations of human rights' cannot appropriately appeal to the principle of communal self-determination. 'That appeal,' according to Walzer, 'has to do with the freedom of the community taken as a whole; it has no force when what is at stake is the bare survival or the minimum liberty of (some substantial number of) its members.'[82] If gross human rights violations invalidate a government's claim to self-determination, the moral barrier against intervention is also thereby negated. Consequently, in such situations, the moral burden of proof must clearly *shift* from external actors who might intervene to the internal actors who must provide reasons other than self-determination (which has no force) to defend their claims to nonintervention. It is not *always* the case, then, as Walzer claims at the beginning of his discussion of intervention, that the 'burden of proof falls on any political leader who tries to shape the domestic arrangements or alter the conditions of life in a foreign country.'[83]

The idea that respecting communal autonomy in situations of violent civil conflict requires external neutrality, most often expressed through nonintervention, is also a suspect claim. As feminist theorists have asserted, a policy of nonintervention in families does not produce neutral consequences. In patriarchal societies, for example, it is assumed that fathers or husbands are the heads of households and the decision-makers for the family. Respecting family privacy in such societies can lead to an implicit endorsement of patriarchal conceptions of authority in the household, and to a denial of the claims to decisional agency of other individuals within the household. Similarly, the society of states recognizes governments as the official decision-makers of political communities. Respecting state privacy, however, can lead to a denial of the decisional agency of its members. In the realm of domesticity in western societies, the policy of nonintervention served to perpetuate patriarchal and abusive structures of authority within families, and internationally the rule of nonintervention has also served the interests of illiberal, paternalistic, tyrannical and abusive regimes. A policy of nonintervention, in the family or in the state, can hardly be considered synonymous with neutrality.

Walzer argues that in situations of intrastate violence such as a civil war, the role of the international community is to aim at 'holding the circle, preserving the balance, restoring some degree of integrity to the local struggle.'[84] This is a strange prescription if we think of civil war through the family/state analogy, since it seems to suggest that external parties ought to let the members use force to determine the terms of their relationship. In the name of preserving the sovereign community, Walzer seems, in this text, to be arguing that intrastate violence should be considered a private communal matter to be worked out within the community, much as family violence used to be considered 'a private family matter to be worked out within the family.'[85] He may very well be right that the use of force by third parties is likely to have a counter-productive effect on the distressed inhabitants of a divided state. Yet restoring integrity to the local struggle clearly requires more of outsiders than adopting a strict policy of nonintervention, or a policy of counter-intervention to preserve the military balance of local forces. Restoring the physical integrity and moral agency of those in the local struggle, which is essential for any kind of self-determination, individual or collective, would actually require the international community to work towards a cessation of the violence and to assist war-torn societies in post-war reconstruction. In more recent works, Walzer notes that

> faced with the reiterated experience of state failure, the reemergence of a form of politics that European historians call "bastard feudalism," dominated by warring gangs and would-be charismatic leaders, I have become more willing to defend long-term military occupations, in the form of protectorates and trusteeships, and to think of nation-building as a necessary part of postwar politics.[86]

Nonintervention in such cases fails to protect the value of community as Walzer conceives of it, and cannot be neutral in its consequences.

Still, the norms of sovereignty and nonintervention may be important to protecting international social pluralism. It is hard to see, however, how cultural and religious plurality constitute moral goods in themselves if their practices do not protect equally the humanitarian interests of their individual members. In the end, Walzer acknowledges that social diversity is one value among many, including peace, equality and autonomy. His argument in favour of social and political pluralism then becomes an instrumental one: 'My argument is that all these [values] are best pursued politically in circumstances where there are many avenues of pursuit, many agents in pursuit. The dream of a single agent – the enlightened despot, the civilizing imperium, the communist vanguard, the global state – is a delusion.'[87] Similarly, according to Robert Jackson, a pluralist international society that the norms of sovereignty and nonintervention maintain is the most morally defensible political 'arrangement to uphold human equality and human freedom around the world.'[88] Like Walzer, Jackson appeals to the liberalism of John Stuart Mill to argue that the political independence of states guaranteed by the norms of sovereignty and nonintervention is the condition for the exercise of human social and moral agency. These arguments suggest that an agency-based view of humanity, to be discussed in later chapters, can be the moral reason to *uphold* the international norms of state sovereignty and nonintervention. While this argument has some validity, it must be admitted that such norms are imperfect instruments for vindicating an agency-based account of humanity, and sometimes they may serve as perverse instruments for the powerful to evade their moral duties to common humanity. This is particularly likely when the norms of state sovereignty and nonintervention translate into an absolute entitlement of states to privacy or freedom from any external interference.

Ultimately, Walzer's reliance on the sovereign individual/community analogy tends towards a naturalization and simplification of the political community, obscuring the problematic nature of transferring a conception of individual privacy to a collective unit such as the state. A family/state analogy is better able to illuminate the ethical problems associated with the interpretation of state sovereignty as privacy.[89] With such an analogy in mind, Mill himself might also have reached different conclusions about nonintervention in a state's internal affairs, since it was he who wrote in relation to family violence, 'The domestic life of domestic tyrants is one of the things which it is the most imperative on the law to interfere with.'[90]

Intervention and the use of force

Walzer's preoccupation with the value of communal autonomy in *Just and Unjust Wars* lies behind his seeming endorsement of the peculiar argument that 'the citizens of a sovereign state have a right, insofar as they are to be coerced and ravaged at all, to suffer only at one another's hands'[91] rather than at the hands of foreigners. The unjustified use of force by a state against its own population, however, seems no less wicked than the unjustified use of force in other people's countries. The brutalities inflicted on Iraqis by Saddam Hussein's regime are not any less bad than the destruction wrought by US-led forces in the 2003 war against Iraq just because the use of force was carried out by internal rather than external agents. In both cases, it is the unjustifiability of the use of force, rather than the interventionary nature of the latter case, that warrants condemnation. This is not to argue that the grievousness of the unjustified use of force by foreign powers is somehow lessened since it is comparable to the unjustified use of force within a state; it is to argue that the latter deserves the same moral reproach as the former.

Furthermore, if it is the use of force itself that is morally problematic, the use of force by national liberation movements must be seen as part of the moral problem. Walzer, however, like many who opposed the US military intervention in Vietnam, tends to romanticize intrastate violence in the context of a national liberation struggle. An authentic political community, he argues, is one that can pass the test of self-help, defined in terms of its capacity to wage 'a large-scale military struggle for independence.' At the same time he asserts that a 'legitimate government is one that can fight its own internal wars.'[92] It is not clear, however, why the preponderant military strength of a nationalist movement would necessarily add to its moral claim to self-determination or political independence, any more than why a state's preponderant military control would justify its suppression of a nationalist movement. For example, would Quebec have a greater moral claim to secession if the Quebec nationalist movement were to mount a large-scale military struggle against the Canadian federal government? Or, would the Canadian federal government have a greater moral claim to keeping Quebec within Canada because it is able to control secessionist forces through military means? A negative response to both of these questions shows the moral flaws in Walzer's arguments, and leads to a recognition that force cannot determine the rightness of any moral claim, within or between nations and states. In fact, those who resort to the use of force, whether they be states or national liberation movements, tend to undermine significantly the force of their moral claims.

It becomes apparent in Walzer's later replies to criticisms of *Just and Unjust Wars* that the kind of freedom for political communities that he endorses is not so much freedom from intervention as freedom from military invasion. In a footnote, he admits that in supporting a rule of nonintervention, he does not 'mean to rule out every effort by one state to influence another or every use of diplomatic and economic pressure.'[93] Similarly, the high threshold Walzer places on the level of human rights violations necessary to justify intervention stems clearly not so much from the unjustifiability of intervention or violation of sovereignty for humanitarian concerns as from the unjustifiability of the use of force as a means to carry out such interventions.[94] It is important to remember then that Walzer's *Just and Unjust Wars* is primarily about the just and unjust use of force, which is important to, but not exhaustive of, the larger topic of just and unjust interventions.

Walzer has continued to conflate the issues of intervention and the use of force in his later writings. He begins an article on 'humanitarian intervention' with the well-known question, 'To intervene or not?' and then indicates his real concern, noting that 'the use of force in other people's countries should always generate hesitation and anxiety.'[95] Walzer's restrictive interpretation of intervention conforms with most theoretical and practical definitions of intervention in the International Relations literature.[96] One should be careful, however, not to conflate these issues. The interventionary aspect of an activity, the fact that it is done 'in other people's countries,' is distinguishable from the activity itself – in this case, the use of force.

Forceful measures should generate 'hesitation and anxiety' whenever they are considered, such as in domestic relationships, by parents in the disciplining of children, in national politics, by nationalist movements or by the state against civil unrest, as well as in international politics, by states or the international community against another state or political community to effect a change in its internal affairs. In all these cases and levels, the proverbial moral issues related to the use of force apply. Is the use of force prudent, proportional and likely to be effective in terms of a defined goal? The use of force is contentious for the same categories of reasons in all these cases, even though only the last is an incontrovertible case of intrusion by an outside party. The concerns of prudence, proportionality and utility are intrinsic to the moral problem of the use of force in general, whether it be for humanitarian purposes or not, and whether it be interventionary in nature or not, and can be distinguished from the moral issues that are intrinsic to the problem of intervention, military or otherwise. Thinking of intervention in only military terms invariably leads to a consideration of the moral issues related to the use of force in general, rather than the moral issues connected to the issue of intervention.

The question Walzer seeks to answer in most of his writings on intervention is 'to use force or not?' and not 'to intervene or not?' The conflation of these two issues in international theory and practice has meant that governments have been able to claim a much stronger social convention against all types of intervention than is supported even in international law. Indeed, state officials commonly consider any type of unsolicited comment on, or interference in, the internal jurisdiction (political, economic and cultural) of one state by another state or outside party to be unjustifiable violations, in varying degrees of subtlety, of a state's sovereignty and the rule of nonintervention. It is, however, a mistake to advance a general doctrine against intervention, because of the problems associated with a specific and extreme type of intervention. Many situations may justify some kind of interventionary response, while ruling out military intervention. Crucial opportunities to engage in preventive and nonmilitary actions, before a crisis explodes or escalates to the level of mass atrocity, are missed when the concepts of intervention and the use of force are conflated.

IV   Areas of disanalogy

While the family/state analogy provides a compelling way to analyze intervention as a moral problem in domestic and international politics, there is one main area of disanalogy that is worth exploring.

The main area of disanalogy is between the state as a public enforcer in relation to the family, and the various actors that comprise international society as a public sphere in relation to each state. Most states have overwhelming coercive capacity, and tightly structured legal and political systems, giving them more effective control over citizens and families, than international society as a public domain, with diffuse military capabilities and looser legal and political institutions, has over member states – not to mention global nonstate actors. Because of the relatively underdeveloped state of international mechanisms for the use of force, it is unlikely that agents of international society will be able to intervene in cases of intrastate violence as easily as agents of the state (police, social workers, etc.) can in the case of family violence.

Yet one should be careful not to exaggerate the significance of this difference in coercive capacity. It does not seem that the coercive power of the state can alone or even significantly account for the changes in norms that have occurred in western societies about the proper scope and limits of parental authority, and the legitimacy of public intervention in families, in the last three centuries. Indeed, in the twentieth century, even when state power was quite capable of forcibly intervening in families, the normative interpretation of family privacy supported a public and social policy of nonintervention in intrafamilial relations. The question of intervention is thus not determined solely by capabilities, but more fundamentally by normative understandings of the public/private distinction. In world politics, similarly, the battle over ideas and attitudes about the moral basis, scope and limits of sovereign authority is at least as important as the battle over material resources and capabilities. Even if international society acquired the capacity to intervene effectively in intrastate relations, without an altered normative understanding of state sovereignty as privacy, it is unlikely that a change in coercive capacity alone will alter the norm of nonintervention.

The preoccupation with military capabilities also privileges the state as an actor in world politics, for it is states that currently possess the most organized concentration of military force. The focus on states, however, reaffirms the subordinate status of other actors, such as the individual men and women whose victimization ultimately provides the justification for 'humanitarian intervention,' as well as those nongovernmental organizations and international institutions that may possess greater capacities and legitimacy to engage in more effective types of intervention to address humanitarian concerns. Just as there are other options besides calling the police in response to familial violence and abuse of parental authority, there are options other than military force as well for confronting intrastate violence and abuse of sovereign authority which we may attack with more imagination given a better understanding of the moral basis for intervention. Clearly, however, in the case of family violence, as well as state terror and violence, one will not be predisposed to legitimizing other kinds of intervention or thinking about how to intervene if one accepts the view that a family or state, by virtue of its private or sovereign status, is acting within its rights.

International intervention to address intrastate violence at this time perhaps more closely resembles intervention by nonstate persons in cases of child maltreatment. In both cases, 'where [social respect for] privacy is high, the degree of social control will be low.'[97] In both contexts, the absence of a common overarching authority to fix a common definition of maltreatment means that pluralistic standards can vie for legitimacy. That is, the intervenor often has a different standard than the allegedly abusive party. Thus Bull argues that the lack of international consensus on the basic concept of 'human rights' makes it a shifty and unreliable source for justification of intervention.[98] It is interesting to note, however, that substantive debate in international politics about human rights is pre-empted when sovereignty as privacy is understood as an absolute and alienable right of statehood. Domestically, for example, a parent faced with a stranger intervention might be more likely to say 'Mind your own business,' than argue that her actions were justified. Similarly, when states adopt a strict view of sovereignty as privacy, they seldom attempt to argue that their treatment of their citizens conforms with a certain interpretation of human rights, or can be justified by other moral considerations.

Rather than making these types of arguments, the merits of which can be debated, abusive parents and sovereigns often appeal to the rhetoric of privacy or sovereignty, asserting not so much that they are justified in their conduct, as that the intervenor has no right to interfere in a private affair. As asserted earlier, the latter type of argument is not enough. It may be undisputed that an act occurred in a sovereign jurisdiction of a state, or that those acted upon belong normally to the domestic jurisdiction of the state. Whether the act should be a private or public concern, however, depends on substantive normative arguments that involve more than a determination of whether the act was committed in a private or public sphere or relationship. It seems to me a good idea to encourage more open and direct international debate and discussion about human rights. Adhering to the interpretation of sovereignty as privacy, however, can only pre-empt that debate.

Ordinary people, without state agents readily available, lack formal protocols, mandated authority and institutional resources to intervene in cases of child maltreatment.[99] States and other actors in global civil society have also lacked these procedures, mechanisms and tools to intervene in cases of sovereign abuse of its own citizens. In the case of child abuse, a stranger who witnesses perceived abuse can in extreme cases notify the public authorities, and involve the state in a process of intervention in the family in question. In the international arena the United Nations is attempting to fulfill this role, but in a context of less developed protocols, more limited or contested authority, and very scarce resources. Again, these deficiencies are unlikely to be ameliorated if state sovereignty as privacy is interpreted in absolutist terms.

The difference between families and states as collective units and the differences between the societies in which they are embedded do not detract from the general utility of the family/state analogy. The use of this analogy has illuminated the moral problem of intervention as an intrusion of the privacy of a collective unit. It leads to an examination of the normative value of state privacy, raising the question: what are the moral foundations and justifications for state sovereignty? For state sovereignty to constitute a normative argument against intervention, we have to examine the particular moral goods, goals and interests that it is intended to uphold or foster, and weigh them against the normative arguments favouring intervention. Thus in the case of the state in international society, just as in the case of the family in domestic society, there may exist morally compelling reasons for intervention which outweigh or transcend the moral considerations favouring nonintervention in any given situation.

V   Conclusion

The idea of the private family and home, however natural and eternal it may seem, has not always been with us. Witold Rybczynski has observed that the idea of a household inaccessible to nonfamily members was unintelligible in medieval times: 'The medieval home was a public, not a private place. . . . In addition to the immediate family [the household] included employees, servants, apprentices, friends, and proteges – households of up to twenty-five persons were not uncommon. Since all these people lived in one or at most two rooms, privacy was unknown.'[100] The idea of home as a private place had to await a transformation of the medieval mind, from a preoccupation with 'the external world, and one's place in it' to an awareness of 'the internal world of the individual, of the self, and of the family.'[101] Some societies have historically lacked 'any articulated distinction between public and private spheres and concerns,'[102] and even within one society, views of the distinction may change, just as the idea of family privacy has varied between and within societies over time.

In international society the interpretation of sovereignty as privacy by scholars and practitioners has been undergoing a significant normative shift in the post-Cold War and post-9/11 worlds. In some ways, this shift does not constitute a dramatic discontinuity in the moral foundation of world order, as theorists of international society have historically admitted normative exceptions and limits, in theory and practice, to the internal liberty of states conceived as a moral good. It is important to remember that the Westphalian conception of sovereignty developed in a context of universals: princes advanced claims for more autonomy for states in an environment of common religious and cultural links. Bodin, a proponent of 'absolute' state sovereignty, clearly viewed state sovereignty in a greater moral and religious context. While he defined sovereignty as 'that absolute and perpetual power vested in a commonwealth,' he stressed that if 'we insist however that absolute power means exemption from all law whatsoever, there is no prince in the world who can be regarded as sovereign, since all the princes of the earth are subject to the laws of God and nature, and even to certain *human* laws common to all nations.'[103]

Vattel similarly championed state sovereignty in its role as a protector of international pluralism, yet he also justified intervention in cases of 'intolerable persecution and evident tyranny.'[104] As Andrew Hurrell has noted, the protection of the autonomy of any particular community has been constantly balanced against 'the protection of certain minimum standards of human rights and by the need to uphold the overall structure of coexistence.'[105] At the genesis of the concept of the state and sovereignty as privacy, the freedom from intervention that states could enjoy as a moral claim in international society and law was not thought to be morally absolute, theoretically or practically. Nicholas Wheeler has harnessed these strands of solidarism in 'international society' theory to argue in favour of the moral permissibility of military interventions in cases of supreme humanitarian emergency, including genocide and other gross violations of human rights.[106]

The argument of this chapter is not that states can make no moral claims to sovereignty as privacy. Indeed, the idea of the abuse of authority (sovereign or parental) implies the possibility of legitimate authority. Intervention to stop the abuse of authority clearly does not undermine in any way the legitimate use of that authority, nor does it necessarily challenge the legitimacy of those in the particular state or family who are vested to exercise that authority. Furthermore, intervention against abusive governments does not undermine the concept of the state as a sovereign institution, but serves to reinforce the moral foundations of the state and sovereign authority. Similarly, intervention in abusive families does not necessarily undermine the family as a social institution; rather, it may be required to reinforce a certain public conception of that institution, which the abusive family is seen to violate.

If these arguments are right, then states' moral claims to sovereignty as privacy in international society must be qualified in certain basic respects, but communitarianism cannot internally generate the grounds for the relevant qualifications, such as consistency with duties of common humanity. Against the interpretation of 'sovereignty as privacy,' a cosmopolitan ethical perspective has generated an alternative interpretation of 'sovereignty as responsibility.' Its implications for the meaning, evaluation and significance of theories and practices of intervention in world politics will be the subject of the rest of this work. Before considering the ethics of cosmopolitan intervention, I want to clarify our understanding of cosmopolitanism as an ethical perspective and consider some challenges from its realist and communitarian critics.

5
The One and Many Faces of Cosmopolitanism[1]

What a piece of work is a man, how noble in reason, how infinite in faculties, in form and moving how express and admirable, in action how like an angel, in apprehension how like a god: the beauty of the world, the paragon of animals; and yet to me what is this quintessence of dust?

Shakespeare, *The Tragedy of Hamlet*[2]

I Introduction

In both ancient and modern worlds cosmopolitan ideas have developed alongside, if not directly in response to, the posited social, political, economic and ethical imperatives of a divided world. Consequently, the salience of such ideas may be measured more by the level of contestation than of acceptance. Despite its long history, an uncontentious account of the implications of a cosmopolitan ethical perspective still eludes political and moral theorists. Part of the difficulty of understanding the precise nature of cosmopolitanism, as well as its relationship with other perspectives, lies in the myriad ways it has been understood or, perhaps more accurately, *misunderstood*. A plethora of images, many inconsistent if not altogether contradictory, confront students of cosmopolitanism. Critics target its various alleged manifestations – as political visions,[3] ethical commitments[4] and economic agendas[5] – without being entirely clear about how these disparate expressions of cosmopolitanism cohere under a single paradigm.

My aim in this chapter is to clarify our understanding of cosmopolitanism as an ethical perspective, which will aid our development in the next chapter of a cosmopolitan account of the public/private construct at the global level, the moral foundations of state sovereignty as privacy, and the ethics of intervention, especially 'humanitarian intervention,' in world politics. A cosmopolitan ethic is commonly understood to refer to a universalistic morality that eschews parochial, especially national, limitations or prejudices.[6] More positively, a cosmopolitan ethical perspective entails the acknowledgement of some notion of common humanity that translates ethically into an idea of shared or common moral duties towards others by virtue of this humanity.[7] H.C. Baldry refers to it as an 'attitude of mind' centered on the notion of human unity.[8] Martha Nussbaum defines a cosmopolitan as someone 'whose primary allegiance is to the community of human beings in the entire world.'[9] The universality and generality[10] of a cosmopolitan ethical orientation ultimately have their roots in a universalist conception of the right and the good. As Nussbaum states elsewhere in her influential article, the cosmopolitan stance asks us 'to give our first allegiance to what is morally good – and that which, being good, I can commend as such to all human beings.'[11] Cosmopolitanism so conceived as ethical universalism presents a clear and provocative challenge to the ethical particularism of national and other more parochial sources claiming our moral allegiance.

Critics find radically diverse faults with the cosmopolitan perspective. As part of our goal to understand cosmopolitanism, it may be fruitful to examine the points of contention between it and its competing perspectives. I will be especially concerned with the challenges posed by realist and communitarian perspectives. Realists regard cosmopolitan claims as too optimistic for a divided humanity, while communitarians generally find them too threatening to key moral goods, such as communal autonomy and plurality. A cosmopolitan perspective is thus at best utopian, and at worst dangerous, for imperfect and diverse humanity. It assumes too much of the natural bond between human beings, tips the moral balance too much in favour of cold universal reason at the expense of more partial sentiment and cares too little about the boundaries that preserve individual, but especially collective, integrity. These critiques reveal distinct but related negative images of cosmopolitanism as idealism, rationalism and imperialism. For cosmopolitanism to claim any moral force, it must refute these portrayals. Let us begin, then, with a view of cosmopolitanism through the eyes of its critics.

II   Critiques of cosmopolitanism

The perils of utopian idealism

International realists have characterized the defining divide in twentieth-century international relations as an antithesis between idealism and realism.[12] E.H. Carr focuses on this dichotomy in his classic work, *The Twenty Years' Crisis*, asserting that the contest between idealism and realism represents the enduring and intractable conflicts between free will and determinism, theory and practice, and ethics and politics. As we have noted earlier, 'realism is founded on a pessimism regarding moral progress and human possibilities;'[13] in contrast, idealism is sustained by a naïve optimism that involves undue faith in the inevitability of moral progress and human perfectibility. Realist critiques of cosmopolitanism have consistently been bound up in this posited dichotomy. They consistently portray cosmopolitan ideas as belonging in the realm of idealism, from political visions of world government, collective security and global distributive justice to the ethical arguments appealing to a notion of common humanity that underlies them.

The universalist implications of the idea of common humanity, expressed in such phrases as 'all men are brothers,'[14] seem utopian in a world marked by fragmentation, discord and conflict. Far from a unity or community of humankind, realists such as Gilpin see 'a world of scarce resources and conflict over the distribution of those resources,' where 'human beings confront one another ultimately as members of [non-universal] groups.'[15] The moral community of humankind, posited by Nussbaum and other cosmopolitan theorists, does not accord with the reality of the human condition. Because we live in a broken rather than united world, amongst self-interested rather than altruistic groups, no harmony or reconciliation of universal and particular, public and private, or international and national, interests can be assumed or, perhaps, even attained.

Realists have targeted idealism not only because of its intellectual failings, but also because, as Gilpin has stated, 'a moral commitment lies at the heart of realism.'[16] Realists believe that idealizing humanity and the human condition, resulting in utopian views of the nature of politics and the possibility of its transcendance with a more harmonious ethic, will only undermine international and human security. The realist in Hedley Bull asserts that in positing a community of humankind that is 'destined to sweep the system of states into limbo,' cosmopolitan ideals threaten international order and stability. In their 'aim at uniting and integrating the family of nations' such ideals 'in practice divide it more deeply than ever before.'[17] Idealistic cosmopolitanism thus produces no ideal, but its antithesis. Its denial of the facts of human existence makes cosmopolitanism a misleading compass for action. Realists thus fear that adopting a cosmopolitan ethical orientation would lead many individuals, and states, to ruin.

That idealism and realism are polar opposites is clear; what requires further examination in the realist critique is the posited connection between idealism and cosmopolitanism. Is the idealistic foundation targeted by realists intrinsic to cosmopolitanism as an ethical perspective? As we shall see, a realist view of the human condition can lead us towards rather than away from embracing cosmopolitanism as a moral orientation. We can agree with realists that moral theories relying on a misplaced faith in human perfectibility or moral progress or a natural harmony of interests are superficial and practically untenable, without agreeing that a cosmopolitan moral perspective necessarily suffers from these failings.

We should acknowledge, of course, that some historical conceptions of cosmopolitanism have indeed been guilty of utopianism.[18] Idealistic cosmopolitanism is intricately associated with expressions of the cosmopolitan ideal in European Enlightenment thought, which stressed the significance of human reason in the advancement of civilization. A belief in the 'unity and immutability of reason,' that it was 'the same for all thinking subjects, all nations, all epochs, and all cultures,'[19] gave the eighteenth century a complacent attitude about the inevitability of moral and intellectual progress guided by reason. According to Enlightenment rationalists, Reason's 'province was to lay down certain definite, incontrovertible principles, and then, in the light of those same principles, to deduce conclusions equally definite and incontrovertible.'[20] Carr mocked this Enlightenment faith in universal reason, especially in the domain of International Relations: 'Reason could demonstrate the absurdity of international anarchy; and with increasing knowledge, enough people would be rationally convinced of its absurdity to put an end to it.'[21] Critiques of cosmopolitanism as idealism thus share key points of affinity with critiques of cosmopolitanism as rationalism, to which we now turn.

The cold and lonely road of rationalism

Along with their disparagement of cosmopolitanism's misguided faith in human unity, critics also decry its adherence to a concomitant ideal of universal human reason. For cosmopolitan rationality, with its abstract and impartialist airs, is either illusory or cold and alienating if realized.

The critique of the posited impartiality of cosmopolitan rationality has special force when we consider the cultural plurality, as well as the economic disparity, in the world. The impartialist claims of cosmopolitanism have, since ancient times, clashed with critics' portrayals of cosmopolitanism as paternalistic and elitist, an ethic formulated by a small privileged group of intellectuals.[22] Its universalist and impartialist pretensions obscure the fact that cosmopolitans of the past spoke only to the experience of a minority of people in the world, or even in their own society. Indeed cosmopolitan thinkers of the eighteenth century were known 'unconsciously [to] measure mankind by criteria of their own rationality'[23] in their development of a cosmopolitan ideal. As Sheldon Hackney has asked, 'can any conception of universal reason escape being culture bound?'[24]

Since people cannot escape from involvement in particular families, cultures and societies, critics of the abstraction of cosmopolitan rationality also focus on its psychological tenability. As Nussbaum has put it in describing this line of criticism, 'cosmopolitanism seems to have a hard time gripping the imagination.'[25] Humanity is too large and abstract a category with which to evoke the passions of moral commitment, obligation and loyalty. Reason may posit a community of humankind, but most people live in much more parochial communities, bounded by kin, culture and state. The human being is an abstraction compared to my brother, my cultural community or my country.[26] As Walzer has put it, 'our common humanity will never make us members of a single universal tribe. The crucial commonality of the human race is particularism: we participate, all of us, in thick cultures that are our own.'[27] Cosmopolitanism does not adequately accommodate the human need to belong to communities of meaning and purpose.[28] As the world becomes more vast, impersonal and anonymous, people will seek more bounded, intimate and intelligible communities.[29] Furthermore, as Gilpin has argued, 'Homo sapiens is a tribal species, and loyalty to the tribe for most of us ranks above all loyalties other than that of the family.'[30] This critique thus challenges the view that a common moral identity can develop out of more intense interaction between individuals and cultures. Historically, at least, cosmopolitan claims have lost to those embodied by more parochial sources of identification; thus, the posited community of humankind has been eclipsed by the rise, in ancient Greece, of the *polis* and, in Enlightenment Europe, of the nation-state.

Not only are critics sceptical about the empirical feasibility of cosmopolitan rationality, they also question its moral desirability. Communitarians tend to argue not only that loyalty to our particular 'tribe' *does* rank above all other loyalties, but that it *ought* to be privileged, because membership and participation in our 'tribe' is the very source of moral life as most of us know it. The highly particularistic sources of identity must have more weight in the creation of the self, including the moral self, than the category of common humanity. According to MacIntyre, communitarian morality posits that membership in a bounded political community is 'a prerequisite for morality,' and that if 'it is the case that I am characteristically brought into being and maintained as a moral agent only through the particular kinds of moral sustenance afforded by my community, then it is clear that deprived of this community, I am unlikely to flourish as a moral agent.'[31] Loyalty to one's particular political community, rather than to some abstract community of humankind, should thus be every individual's highest moral obligation.

Ultimately these critics worry about whether cosmopolitanism can give more particularistic attachments and loyalties their due. Max Boehm defined cosmopolitanism as 'a mental attitude prompting the individual to *substitute* for his attachments to his more immediate homeland an analogous relationship toward the whole world, which he comes to regard as a greater and higher fatherland.'[32] Martin Wight similarly faults cosmopolitanism for 'proclaiming a world society of individuals, which *overrides* nations or states, diminishing or dismissing this middle link.'[33] Implicit in their characterizations of cosmopolitanism is the assumption of a dichotomy between the one and the many, the universal and the particular, humanity and community, reason and sentiment, obligation and loyalty. While idealistic cosmopolitanism can be faulted for assuming an unproblematic harmony between these, the critique against rationalistic cosmopolitanism is that, given a recognition of their incompatibility, a cosmopolitan ethic errs in granting priority to the one over the many, to abstract universal obligations at the expense of concrete particular loyalties and affiliations.

The idea that a cosmopolitan perspective necessarily denigrates or dismisses more particularistic ethics is indeed encouraged by some conceptions of cosmopolitanism. This impression has grown partly due to a literal reading of the provocative expressions of cosmopolitan sentiments by those such as the Cynic Diogenes, who claimed to be a 'wanderer' with 'no city, no home, no fatherland.'[34] Amanda Anderson notes the popular use of cosmopolitanism 'to denote cultivated detachment from restrictive forms of identity.'[35] Jeremy Waldron once mistakenly embraced this notion of rootlessness instead of challenging its appropriateness as a description of the cosmopolitan identity.[36] The phrase 'rootless cosmopolitan,' however worn, reveals what critics perceive to be a deficiency of the cosmopolitan self.[37] A cosmopolitan, by being able to be many things, 'we fear, is really no one, a man without allegiance' – 'He is not, in positive terms, *a friend* to all, but merely *not a stranger*.'[38] The cosmopolitan is fated to a world of superficiality, far from the real world of blood and belonging.

In fact, critics argue that the ethical implications entailed by a cosmopolitan perspective are largely hypocritical. Boehm put the point cogently:

> on the whole the actual obligations which cosmopolitanism lays upon its adherents are comparatively negligible – the more so because in practise it seldom goes beyond demonstration, sentimentality, propaganda and sectarian fanaticism. Hence it often exists among persons whom fortune has relieved from the immediate struggle for existence and from pressing social responsibility and who can afford to indulge their fads and enthusiasms.[39]

Cosmopolitanism may be an ambitious ethical perspective, yet ironically, perhaps precisely because of its worldly aspirations, it has virtually no real-world application.

The inevitable dichotomy and ethical contrast between the universal and the particular, however, is more often assumed than explained or examined. Understanding the normative relationship between them is crucial to a morally viable and coherent conception of cosmopolitanism. For now, however, let us continue with the critics' line of argument.

The logic of imperialism

Cosmopolitan views of human unity and rationality, unable to account for deep difference,[40] tend towards a monistic vision of humanity. Indeed, Enlightenment rationalism carried a revolutionary impulse in its critique of tradition, for according to Reason the 'world was full of errors, errors born of human self-illusion and encouraged by irresponsible authority... The first thing then [Reason] had to do was to effect an enormous clearance, to get rid of that gigantic mass of error.'[41] The cosmopolitan penchant for monism leads to the third critical image of cosmopolitanism.

By imagining humankind to be 'a unity, united by the faculty of reason, capable of pursuing the same ends through the same channels,'[42] cosmopolitanism naturally fosters aspirations for a universal state and attempts at world conquest. 'Scratch a cosmopolitan and you'll find an imperialist just below the surface,' as Ronald Beiner has put it in describing this line of criticism.[43] We can trace in Wight's understanding of cosmopolitanism the essential continuity of the seemingly diverse critiques of cosmopolitanism as idealism, rationalism and imperialism. According to Wight, cosmopolitanism begins with an ideal of human unity, but because not all men are brothers, nor all women sisters, they will have to be forced to be so. Because humankind is not a unity, a cosmopolitan ethical perspective begets a politics that must rely on coercion to bring about its vision of human harmony. The idealism of cosmopolitanism thus ends with a nightmarish quest for hegemony; in assuming the best of humanity, cosmopolitanism becomes its worst enemy.

Wight prefers a society of states, with all its failings, to a cosmopolitan revolution that will destroy not only that society but the order and stability that it provided to international as well as domestic scenes. His discomfort with cosmopolitanism ultimately reflects a deeper and larger concern about the effect of radical normative change on the lives of ordinary men and women. While we can agree with Wight that taking cosmopolitanism seriously might entail a revolution in perspective affecting all realms of human conduct, we need not assume that such a revolution will necessarily occur suddenly or violently. Indeed we can think of some 'revolutionary' changes in ethics, politics and economics that have occurred in human histories that did not entail massive violent upheaval and wholesale destruction of previous social, political or economic structures. We can condemn, in agreement with Wight, methods of change that inflict unnecessary and excessive hardships on people here and now, without going so far as to deny the moral short-comings of existing arrangements, and the need for their amelioration.

While the conservative critique of cosmopolitanism focuses on its revolutionary propensities that threaten to subvert established modes and orders, radicals view cosmopolitanism as an ethical doctrine that too easily plays into the hands of the powerful, be they states, cultures or multinational corporations, providing an ideological basis for the maintenance or enhancement of their dominance. Sun Yat-Sen, China's first modern revolutionary, for example, saw cosmopolitanism as imperialism, from a rather different perspective than Wight: 'Cosmopolitanism...is the same thing as China's theory of world empire two thousand years ago....China once wanted to be sovereign lord of the earth and to stand above every other nation, so she espoused cosmopolitanism.'[44] In this vein, Carr argued that international 'order' and 'international solidarity' 'will always be slogans of those who feel strong enough to impose them on others.'[45] Immanuel Wallerstein has thus commented that cosmopolitan ideals 'can be used just as easily to sustain privilege as to undermine it,'[46] rendering it useless to those who seek to draw from it a consistent political agenda for change.

Given this ambiguity, cosmopolitanism can claim no clear moral superiority over other more parochial ethical doctrines. Thus Michael Walzer has argued that 'perverted cosmopolitans' have been responsible for as many crimes of the twentieth century as 'perverted patriots.'[47] We cannot deny the cogency of this critique when we consider those religious, political and economic ideologies in human history that have attempted to universalize their doctrines through violent or coercive means in the name of some grand universal aim, be it spiritual salvation, civilization, freedom, free trade or even justice.[48] A militant cosmopolitanism might indeed breed global slavery rather than freedom. The image of cosmopolitanism as imperialism leads us to address the issue of the role and use of coercion in the advancement of ethical goals. Do cosmopolitan truths justify the use of coercion? If not, can they ever be effectual? If justice without force is a myth, what is the ethical value of justice with, or perhaps *through*, force?

Indeed, this image casts grave doubts on the tenability of cosmopolitanism as an *ethical* perspective. To address this critique, we might ask whether the universalism entailed by a cosmopolitan ethical perspective need be absolutist. Cosmopolitanism, as a viable ethical perspective, depends on a distinction between universalisms that are absolutist and those that are not. Walzer's critique of cosmopolitanism inadvertently leads us to acknowledge that it is not only universal perspectives like cosmopolitanism that can suffer from absolutism; parochial doctrines like ones that espouse the inherent superiority of a certain racial or national group, for example, have also been known to breed imperialistic and totalitarian enterprises.

III Re-imagining cosmopolitanism

Given the seriousness of the critics' charges, one might be tempted to pronounce cosmopolitanism dead as an ethical perspective. Can cosmopolitanism as a moral orientation escape utopian idealism, rootless rationality and brutish imperialism? Are cosmopolitan projects doomed to bring disaster onto humanity?

Our response to these critics might begin with the observation that no ethical perspective – realist, communitarian or cosmopolitan – can be free from moral danger, for whichever ethical perspective we might adopt, all are corruptible. To paraphrase Tolstoy, each perspective, like a family, when flawed is 'unhappy in its own way,' but when rightly conceived, all perspectives like all happy families, 'resemble one another.'[49] When properly understood, these perspectives can all be enlisted to aid the betterment of the human condition, but when ill-conceived, they go wrong in various ways that unleash different but equally devastating plagues upon humanity. To salvage cosmopolitanism as a moral perspective, we need to illuminate different images of humanity.

The fragility of being human

Critics have asserted that the cosmopolitan idea of humankind as one family or community is utopian. Yet this idealistic reading of phrases like 'all men are brothers' is a surprising interpretation, given universal experiences of sibling and familial discord. Indeed, much of literature ancient and modern, not to mention post-modern, find within the subject of the family all the conflict and failings of human relations outside the family. The stories of Cain and Abel, King Lear and his daughters, and Dostoyevsky's brothers Karamazov, to note some well-known examples, all depict family relationships in less-than-ideal and certainly not harmonious terms. The mere assertion that all human beings comprise a unity like a family would not seem then to lead to any automatic conclusions about the harmony of human relations, unless one holds excessively idealistic assumptions about families and other group relations. Yet a cosmopolitan view of human unity need not be utopian.

The idea of common or shared humanity entails common circumstances that make the idea of a *human* condition intelligible. In the works of Homer, these common circumstances defined who was human and who was not. As Baldry notes, Homer's normal word for a human being was not *anthropos*, but 'mortal,' *brotos* or *thretos*,[50] a condition that separated humanity from the gods. Human beings, children of one of the lesser gods, were far from being the 'paragon of animals' and closer to being the 'quintessence of dust.'[51] Not surprisingly the earliest cosmopolitans were medical writers such as Hippocrates, habitually exposed in their work to the physical and mental frailties of the human body and mind. The unity of humankind consists in this common human condition: a wretched, feeble and pitiable existence, marked by uncertainty, insecurity and eventually death. Thucydides's description of the plague's effects in Athens in the second year of the Peloponnesian War also shows an awareness of this natural equality of human vulnerability.[52] In modern times, Albert Camus has offered us a similar view of humanity, united in our common capacity to suffer.[53] The idealistic cosmopolitanism of eighteenth- and nineteenth-century Europe thus competes with a more ancient cosmopolitanism based on sadder truths about the human condition.

A keen awareness of the fragility of being human is not an exclusive preserve of realists. It is precisely this view of the human condition that underlies Judith Shklar's liberalism of fear.[54] Her assertion that cruelty is the primary human vice evokes not the idealistic image of humanity as a harmonious unity, but forces us to pay attention to human conflict, insecurity and suffering. Quintessentially cosmopolitan in her moral outlook, since 'putting cruelty first' appeals to a universal human capacity to inflict and suffer harm, Shklar's morals are nevertheless wholly free of idealist assumptions. For Shklar does not begin with a utopian vision of what can be achieved given a belief in the perfectibility of human nature or the inevitability of moral progress; instead she begins 'with what is to be avoided.'[55] Far from holding an optimistic view of human possibilities, Shklar's liberalism of fear becomes 'more *a recipe for survival than a project for the perfectibility of mankind.*'[56] Shklar's work is valuable to the debate in International Relations theory between idealism and realism precisely because her arguments constantly expose the falseness and inadequacy of this posited dichotomy in characterizing the nature of the distinctions between various ethical perspectives.

While putting cruelty first for its affront against our common humanity may be distinctively cosmopolitan, all ethical perspectives can condemn cruelty, or the act of taking delight in, or being indifferent to, the unjustified pain and suffering of others. Thus realists should want to avoid it because, given the fear and mistrust it inspires, cruelty breeds insecurity, and communitarians would condemn it for inhibiting mutual caring and fellowship. For liberals, as Shklar has pointed out, cruelty 'is often utterly intolerable . . . because fear destroys freedom,'[57] and not, as John Kekes has speculated, because cruelty is the opposite of benevolence.[58] Different ethical approaches may value differently moral goods such as freedom, humanity, community and security, but in acknowledging that all these goods can be destroyed by cruelty and fear, ethical perspectives may be united in their condemnation of cruelty. The moral commitment that Gilpin asserts lies at the heart of realism is thus not incompatible, but has deep resemblances, with the moral commitment at the heart of cosmopolitanism. Focusing on cruelty rather than insecurity, however, reminds us that our commitment is a *moral* one, and makes us less inclined to solve the problem of insecurity through means that are themselves morally questionable.

Recognizing the significance of cruelty as a moral vice, public and private, not only forces us to see humans as potential victims and sufferers, but also requires us to confront the unpleasant reality of humans as agents responsible for such vice and malice. Thus Shklar warns that putting cruelty first 'dooms one to a life of skepticism, indecision, disgust, and often misanthropy.'[59] Indeed the loathing of human cruelty itself can generate a misanthropy that motivates the worst cruelties committed by humankind. Realists, 'overwhelmed like Hamlet by the density of evil,'[60] perhaps have more often fallen prey to this danger. Realist pessimism tinged with misanthropy accounts for the moral failings of classical and contemporary realism. Crushed by the ubiquity of cruelty and consumed by misanthropy, some realists are led to reject all morality as a sham, and to advocate a politics of power. Yet Shklar shows us that our survival, individual and collective, depends on our resolve to avoid misanthropy and confront the worst of human vices without moral despair or resignation.

Cosmopolitanism's moral condemnation of cruelty translates at a minimum into a moral obligation to uphold the principle of humanity, to do our best 'to prevent and alleviate human suffering wherever it may be found.'[61] Cosmopolitanism requires us to pay attention to the cries of victims in the flesh, a difficult task given how suffering usually takes place, 'while someone else is eating or opening a window or just walking dully along.'[62] Individuals and societies attempt to manage personal and public responsibility for suffering by making a distinction between misfortune and injustice.[63] At the international level, until very recently, the suffering of individuals and some groups – whether the cause be famine, civil war or pestilence – tended to be discounted as misfortunes, for international society could only admit claims of justice and injustice between states. The normal model of justice in international as in domestic society, however, can be a terrible burden to anyone whose suffering cannot be acknowledged or redressed within its bounds. Shklar's appeal to 'take the victim's view'[64] is thus at least potentially cosmopolitan in enabling us to recognize the suffering of the exile, refugee, enemy and stranger.

IV Cosmopolitan unity and diversity

Focusing on cruelty, especially the physical kind, also challenges the critics' image of cosmopolitanism as rationalism in putting our sentient aspect to the fore, the feeling rather than thinking human being. As Shklar has observed, 'Putting cruelty first ... is too deep a threat to reason for most philosophers to contemplate it at all.'[65] This is because the fear engendered by cruelty 'reduces us to mere reactive units of sensation.'[66] Yet it is a view of humans as more than sentient beings that inspires a moral condemnation of cruelty.

Of course, common sentient vulnerability does not completely define the human condition. For the ancient Greeks to be human was not to be a god; however, it was also not to be a beast. While the fleeting and uncertain nature of the human condition distinguishes humans from the gods, articulate reasoned speech and skill separates humans from the rest of the animal world.[67] Human beings are imaginative expressive actors who do not merely act according to instinct, but possess the freedom to act according to values, meanings and interpretations of tangible and intangible worlds which they themselves have a role in shaping and developing. Thus humans are part authors of themselves and their world. It is this rational capacity of humans that is threatened by cruelty, for in causing pain and fear, cruelty is 'language-destroying,'[68] unmaking the self and the world it has created. Cruelty therefore has diverse implications, affecting not only physical security, but also human agency and autonomy.

The cosmopolitan image of humanity is thus more complex than its critics have allowed, and involves an irreducible duality. On the one hand, cosmopolitanism is founded on the recognition of a common human condition marked by vulnerability to suffering. In this sense, humanity is one. On the other hand, the unity implied by this common condition does not entail homogeneity or sameness, for to be human is also to be distinctively individual or particular. In this sense, humanity is many. From a cosmopolitan perspective, human beings are one *and* many things.[69]

Critics of cosmopolitan rootlessness imply that this multiplicity of identities constitutes no real identity at all. The criticism betrays a rather singular conception of human rootedness and belonging, and discomfort with the duality of human existence and the potential conflicts it may engender. A cosmopolitan perspective, however, does not assert that individuals should aim to be rootless; rather it portrays individuals as possessing multiple roots.[70] Rather than being alienated or solitary, a cosmopolitan self acknowledges its *solidarity* with a multiplicity of others. From this plurality we derive various sources of obligation and loyalty, affinity and difference. To those who want to assert the moral primacy of an unproblematic allegiance to a single community, such as one's country, the cosmopolitan identity must be disconcerting, for multiple roots translate into divided loyalties. Thus to a cosmopolitan such as Shklar, betrayal cannot be the primary vice, for given the plural nature of human rootedness and belonging, disloyalty or betrayal may be regrettable but is necessarily common.[71] In misportraying a cosmopolitan as a person 'without allegiance,' critics evade the cosmopolitan challenge of conceiving of the self as one *and* many things, a divided but single whole. A person without roots or allegiances is certainly doomed to superficiality, but a cosmopolitan, with multiple roots and bound by diverse compelling obligations, almost certainly is not.

With this awareness, individual integrity and communal authenticity cannot mean an unambivalent attachment to a singular conception of the self or community; rather what may be required is a recognition of their inherent complexity and a permanent state of inner doubt and contestation rather than harmony. The desire to reduce this conflict, and to solidify loyalty to one cause or group, leads to attempts to reduce the multiple sources of the self and of societies; historically and in our own time, this has resulted in the forced uprooting of entire groups and the whittling down of complex individual personalities into thin shadows. Thus one of the first casualties of war is the ability to acknowledge the plural roots and divided loyalties of selves and of communities. One can be identified as an ethnic Albanian or a Serb, a Tutsi or a Hutu, but not as a Tutsi and a teacher and a mother of four, or a Serb and a pacifist who is married to a Croat. Inhumanity consists not only in denying the fact that one's victims are human beings, but also in severing the multitude of roots that embed them in a particular but common set of human relationships, producing an unaccommodated humanity deprived of names, nationality, citizenship, religion, ethnicity, ethical convictions, political, economic or social position.[72]

Far from denying human diversity, then, a cosmopolitan perspective makes us only too keenly aware of it, at all levels, within individuals and between them, as well as within communities and between them. A cosmopolitan understanding of the dual nature of human rootedness and belonging paradoxically allows us to recognize not only human plurality, but also the bonds of affinity between individuals and groups that are diverse in other respects.

Critics still worry that despite its acknowledgement of our more parochial selves, cosmopolitanism's commitment to universal justice necessitates a denigration of particular attachments. The idea that our more parochial loyalties constitute sources of morality should lead us to examine the ways in which they are morally relevant. How would a cosmopolitan ethic address the common sentiment that we do owe more to our family members, friends and fellow citizens than to others, and that the world would be a lesser place if we all lost this special sense of loyalty towards our own, however that is defined?

The quarrel between loyalty and obligation is not new. The two concepts are qualitatively different when we define obligation as 'rule-governed conduct' emanating from principles of justice, and loyalty as an emotional 'attachment to a social group.'[73] This distinction between loyalty and obligation, however, does not entail their mutual exclusivity. Indeed, group loyalty and the feeling of belonging engendered by it can serve as powerful motivations for people to fulfill their public or private moral obligations. Shklar argues, however, that the unavoidably exclusive nature of this kind of loyalty makes problematic those obligations we may have beyond our circles of loyalty and belonging. This is a great defect of basing moral obligation on centers of loyalty so conceived, since sociologically, cruelty, inhumanity and injustice are more easily perpetrated against 'others,' who cannot claim our emotional loyalty and who would thus by definition fall outside of our universes of obligation.[74]

While affective loyalty may establish a bond between some derived from common group membership and fellowship, it is qualitatively different from the bond created by moral obligation and justice, which connects us not only to those with whom we share a sense of loyalty and belonging, but more importantly, to those with whom we do not. While we may feel that we owe more than justice requires to those with whom we have special attachments, we must, in the interest of justice, fulfill moral obligations sometimes at the expense of such attachments. Thus the bond of loyalty may reinforce the bond of justice, but should not replace it.

Richard Rorty has provocatively challenged this distinction between loyalty and obligation by characterizing justice 'as a larger loyalty.' Rorty thinks it would be more useful to describe conflicts between loyalty and justice as 'conflicts between loyalties to smaller groups and loyalty to larger groups,' with justice as merely 'the name for our largest current loyalty.'[75] A cosmopolitan conception of justice requires us to expand our circles of loyalty to include the human species or all living things, while a communitarian conception of justice may only require the expansion of our circles of loyalty to include one's fellow citizens. Ironically, although Rorty intends to challenge proponents of Kantian reason and justice, it is not only his understanding of justice that is problematic here, but his understanding of loyalty.

Consider the case of conscientious objectors, such as those Americans who protested against the Vietnam War. If we follow Rorty, American protestors were faced with conflicting loyalties between a smaller loyalty for their own country and fellow citizens, and a larger loyalty that included the Vietnamese. And yet, this characterization would be unsatisfactory to those who saw their protest as an expression of their loyalty, not to the Vietnamese people or government, whom they could hardly know, but to their own country. If we cast the debate about the Vietnam War in terms of loyalty, it was not a conflict of loyalties between a smaller and a larger group, but a contest between two competing visions of what it meant to be loyal to one's smaller particular group. Rorty's argument does not capture a concept like the 'loyal opposition,' and yet some of the most loyal characters in literature exhibit this quality. King Lear's servant Kent, for example, expresses his undying loyalty to the king by warning him of his folly. It is clear that Kent's primary motive in arguing with the irascible king is his loyalty to Lear's particular well-being, and not for any larger group.[76]

Similarly, even if we concede the claim from the 'morality of patriotism' that individuals have a moral obligation to be loyal to their particular political community, we are still left with the question of how loyalty is best expressed. MacIntyre cautions near the beginning of his essay on patriotism that the concept 'is not to be confused with a mindless loyalty to one's own particular nation which has no regard at all for the characteristics of that particular nation.'[77] Yet if patriots must view the nation as the very source of morality, then they leave nations judges of the moral desirability of their own characteristics. If one accepts this view, patriotism would come close to being a mindless loyalty to one's own particular nation, since the individual who belongs to a nation cannot have any other standpoint from which to evaluate her national characteristics. Loyalty as a moral virtue is more than mere obedience or 'the habit of identifying oneself with a single nation or other unit, placing it beyond good and evil.'[78] If being moral is to be loyal to our particular attachments, as the morality of patriotism asserts, and if being loyal to them is to be moral, then we must fulfill our moral obligations not only in the interest of justice, but also in the interest of our loyalty to our particular groups. If justice were a kind of loyalty, it would not necessarily be a larger one, but a moral one.[79]

While the irreconcilability of some demands for loyalty with moral obligation may be morally unproblematic, a similar irreconcilability between particular and universal obligations would be deeply troublesome.[80] The dichotomization of loyalty and obligation tends to lead to a dichotomous view of particular and universal obligations. How should we conceive of their relationship? Danish director Kaspar Rostrup's film *Memories of a Marriage*[81] offers a compelling view of their moral reconciliation. The film recounts the joys and sorrows in the life of an ordinary working-class couple, Karl and Regitze Aage. In one scene, Karl returns home to find that his young son has been unjustly punished at school by a teacher. Karl views it as a misfortune, saying, 'That's too bad,' and 'What's done is done.' Regitze, unwilling to put up with the injustice, storms off to the bus stop, committed to making her protest alone. As she is getting ready to leave, her son pleads with her not to go, arguing, 'That'll only make things worse.' When she has left, the boy laments to his father, 'I think she's mad too.' The father then replies, 'Your Mum is absolutely right. She's not doing this for your sake alone, get it? She's thinking about all the other kids he might some day beat up.' Angry at his own cowardice, he leaves the house to join his wife.

In this case the particular affection a mother has for her son makes Regitze's outrage understandable. We feel the father is a bit too humble for not wanting to protest officially against the ill-treatment of his own son. If Regitze went to protest only out of personal fidelity to her son, we would admire her maternal pride and loyalty, but it would be difficult to see her action as cause for moral praise. However, Karl's explanation of Regitze's action shows how our particular attachments gain moral significance or worth when they are a window to our moral responsibilities, universal and particular.

In this case, personal fidelity and family loyalty as well as parental obligation may all sustain a universal moral obligation to protest against injustice, but in some cases these may all conflict. Kristin Renwick Monroe gives us tragic examples of conflicts between obligations in her narratives of people who rescued Jews during the Holocaust.[82] Many rescuers exposed not only themselves, but also their own families, to grave danger by hiding Jews in their homes. Monroe gives us compelling evidence that rescuers consistently, if not altogether consciously, gave priority to strangers' lives even at the expense of the safety of their own children. Rescuers knew of the dangers but did not do a cost–benefit analysis; rather, compelled by moral obligations derived from their perceptions of a shared humanity, rescuers acted to help those in the direst need. As Bethe, a rescuer in Berlin who had three small children, put it:

'We knew what could happen. If they had caught us, we would have been taken away. The children would have been taken away. We absolutely knew this. But when they're standing at the door, and their life is threatened, what should you do in this situation? You could never do that [turn them away].'[83]

The supererogation of the rescuers, their sacrifice of their basic interests and needs for the basic moral claims of others, may be morally praiseworthy, but this extreme form of altruism would be a problematic basis for a theory of moral obligation. This is not mainly because such a theory would be unappealing to self-regarding human beings and therefore ineffective, as realists have argued, but because supererogation, in necessitating the possible sacrifice of one's very survival, cannot serve as the central virtue underlying any theory of moral obligation.

To identify this central virtue, we might note that while conflicts between loyalty and obligation may be unavoidable in the most well-ordered of societies, and perhaps an occasional feature of any enduring human relationship, the exceptional conflict *between obligations* ultimately reflects the extreme injustice of a regime. When rescuers must risk harm to themselves and their families in order to do right by imperilled Jews, the conflicts between obligations that they face indicate a context of extreme injustice in which no available choice can be morally unproblematic.[84] Simone Weil therefore identified the paramount importance of 'order,' or 'a texture of social relationships such that no one is compelled to violate imperative obligations in order to carry out other ones.'[85] We might call this right ordering *justice*. A world in which our universal and particular obligations were in perpetual conflict would not only be a deeply tragic world, but a grossly unjust one.

A cosmopolitan acknowledgement of our universal and particular obligations makes intelligible cries of injustice, inhumanity and intolerance beyond our own spheres of affection, and requires those of us who are more fortunate to do what we can to combat them. Myopic communitarians or realists who are blind to our humanity, in its commonality as well as its diversity, are more likely to see misfortune instead of injustice beyond the gates of their own community and, in their resigned acceptance of a world of suffering, are more likely to commit passive injustice. From a cosmopolitan view, the fact that our obligations do conflict greatly at the international level should indicate to us the moral untenability of the existing state of global arrangements. While social and political psychologists may want to focus on illuminating the logic of altruistic behaviour, political theorists should perhaps concentrate on resolving contexts of injustice which make not only altruism, but supererogation, necessary. For it is not altruism, but justice, that is wanting in the world.[86]

Ethical tolerance, active not passive

The complex understanding of humanity, community and the self at the heart of a cosmopolitan ethical perspective, its twin focus on the one *and* the many, removes it further and further away from ideological absolutism and the critical image of cosmopolitanism as imperialism. Absolutism as an ideal involves the assumption that human diversity and difference inevitably lead to conflict. An absolutist seeks to eliminate conflict by reducing this pluralism. Yet no ethical perspective can avoid some form of despotism if it does not acknowledge the essential duality of the human condition. The noblest of motives may be corrupted by ideological absolutism, which has always excused cruelty and every other kind of injustice, public and private, against its enemies – the defective, the infidel, the heretic or dissident, the moderate and the tolerant.

The critique of cosmopolitanism as imperialism, however, seems puzzling if we remember the use of the word 'cosmopolitan' in ordinary discourse to describe peaceful social *plurality* rather than homogeneity. A cosmopolitan city, after all, is a place where people and cultures from many or all parts of the world cohabit in more or less peaceful co-existence.[87] Cosmopolitanism so conceived is antithetical to absolutist universalism and 'implies tolerance.'[88] Indeed, as I have suggested, a cosmopolitan ethical perspective sees human pluralism as a source of reconciliation as well as conflict. Diversity alone therefore cannot account for human conflict; as John Locke put it with respect to the religious wars plaguing the Christian world, 'it is not the diversity of opinions but the refusal of toleration to those that are of different opinions that has produced all the bustles and wars.'[89]

Toleration as an ethical virtue requires us to forbear from the use of violence and coercion to promote our view of the right, the good or the truth. Force is a counterproductive method because the virtues that comprise the right and the good depend on the exercise of moral will, intention and agency, which render them intelligible. Someone who is coerced to do the right thing can be called 'compliant' but not 'just' or 'virtuous.' A person who is forced to subscribe to a belief may be a conformist, but not a true believer. Coercion, then, corrupts the very accessibility of the right, the good and the truth.

Some have sought another route to tolerance and the mitigation of human conflict, by positing a profound scepticism of all human knowledge, and asserting the relativity of all conceptions of the truth, the right and the good. Moral relativism is of course the medicine realists have prescribed for taming cosmopolitanism's missionary and coercive proclivities. If we give up the idea of universal truth or morality, realists argue, we may be less inclined to kill each other over conflicting conceptions of it. Yet there is a difference between arguing that truth and morality are not promoted well through coercion, and arguing that coercion is unjustified because there is no universal truth or morality. The latter argument breeds relativism, which is antithetical to tolerance. As Samuel LaSelva has cogently argued, 'What relativism produces is not tolerance but an abdication of responsibility for basic human values,' for ultimately 'relativism is incapable of sustaining any values at all.'[90] Both ideological absolutism and relativism undermine tolerance, the foundation of peaceful co-existence. This is because relativism tends to breed passive indifference and unbridled licence, but not active tolerance.

It is important to note a common confusion between tolerance and passitivity. A cosmopolitanism that promoted passive indifference to the right, the good or the truth would hardly deserve the name of an *ethical* perspective. The importance of tolerance as a virtue to a cosmopolitan moral orientation, however, reveals the active and interventionary nature of this perspective, necessitated by its perception of a shared moral obligation to resist injustice. Because injustice and cruelty occur in every sphere of human relations and in all societies and cultures, a cosmopolitan ethic entails interventionary action to resist them in public as well as private life, at domestic and international levels. Yet a cosmopolitan approach also recognizes the inherent limits of coercion as a means to promote its ethical ideals.[91]

Cosmopolitanism's recognition of a shared moral obligation to combat cruelty and injustice commits us not only to refrain from doing injustice ourselves. Indeed, the world would still be a morally defective place if people merely avoided committing active injustice. A cosmopolitan ethic requires us to attach moral blame to 'passive injustice,' which is 'the refusal of both officials and of private citizens to prevent [or stop] acts of wrongdoing when they could and should do so,' or 'a failure to mitigate suffering that could have been alleviated.'[92] Shklar's concern for victims led her to highlight this Ciceronian insight, for victims often cry 'Injustice!' not only against those directly responsible for it, but also against those who stood by and did nothing to stop it. We see the sinister force of passive injustice at work in the fictional scene described earlier involving the Aage family. In defence of his passitivity about his son's ill-treatment at school, Karl points out to Regitze that he was not the one who slapped his son. While true, we understand Regitze's moral reproach of his behaviour since his failure to stand up to injustice or attempt to make the guilty account for it makes him morally culpable. The example also shows how even the bonds engendered by family love and loyalty do not prevent us from committing passive injustice. Indeed, a sense of loyalty can assuage our sense of injustice, so that loyalty can overcome even active injustice, to the detriment of justice, indicating the larger role that affective loyalty may play in contributing to the wide acceptance of passive injustice.[93]

Regitze's character exhibits a quintessentially cosmopolitan ethical perspective in her passionate resistance of both active and passive injustice, although she is far from the superficial worldly cosmopolitan individual described by Waldron.[94] She is not a woman of the world, she has not travelled much or experienced many cultures, she is a woman of limited means, but she does not forget to do the little good that lies within her powers. While we can see a cosmopolitan stance in Regitze's moral attitude, we are also given a mirror of our less courageous selves in the character of Karl Aage, whose reluctance to help others arises not out of malice, but mostly out of fear, cowardice or narrow-mindedness. As Shklar has warned, 'we commit and permit a mass of injustice because we are lazy or lack courage or both.'[95] Contrary to Boehm and other critics, cosmopolitanism, rightly conceived, is neither lazy nor cowardly; rather, in requiring us to acknowledge the humanity of others, to intervene against active and passive injustice *and* to forbear from using coercion to promote ethical ideals, cosmopolitanism makes difficult but possible demands on us all.

V   Conclusion

A cosmopolitan ethical perspective as I have construed it can be distinguished from a common conception of cosmopolitanism in International Relations. In terms of political order, cosmopolitanism has been typically associated with visions of world government and a concomitant idea of universal world citizenship. So construed, cosmopolitanism appears to clash with a world organized into territorially distinct and politically independent states, as well as subvert the more bounded notion of national citizenship.

We might, however, be cautious about drawing any automatic linkages between a vision of political order in the form of a universal world government – a state writ large to encompass the entire earth and its population – and a vision of world order guided by cosmopolitan moral principles. For nothing in the idea of a world state can guarantee cosmopolitan morality as I have outlined it.[96] Linking a cosmopolitan ethical perspective with a world government agenda also misidentifies the barrier to the realization of a cosmopolitan moral order. A world government or universal state would certainly eliminate the political, if not cultural, plurality that is a hallmark of a society of states, but this change would not necessarily lead to the validation of cosmopolitan morality. The barrier to the realization of a cosmopolitan moral order, then, lies not in the size of the state that claims our moral allegiance (parochial or universal in scope), but in how we characterize the normative agency and structure of the state or political unit, whatever its scope or domain. This means that we cannot dismiss a cosmopolitan ethical perspective as an irrelevant, misguided or unrealizable dream in a world lacking a central and universal political authority; rather we need to explore how the norms generated by such a perspective would re-shape our understandings of the moral status, rights and obligations of existing agents and structures of domestic and international societies.[97]

A cosmopolitan ethical perspective allows us to recognize that as individuals and as members of groups, we are all 'involved in a multiple scheme of relationships'[98] which are diverse yet share a common moral core. Cosmopolitanism encourages a moral allegiance not to an abstract community of humankind, but to the humanity in all those with whom we associate who can claim to be human, friend, stranger or foe. So construed, cosmopolitanism comprises a core normative orientation upon which the ethical quality of our various commitments depend. Whether we seek to build a stable world order, strong communities or robust individuals, a cosmopolitan ethical perspective of the kind I have constructed in this chapter is vital for their realization. Cosmopolitanism thus constitutes an ethical primer coat of sorts; it is not the be-all and end-all of moral life, but without it our most noble and well-meaning moral masterpieces will peel and crumble.

Contrary to the images of cosmopolitanism put forward by its critics, we can conceive of a cosmopolitanism that is nonidealist, nonalienating and noncoercive, which nevertheless also eschews the opposite vices of cynical misanthropy, unreflective obedience and indifferent passivity. A cosmopolitan ethical perspective, rightly understood, is realistic in its recognition of a common human condition marked by frailty and falli-bility, faithful not only to the one but also to the many, and tolerant in its nonviolent promotion of ethical understanding. It provides us with a morally compelling view of how our many worlds may meet, as they inevitably will, on terms of humanity, justice and tolerance, which are the foundations of perpetual peace and friendship, rather than on terms of cruelty, inequity and violence, the foundations of perpetual war and animosity.

Cosmopolitanism requires us to practise the virtues of humanity, justice and tolerance not only among our fellow citizens, compatriots or believers, within our own families or circle of friends, but also among strangers, enemies and infidels – those who typically fall outside of our matrices of habitual loyalty and belonging. Cosmopolitanism does not require us to deny our particular loyalties and affiliations, but nourishes a sympathetic if critical approach towards them. It does not entail the abolition of the society of states, only that such a society should recognize, endorse and uphold cosmopolitanism's ethical commitments to humanity, justice and tolerance. Although we live in a world full of pluralism, this diversity paradoxically is the stuff of which not only the borders, but also the bridges, between individuals and collectivities are made. These borders and bridges are neither fixed nor natural, but have evolved and are evolving as human beings, at a material and a mental level, continue to interact with each other.[99] A cosmopolitan ethic guides us in this evolution, leading us to seek a balance between the bonds and boundaries of our public and private universes of obligation, respecting both our common humanity and the rich variety of differences that animate human life.

As Amanda Anderson has put it, 'cosmopolitanism endorses reflective distance from one's cultural affiliations, a broad understanding of other cultures and customs, and a belief in universal humanity.'[100] A cosmopolitan recognition of the one *and* many faces of humanity allows us to appreciate the value of both universal and particular moral obligations, rather than posing their dichotomization and exalting one at the expense of the other. For without a universal face, our ethics will remain vulnerable to the question, 'Justice for whom?' And without particular ones, the duty to fulfill our moral obligations, universal or particular, will be defeated by the perennial question asked by Karl Aage and most of us who lack the moral courage to combat injustice, 'Why me?' The critics of cosmopolitanism are thus misguided in their singular conceptualizations of cosmopolitanism, which miss its eclectic and syncretic nature.

Critics might respond that cosmopolitanism is not so much eclectic and syncretic as confused and schizophrenic, for inherent tensions exist between the principles of humanity, justice and tolerance, which may occasion hard trade-offs between them rather than harmonious accommodation. Yet while critics might argue that cosmopolitanism cannot have it all, its defenders might argue that one cannot have any one without the others. From a cosmopolitan view, a justice that is intolerant or inhumane constitutes a defective form of justice. Similarly, a humanitarianism uninformed by tolerance breeds the worst form of tyrannical universalism, while one ignorant of justice risks becoming a naïve pawn of the unjust. Finally, tolerance of the inhumane or unjust leads to licentiousness and the forfeiture of any moral life. These ethical commitments must be pursued together rather than as ends-in-themselves, for their moral worth relies on their mutual interconnection.

None of this means to deny the moral complexities that confront us all in our attempts to reconcile and fulfill our international, domestic and personal responsibilities. On the contrary, it is only with a cosmopolitan appreciation of the one and many faces of humanity that our moral difficulties become most apparent. Cosmopolitanism does not ignore the need for hard choices but accentuates just how hard they should be. In enabling us to feel the real weight of hard moral choices and tragedies that inevitably arise in contexts of pervasive injustice and widespread misery, a cosmopolitan ethical perspective should lead to greater efforts to prevent the perpetuation of such contexts in which only hard choices remain. The responsibility to engage in these efforts rests on us all, and especially on those 'whom fortune has relieved from the immediate struggle for existence.'[101]

Despite the long history of cosmopolitanism, its implications for our understanding of the individual self, for political community and for world order have so far received only a faint, wavering light. Baldry observed that cosmopolitan ideas in ancient Greece 'had no more than a reforming effect on human relations.' Indeed, the world of the ordinary Greek person in the late fifth century B.C. was still dominated by cleavages between rival city-states, and assumptions about the natural superiority of men over women, free men over slaves, high over low and Greeks over barbarians. This might allay the fears of some critics of cosmopolitanism, but its modern proponents should find this sobering. Although we live in an era of increasing globalization, most of us today are still like 'the most enlightened of the [ancient] Greeks,' far 'from full understanding of its [moral] implications.'[102] So long as the age-old scourges of inhumanity, injustice and intolerance have their say in the world, however, cosmopolitanism as an ethical perspective will endure as a pertinent, if not pervasive, feature of our moral life in a brave new millennium.

6
Cosmopolitanism, Liberalism and Intervention

> We will not enjoy development without security; we will not enjoy security without development, and we will not enjoy either without respect for human rights.
>
> Kofi Annan, *The New York Times*[1]

I Introduction

The New Zealand film, *Once Were Warriors*, recounts the private cycle of violence plaguing one family, and the external social circumstances that contribute to its perpetuation.[2] In one scene during a party involving several other drunken friends, the couple have an argument that turns into a physical fight in which the husband dominates. The friends respond by fleeing the house *en masse*, leaving the couple to themselves, while the children are left to witness the violence and deal with the aftermath. No one, individually or collectively, takes it upon themselves to break up the fight, or stop the assault, and no one calls the authorities. Nor do any of the friends return the next day to enquire about the welfare of the family or to offer any kind of support or assistance. The private torments of one family mixed with social indifference and even endorsement lead tragically to the violation and death of an innocent child. Historically, the society of states has often acted like the drunken friends who desert the scene when violence breaks out. In the face of inhumanity confined within sovereign borders, nonintervention was the norm required by an absolutist interpretation of 'sovereignty as privacy'; not only the use of force, but all kinds of interventionary actions by other states or the United Nations received little endorsement from the society of states because they were seen to challenge the normative foundations of that society.

110

Communitarian perspectives have contributed to this historical privatization of intrastate violence by giving the notions of communal integrity and, by extension, state sovereignty more moral weight than they deserve. By implication, communitarians need to assume an excessively opaque view of the public/private or international/domestic distinction at the global level. In contrast, cosmopolitan perspectives begin with an acknowledgement of the deep interconnection between international and domestic realms, and note the porous quality of the international/domestic distinction. Empirically, an opaque or dichotomous view of the distinction has been harder to sustain as scholars and practitioners of international politics increasingly acknowledge the 'existing pattern of interstate influence and interpenetration.'[3] Contemporary cases of intrastate violent conflict that give rise to calls for international intervention do not conform to the neat international/domestic dichotomy posited by realist and communitarian images of international relations. Conflicts that invite considerations of international intervention more typically traverse this divide, resulting in what Oliver Ramsbotham and Tom Woodhouse have called 'international-social conflicts' (ISCs), 'communal conflicts which become crises of the state' and 'thereby automatically [involve] the wider society of states.'[4] Not only do such conflicts involve the society of states, its member states and international institutions, they also involve a wider global civil society of individuals and nongovernmental organizations and institutions such as religious groups, corporations, human rights advocacy groups, as well as humanitarian relief organizations.

Given the interconnectedness of global, international and domestic spheres, it would be misleading to portray cases of political violence that occur within sovereign boundaries as isolated expressions of national deviance. Intrastate violence, like family violence, does not occur in a social, political and economic vacuum. The mutual interplay of internal and external factors in intrastate violent conflicts ultimately demonstrates the limited utility of focusing on the question of whether or not to intervene. In his account of the 1994 Rwandan genocide, for example, Gérard Prunier points to the idea of a 'special relationship,' based on language and culture, that France had cultivated with its former African colonies and other francophone states. This meant that 'within the mutually-accepted Franco-African political culture, "it is not when the French government intervenes that he [a French official] has some explaining to do, it is when it doesn't."' In the crucial months leading up to the genocide, France gave unquestioning support to the Habyarimana government, despite its poor record of human rights and treatment of Tutsi refugees. Prunier observes, 'This blind commitment was to have catastrophic consequences because, as the situation radicalised, the Rwandese leadership kept believing that no matter what it did, French support would always be forthcoming. And it had no valid reasons for believing otherwise.'[5] Once we acknowledge the historical web of social entanglements between states, and recognize that domestic and international structures of norms, power and authority are mutually interconnected rather than mutually exclusive, the issue becomes not whether, but how to intervene or, simply, how to act.[6]

Recognition of the mutual interconnection of international and domestic realms allows us to move beyond blaming 'bad' states or governments, and to investigate deficiencies in the international normative and institutional framework that might protect or even create and promote them. A cosmopolitan perspective, in positing the interconnection of public and private global, international and domestic orders, holds that intrastate violence and the human suffering it spawns are legitimate concerns of individual men and women everywhere, communities in all parts of the world, and the society of states as a whole.

As the previous chapter revealed, however, many critics of cosmopolitanism are sceptical about the philosophical and practical tenability of making such universalist moral claims in a pluralistic and divided world. On what grounds can any framework of moral rights and obligations be considered common to all human beings? Can the idea of 'common humanity' be a practical motivating force in a diverse and divided world? In Section II of this chapter, I defend a liberal cosmopolitan approach to understanding the claims of common humanity. Although my account is inspired by liberal political philosophy, I argue that it is not parochial to liberalism.

A cosmopolitan view places duties of common humanity at the foundation of domestic, international and global orders. Such a perspective is able to recognize the normative interconnectedness of these diverse orders. In Section III of this chapter, I will explore developments in international law that endorse a cosmopolitan view of state sovereignty as primarily the authority and responsibility of political agents to promote or secure conditions for the exercise of accountable power and authority that affirm rather than subvert human (moral and social) agency, dignity and responsibility. Whereas the communitarian account of 'sovereignty as privacy' emphasizes the exclusive power of sovereigns to order their domestic realms and entails their right to noninterference in this respect, the alternative cosmopolitan account of 'sovereignty as responsibility' highlights the conditional nature of state sovereign authority and its embeddedness in a global normative structure that is morally responsive to the claims of common humanity. According to this liberal cosmopolitan view, sovereign borders in principle should pose no normative barrier whenever and wherever the claims of common humanity are violated or disrespected. Cosmopolitanism as an ethical perspective thus endorses the potential legitimacy in principle of a wide-ranging set of interventionary activities; 'cosmopolitan interventions' are not exhausted by the concept of 'humanitarian interventions,' or military actions for humanitarian purposes.

How should we define the claims of common humanity that are to inform our conception of the normative basis of sovereign authority? In Section IV of this chapter, I examine the debate among liberals on this theme, which has focused on how to conceive of 'human rights' as a standard of legitimacy for domestic political authority. Of particular interest is the debate between social liberals, such as John Rawls, and cosmopolitan liberals, such as Charles Beitz. The main conclusion of this chapter is that the issue of human rights ought to be a subject of reflection, dialogue and debate at all levels of political governance and among all members of global political and civil societies. It is the active engagement of these larger societies that has historically prompted and directed the development of human rights norms and standards within states in the society of states. The content of such norms has evolved from the mutual interplay of various types of actors in global society, and the public/private distinction is helpful for thinking about the different kinds of moral space afforded to (private) nongovernmental and transnational agents and organizations, as well as to (public) governments and international institutions, in the continuing evolution of human rights norms. Ultimately, a cosmopolitan conception of 'sovereignty as responsibility' encourages an open and potentially transformative dialogue on the substance of human rights, whereas the traditional interpretation of 'sovereignty as privacy' tends to pre-empt any substantive debate about human rights norms.

II Claims of common humanity: An agency-based view[7]

Rather than transcending or disciplining political, religious, economic and social divides and conflicts, the claims of common humanity have historically been subordinated to them, or at least heavily mediated by them, so that entitlements based on the status of being human were rarely, reluctantly or only instrumentally extended to the enemy, infidel, refugee and stranger. In modern times, as Martha Finnemore has shown, the 'humanitarian interventions' practised by nineteenth-century Europe were nonuniversal in that the only 'humanity' considered worthy of protection was limited to Christians: 'there were no instances of European powers considering intervention to protect non-Christians.'[8] More recently, nonuniversal 'humanitarian intervention' was exemplified in the evacuation of foreign nationals by French and Belgian soldiers in the early days of the 1994 Rwandan genocide.[9] Part of the controversy surrounding 'humanitarian intervention' as a concept and practice results from disputes about the claims of common humanity itself. The moral legitimacy of 'humanitarian intervention' partly depends on the intelligibility of making universalist moral claims. If political divisions or cultural pluralism deprive such claims of their very intelligibility, it is hard to see how any practice founded on them can ever be legitimated.

My answer to this line of argument is to distinguish between cultural or political pluralism, and political or cultural relativism. While norms and ideas are inevitably contextualized, this does not negate the possibility or utility of constructing from diverse philosophical, ethical and religious foundations, moral claims or norms that are broadly universalizable in our contemporary world.[10] In addition, as I will elaborate in Section IV of this chapter, part of the contemporary context in which moral ideas and claims are generated and developed, contested and validated, and entrenched and enforced involves cross-cultural, international and global initiative, debate and action. It would therefore be misleading to hold a simplistically insular or atomistic view of the relations between ethical, philosophical or religious perspectives and traditions, and the communitarian tendency to do so obscures the interactive sources of their development.

In the 1990s state representatives from a wide variety of cultures affirmed claims of common humanity in their recognition of the intolerable *inhumanity* of certain situations. In supporting UN Security Council Resolution 794 authorizing the use of military force in Somalia in 1992, for example, the Zimbabwean Ambassador declared, 'we cannot countenance this untold suffering of innocent men, women and children from starvation and famine.' The Moroccan Ambassador similarly talked of 'the universal conscience' being aroused by the desperate plight of Somalis.[11] Although there are compelling reasons to question whether the use of force was a necessary or appropriate means of alleviating the humanitarian catastrophe in Somalia, few would deny the moral cogency of the claim that the situation constituted an affront to 'our common humanity.'

The idea of common humanity entails an account of what is common and distinctive about being a human agent. To capture this quality, consider an image from Shakespeare, of human beings being treated like flies in the hands of wanton schoolboys.[12] What is so morally offensive or disturbing about this depiction? I believe such an image violates our common self-understandings of what it means to be a human agent. To treat people like flies is to deny their personhood. The fly is a metaphor for powerlessness; to be treated like a fly is to be treated like an object without agency or significance. People who are placed in the position of a fly are deprived of effective social, political or moral agency. As they also lack social standing, their need to feel a sense of belonging and purpose in the world is similarly unacknowledged. Constant anxiety and alienation are thus the tragic universal hallmarks of being powerless.

An agency-based account of personhood recognizes human agency, and especially the capacity for social and moral agency, as common and distinctive to all human beings. What makes practices such as torture, and structures such as slavery, and Nazi concentration camps inhuman is that they deprive their human victims of their agency or their ability to engage in meaningful self-interpretation and moral evaluation.[13] According to Judith Shklar, fear of agency-depriving practices and conditions animates liberalism as a political doctrine, which aims to secure 'the political conditions that are necessary for the exercise of personal freedom.' Shklar's 'liberalism of fear' is a response to the tragic histories of human conflict and cruelty, in which the institution of systematic fear annihilates the security and 'dignity of persons,' vital conditions of human agency.[14] Shklar's condemnation of cruelty clearly derives from a concern for the agency of the person. Ultimately, cruelty destroys more than individual bodily integrity; by reducing individuals 'to mere reactive units of sensation,' it undermines individual personhood and agency.[15] She shared this preoccupation with Hobbes, whose justification of political authority and obligation was conditional on the sovereign's provision of conditions basic to respect for individual personhood and agency. Hobbes thus asserted that public power could not demand an obligation on the part of its subjects to submit to violations of bodily integrity:

> there [are] some Rights, which no man can be understood by any words, or other signes, to have abandoned, or transferred. As first a man cannot lay down the right of resisting them, that assault him by force, to take away his life; because he cannot be understood to ayme

thereby, at any Good to himselfe. The same may be sayd of Wounds, and Chayns, and Imprisonment.[16]

To Hobbes, persons have no obligations to submit to coercion that threatens their bodily integrity, whether the agent of coercion is public or private. His political philosophy sought ultimately to guarantee persons security with respect to their natural vulnerabilities, which is a key precondition for social and moral agency.

From a liberal perspective, social and political structures can guarantee the conditions of free human social and moral agency by granting each individual 'enough equality of power to protect and assert one's rights.' In liberal polities this insight is translated into individual legal equality as a check on 'arbitrary, unexpected, unnecessary, and unlicensed' institutionalized violence; and social pluralism and equity, or 'the elimination of such forms and degrees of social inequality as expose people to oppressive practices.'[17] On this account, as a political doctrine that affirms an agency-based view of the claims of common humanity, liberalism militates against great concentrations or disparities in social, political and economic power that create structures and climates in which some people can count for nothing.

While this account of the claims of common humanity draws its inspiration from liberal political philosophy, it does not seem unreasonable to assert that all human agents, whatever their culture and history, depend on societies regulated by social and political authority and power, and all can fear abusive or neglectful agents and structures of power that, in the extreme, obliterate personhood and the conditions for human moral and social agency. The unfortunate reality is that it is not difficult for an ordinary person to imagine being treated like a fly, because all human beings share natural vulnerabilities, and without the shelter of socially acknowledged and enforced rules of protection, a human being is little more than a 'poor, bare, forked animal.'[18] A social structure, however, may impose different levels of social vulnerability, making some more susceptible to domination, coercion or exploitation by others. It is especially clear to historically oppressed groups such as the poor, women and minorities that societies create different levels of social vulnerability between individuals and groups. The difference between natural and social vulnerability is that the latter is entirely socially constructed. For example, children may be naturally vulnerable, physically and mentally, because of immature biological development, and they may also be placed in a position of social vulnerability when the social structures in which they develop, such as their family, cultural community, political community or legal order, denies them independent personal rights, or grants parents absolute control over their welfare. Similarly, what made black slaves vulnerable in American society was not their innate or biological capacities, but social, political and legal rules that placed them in near absolute subjection to their owners. Political, legal, and social institutions and norms can thus create and sustain unequal or distinct social vulnerabilities that may, at the extreme, deprive some people of protection from direct and indirect assaults against their natural vulnerabilities.

From an agency-based account of personhood and politics, we can view the development of cosmopolitan humanitarian norms and practices in world politics as part of a process of establishing global conditions for the exercise of accountable power and authority that support rather than undermine individual human (social and moral) agency, dignity and responsibility. Ramsbotham and Woodhouse have identified three expressions of humanitarianism at the international level: international humanitarian laws governing armed conflict, such as the Geneva Conventions; the work of international and nongovernmental organizations and structures that deliver international humanitarian assistance; and the international human rights regime.[19] All three dimensions of cosmopolitan humanitarianism are primarily concerned to guarantee the security and dignity of the person, fundamental conditions for human moral and social agency and responsibility. The law of armed conflict, for example, reflects the significance of such concerns – especially of noncombatants, as well as of sick and wounded combatants, and prisoners of war – even in contexts of politically organized and legally sanctioned violence.[20] International humanitarian assistance promotes the security and dignity of persons by aiming 'to prevent and alleviate human suffering wherever it may be found' through the provision of food, clothing, shelter and medical assistance.[21] In a human rights framework, these concerns are expressed through covenants and conventions affirming the equality of persons, and prohibiting practices that undermine human (social and moral) agency such as torture, genocide, slavery and racial discrimination.[22]

An agency-based account of the claims of common humanity provides humanitarian laws of war, the practice of humanitarian assistance and the doctrine of human rights with their moral logic and legitimacy. Evaluating the legitimacy of any interventionary practice, including 'humanitarian intervention,' also involves an examination of how the proposed action serves to promote or secure the claims of common humanity for all those who can claim to be human.

III   Sovereignty as responsibility: Cosmopolitan intimations in international law

My arguments against some realists and communitarians have been that the atomistic and organic accounts of the state or political community that they assume are untenable. Feminist theorists have also had problems with the public/private constructs generated by both atomistic and organic frameworks, particularly as they are applied to family–state relations. According to some feminist theorists, the atomistic conception of freedom as the absence of external (especially public state) intervention is especially misleading as it obscures the social construction of any conception of individual or family privacy. The interpretation of the individual or family as a private entity or sphere beyond state intervention denies the extent to which the definition of an inviolable individual or familial sphere is itself socially constructed and supported through law. Individual and family privacy, as well as concepts such as private property, can only exist in the embrace of community norms. In this vein, a Lockean liberal conception of the 'private sphere' as a pre-political realm of relations between consenting free and equal adults is conceptually flawed.[23] Contemporary realism's atomistic conception of the state and the public/private or international/domestic distinction is incoherent and cannot sustain a *normative* right of states to privacy vis-à-vis international or global societies.

At the same time, feminist theorists note that organic conceptions of the public/private construct have failed women historically, because of restrictive and gendered notions of citizenship that relegated women to the private sphere of the household and denied them freedom to participate in the common political life of the community. This also had the effect of depriving women's issues and concerns within the family of public attention and political remedy. An organic conception of the family, in tending towards its idealization, hides issues of power and control within family relationships that have left individual members in positions of vulnerability within the family. Anita Allen has written that the notion of family privacy is problematic and potentially dangerous. She asks, 'Who is entitled to exercise that right? Who is the spokesperson for the family's interest? What if family members disagree about the desirability of governmental intervention? Of private third-party involvement?'[24] These questions, slightly changed, are equally pertinent in the case of state privacy vis-à-vis international and global societies. Again, organic communitarian conceptions of political community and the public/private construct appear to take us no closer to a morally viable conception of state privacy.[25]

The dual role of privacy as a vehicle for oppression as well as liberty in domestic relations has led political theorists to re-examine the question of how to conceive of the moral value of privacy rights in domestic society.[26] Due to the moral inadequacy of both atomistic and organic accounts of privacy, some feminists argue that no coherent and morally viable distinction can be made between public and private. In this vein, Catharine MacKinnon has called for the abolition of the distinction as a normative construct because it underpins the morally bankrupt notion of privacy.[27] Similarly, Frances Olsen has argued that given the mutual interconnection of the private family and the public state, the characterization of state intervention in the family as a moral problem is a myth that obscures substantive debates about ethics and social policy.[28] As Annabelle Lever has described this line of thought, 'once one grants the claim that the personal is political, it is hard to see what the public/private distinction could be referring to, or what could possibly be the point and justification of privacy rights.'[29] Ruth Gavison, however, argues that jettisoning the public/private distinction altogether would lead to a total denial of the values of privacy and intimacy, which most people, including women, would find problematic.[30] Clearly, although feminists have been united in condemning traditional patriarchal liberal and republican conceptions of the public/private construct, they disagree over how to reconceive it, or whether it has any use at all.

These controversies can be translated with equal force to the interpretation of state sovereignty as privacy in international society. The emergence of social constructivist theory in International Relations has begun to highlight the social foundation of international norms, such as state sovereignty and nonintervention.[31] States enjoy a certain kind of internal sovereignty because of international and global acceptance of its practice, just as individuals and families in western societies enjoy a certain kind of privacy because of societal acceptance and legal codification of individual and family boundaries. Once this is acknowledged, disputes continue over how to characterize the distinct moral value of state sovereignty as privacy, and whether to accord state sovereignty any moral value at all. Jean Cohen has recently criticized 'theorists of cosmopolitan law and justice without state sovereignty' for undermining an important component of a counterproject to imperialistic tendencies in contemporary world politics. She defends the principle of sovereign equality, arguing that its destruction in the current context would spell 'the loss of the autonomy of the political, *the elimination of the distinction between public and private*, and the disintegration of a distinctive political relationship between a polity or government and its citizenry.'[32] These contemporary debates reveal a need to clarify the distinct moral values and foundations of the sovereign state.

International law, for much of the nineteenth and twentieth centuries, historically assumed this value, admitting only states as members with moral standing, agency and accountability at the international level. If it is states that exclusively form the basic subjects of moral concern in such a society, it is states' integrity, rights and responsibilities that determine the contours of international ethics and morality. Individuals may enjoy standing only through citizenship: 'Citizens of states are members of international society only indirectly through their national governments; they are not members on their own.'[33] This conception of international law actually differs from an older 'law of nations' which admitted individual claims. Under Jeremy Bentham's reconceptualization of 'international law,' however, individuals could no longer claim to be subjects in their own right: 'Hence, it was thought to be antithetical for there to be international legal rights that individuals could assert against states, especially against their own governments.' As Mark Janis has put it, 'Positivist legal theory had taken the law of nations of the seventeenth and eighteenth centuries, a law common to individuals as well as to states, and transformed it into two international law disciplines, one "public," the other "private." '[34] Legal positivism in the realm of international law thus constructed a world of public states and private humanity.

Contemporary international law, however, has given increasing public recognition to the claims of common humanity. Menno Kamminga notes, for example, that Article 2(7) of the UN Charter, which prohibits UN intervention in matters essentially within the domestic jurisdiction of states, leaves unspecified the meaning of 'intervention' and 'domestic jurisdiction.'[35] With the development of international human rights law, international law now addresses not only relations between states or sovereigns, but also sovereigns' treatment of the citizens of other states as well as their own citizens: 'individuals, regardless of strict positivist doctrine, are now to be properly considered subjects not only of private, but also of public international law.'[36] Under a cosmopolitan view, it is states, rather than individuals, that are not 'members on their own,' for a state's moral standing and agency rest not only on its unique representation of a particular constituency of members, but also on its contribution to a universal moral order that is respectful of the claims of common humanity. States, as representatives of a particular group of people, not only have responsibilities to safeguard their particular welfare, they are also agents of a wider conception of the common good at the international level, and therefore have common responsibilities towards noncitizens as well.

In recent decades the traditional consensus on interpreting 'sovereignty as privacy' has undergone significant contestation and revision within the society of states itself. Most significantly, as the ICISS put it in 2001, 'Where a population is suffering serious harm, as a result of internal wars, insurgency, repression or state failure, and the state in question is unwilling or unable to halt or avert it, the principle of nonintervention yields to the international responsibility to protect.'[37] Under this view, the internal dimension of domestic political authority and agency is tied to certain international standards of accountability. Sovereignty so conceived still empowers states to order their internal affairs, but it also obligates them to exercise that power in ways that meet the human rights and humanitarian interests of their members. In the case of the genocide-inciting radio station during the Rwandan genocide, for example, an alternative interpretation of 'sovereignty as responsibility' would have justified, and even required, international action to abrogate Rwandan state sovereignty over airwaves, since the state itself was either unable or unwilling to halt the broadcasts.

There have been many recent changes at the international level that indicate a growing endorsement of a cosmopolitan interpretation of 'sovereignty as responsibility.' For example, states adopted the international humanitarian law of armed conflict in 1949 primarily to control state conduct in interstate wars, while leaving states a relatively free moral hand in controlling internal discord. The Geneva conventions thus draw sharp distinctions between 'international armed conflicts' and other violent situations. Recent legal arguments have directly challenged the moral coherence and sustainability of this posited distinction between international and internal armed conflicts. The International Criminal Tribunal for the former Yugoslavia (ICTY), for example, stated: 'elementary considerations of humanity and common sense make it preposterous that the use by States of weapons prohibited in armed conflicts between themselves be allowed when States try to put down rebellion by their own nationals on their own territory.'[38] The principle of holding sovereigns accountable for the violations of genocide, crimes against humanity, war crimes and aggressive war has also gained widespread international legal and political endorsement through the development of international criminal tribunals with universal jurisdiction to try such practices.[39]

Indeed, the recent establishment of the ICC is an institutional manifestation of the movement towards a cosmopolitan conception of 'sovereignty as responsibility.' Although its *ad hoc* predecessors, the International Criminal Tribunals for the former Yugoslavia and Rwanda (ICTY and ICTR) enjoyed 'primacy,' the ICC's jurisdiction is limited by the concept of 'complementarity.' This means that the Court can only exercise jurisdiction when domestic courts fail to prosecute due to lack of will or incompetence. In principle, then, the ICC does not threaten to undermine the authority of well-functioning domestic legal orders, and may simultaneously limit *and enhance* state rights and responsibilities. The interconnection between international and domestic legal orders is, in this case, indisputable. The Rome Statute establishing the ICC is partly a product of the combined efforts of lawyers and judges of domestic courts from a wide variety of states. States that have ratified the Rome Statute are obligated to introduce legal provisions required by the Statute in their domestic legal systems. Thus, ratifying the Rome Statute took time partly because in order to fulfill their responsibility arising from the notion of complementarity to prosecute suspects in their territorial jurisdiction, many states needed to 'bring their substantive [domestic systems of] criminal law into line, enacting the offences of genocide, crimes against humanity and war crimes as defined in the Statute and ensuring that their courts can exercise universal jurisdiction over these crimes.'[40] The recognition of basic duties of humanity as a basis of international legitimacy is thus beginning to have an impact on domestic spheres of sovereign authority. From the arrest and detention of the former Chilean sovereign, Augusto Pinochet, in Britain, to the trial of Slobodan Milosevic at The Hague, to the creation of the ICC, international political and legal endorsement of the interpretation of 'sovereignty as responsibility' has generated legal arguments and precedents that were unthinkable in a world of public states and private humanity. Domestic tyrants may still have the capacity to practise tyranny in the confines of their home state, but cosmopolitan intimations in contemporary international law mean that, at least from a legal perspective, domestic tyrants are less and less able to feel at home in the world.

The mutual interplay between international and legal orders is apparent not only in cases of war crimes, genocide and crimes against humanity; it is also apparent in the increasing appeal to international law as a source of legal authority in domestic judicial decisions. For example, in the US Supreme Court's decision in the case of *Roper v. Simmons*, about the constitutionality of imposing the death penalty on convicted offenders under the age of 18, Justice Kennedy appealed to international law and foreign legal judgements to support the Court's majority decision to prohibit the juvenile death penalty. 'Our determination that the death penalty is disproportionate punishment for offenders under 18,' he writes, 'finds confirmation in the stark reality that the United States is the only country in the world that continues to give official sanction to the juvenile death penalty.' The controversy generated by Justice Kennedy's claim that the Court could legitimately refer to 'the laws of other countries and international authorities as instructive' in this case reveals a growing debate within the United States about how to draw the distinction between international and domestic law.[41]

A liberal cosmopolitan account of the public/private distinction in world politics recognizes the mutual interrelatedness of international and domestic realms, and grounds a state's right to sovereignty in its ability to promote or secure conditions for the exercise of accountable power and authority that affirm rather than subvert human (moral and social) agency, dignity and responsibility. Whereas 'sovereignty as privacy' emphasizes the exclusive power of sovereigns to order their domestic realms and entails their right to noninterference in this respect, the alternative account of 'sovereignty as responsibility' highlights the conditional nature of sovereign authority, especially with respect to the protection of human rights. When duties of humanity are violated within a sovereign state, the consent of sovereign authorities no longer constitutes a normative barrier to the delivery of assistance to the victims. The moral burden of justification shifts from those who seek to intervene, to those who claim to have a right to be free from intervention.[42] Thus, the normative worth of sovereign consent is lost when sovereigns fail in their responsibility to protect their own citizens' human rights and humanitarian interests, in the same way that parental consent loses its relevance when the issue is the protection of children being abused by their parents, or spousal consent becomes a nonmoral concern in attempts to give assistance to an abused spouse.

A cosmopolitan perspective can accommodate conceptions of state privacy as territorial integrity and political decisional agency, but assesses their moral legitimacy in terms of their consistency with claims of common humanity. How does this condition affect a cosmopolitan assessment of some traditional rights of sovereignty?

Clearly a state's right to territorial integrity cannot mean that it can do whatever it wants on or with its own territory, just as a person's right to bodily integrity does not mean that one can 'claim an absolute right to do with one's body as one pleases.'[43] A state's right to territorial integrity also does not mean that any existing state's territorial configuration is inviolable and unalterable. A cosmopolitan recognition of individual moral and social agency means that state borders are in principle open to revision; thus boundary changes are valid so long as they are negotiated in the spirit of fairness and with mutual acknowledgement of the potentially dire consequences of nonpeaceful resolution. The international community can encourage the development of internal legal and political processes and mechanisms for peaceful and fair boundary changes, recognizing that externally imposed alterations are unlikely to enjoy internal legitimacy or contribute to a stable resolution.

Nor does a state's right to political independence mean that it can decide to do anything it wants with respect to its internal affairs, and do it with impunity. International institutions and agents of global civil society may thus hold state officials accountable for government-sponsored violations of human rights against the state's own citizens or noncitizens, although the actual removal of such officials from their domestic office may only be effected through domestic political processes. For example, Spanish courts might legitimately seek to hold Pinochet accountable for state-sponsored human rights violations committed during his 17-year rule in Chile, but it is up to Chilean citizens to decide whether Pinochet may remain a Chilean senator for life.

IV   Social and cosmopolitan liberalism on human rights and intervention

In cases of genocide and other intrastate scenes of political violence leading to large losses of life, it is difficult to sustain any normative argument in favour of protecting or respecting a regime's entitlements to sovereignty and nonintervention. In such circumstances, a regime loses these entitlements, and the only pertinent questions for potential intervenors have to do with determining the legitimacy of intervenors, and the means of intervention that will most effectively halt the violence. But what if the degree of violation is low level, affecting a small number of people or only one person? Should respect for the norms of state sovereignty and nonintervention hold in such cases? For example, in the aftermath of 9/11, and the London bombings in July 2005, many states, including liberal democratic ones, have used the threat of terrorism as a reason to restrict political and civil liberties, and to grant wider legal liberties to state authorities acting against perceived terrorist threats. Individuals have been held in detention without charges, without access to legal counsel and without a trial. In some cases, individuals have been tortured. One prominent Canadian case involved a 34-year-old graduate of McGill University, Maher Arar, who was apprehended in New York in September 2002, while he was returning from a family vacation in Tunisia. Through a secretive program called 'extraordinary rendition,' US authorities were able to send Arar back to his birth country, Syria, where he was regularly tortured by Syrian interrogators until his release a year later, in October 2003.[44] Should the status of sovereignty protect the Canadian, US, Syrian governments and officials from external scrutiny and criticism of their practices that led to Arar's captivity and torture? Are governments immune from challenges to their sovereign authority and conduct when the human rights violations they commit or condone do not amount to acts that shock the conscience of humankind, but affect only a small number of people?

If we are to take seriously the claims of common humanity, even the means used by a state to fight terrorism within its borders should not be immune from external criticism and review. This means that US treatment of prisoners at Guantanamo Bay, as well as Russian policy in Chechnya, which has included summary executions, torture and arbitrary arrests, are legitimate subjects of concern and critical intervention by various international, governmental and global civil society actors. According to the liberal cosmopolitan view I am defending, external actors have legitimate reasons for abrogating the norms of sovereignty and nonintervention, and expressing in some way their condemnation of the violations, even if they affect only one person.[45] This is because from a cosmopolitan perspective, 'every human being has a global stature as an ultimate unit of moral concern.'[46] It is therefore entirely appropriate for international institutions, or global civil society organizations such as Amnesty International, to call power to account for violating the human rights of small numbers of people. Sovereign authorities can also be called to account for failing to address violations perpetrated by individuals, corporations and others against vulnerable individuals or social groups. International economic institutions, other states and people in general also act legitimately by making loans conditional on respecting human rights or withholding favourable trading terms or boycotting goods from a regime that fails to halt human rights violations within its own borders. The legitimacy of various means of intervention, of course, must be measured proportionately to the offence, and should also be judged by their effectiveness. Thus, in cases of low-level political violence or human rights violations that affect a small number of people, the abrogation of sovereignty through military force is unlikely to be justifiable, given proportionality and prudential considerations. A political community's 'integrity' or 'autonomy,' however, is not a morally compelling consideration, once the community has failed to protect the human rights or humanitarian interests of some of its members.

So far, in describing the claims of common humanity that underlie the moral foundation of any legitimate world order and any legitimate conception of sovereign authority, I have used phrases such as 'human rights,' 'duties of humanity,' 'humanitarian interests' and so on. These terms, however, are not obviously coterminous, with 'human rights' usually conceived more expansively than 'humanitarian interests' or 'duties of humanity.' What exactly is the standard that states must meet in order to enjoy full respect for their rights to sovereignty and nonintervention? Most liberals appeal to the language of 'human rights' in delineating this standard, but there is some contention among liberals about how expansively 'human rights' ought to be defined. The debate is most interesting between social liberals, such as John Rawls, and cosmopolitan liberals, such as Charles Beitz. Should we use the 1948 Universal Declaration of Human Rights as the standard? Should we conceive of 'human rights' as similar to the rights enjoyed by citizens in a liberal constitutional democracy? Or should we think of human rights more restrictively?

This debate took shape with the publication of John Rawls's *Law of Peoples*. The Law of Peoples is a basic charter of normative principles to govern relations between politically organized communities of people in the world.[47] Many aspects of Rawls's account of inter-societal justice merit discussion, but here I will focus mainly on his views on human rights as a standard of political legitimacy, the right of sovereignty and the duty of nonintervention in a society of peoples. It is important, at the outset, to note that Rawls is not a statist, and is a critic of absolutist accounts of 'sovereignty as privacy,' arguing that, 'We must formulate the powers of sovereignty in the light of a reasonable Law of Peoples and deny to states the traditional rights to war and to unrestricted internal autonomy.'[48]

Rawls argues that all liberal societies, as well as nonliberal but 'decent' ones, are capable of forming in their mutual relations a 'decent system of social cooperation.' To be a 'member in good standing' in a Rawlsian conception of the society of peoples, a 'decent' society must be peace-loving; its system of law must honour 'human rights proper'; its laws must follow a 'common good idea of justice' based on an account of the fundamental interests of everyone in society; and its judges and other officials must make decisions guided by a common good idea of justice. The standard of decency serves as a minimum moral floor of a reasonably just society of peoples: 'The decent common good idea of hierarchical peoples is a minimal idea. Its being realized by a society renders [the society's] institutions worthy of toleration.' By toleration, Rawls 'means not only to refrain from exercising political sanctions – military, economic, or diplomatic – to make a people change its ways. To tolerate also means to recognize these nonliberal societies as *equal participating members in good standing* of the Society of Peoples, with certain rights and obligations, including the duty of civility requiring that they offer other peoples public reasons appropriate to the Society of Peoples for their actions.' Liberal peoples cannot therefore morally justify disrespect and intolerance of nonliberal peoples based on the moral superiority of a liberal comprehensive doctrine. Toleration of decent peoples serves to promote moral egalitarianism between peoples, and to establish inter-societal norms of cooperation that all 'can reasonably grant without submitting to a position of inferiority or domination.'[49]

Human rights are clearly foundational to Rawls's conception of a 'decent' society.[50] By human rights, Rawls means 'the right to life (to the means of subsistence and security); to liberty (to freedom from slavery, serfdom, and forced occupation, and to a sufficient measure of liberty of conscience to ensure freedom of religion and thought); to property (personal property); and to formal equality as expressed by the rules of natural justice (that is, that similar cases be treated similarly).' In another complementary account, Rawls explicitly depicts human rights as 'a special class of urgent rights, such as freedom from slavery and serfdom, liberty (but not equal liberty) of conscience, and security of ethnic groups from mass murder and genocide.' Rawls argues that individuals must enjoy these entitlements in *any* system of social cooperation, and a social system that denied or disrespected these entitlements would constitute not a system of social cooperation, but of social exploitation, oppression and tyranny. Human rights, so conceived, are universal in the sense that they 'cannot be rejected as peculiarly liberal or special to the Western tradition. They are not politically parochial.' They are also universalizable in the sense that 'they are intrinsic to the Law of Peoples and have a political (moral) effect whether or not they are supported locally. That is, their political (moral) force extends to all societies, and they are binding on all peoples and societies, including outlaw states.'[51]

Human rights are thus central to a regime's political legitimacy in the society of peoples, for they 'specify limits to a regime's internal autonomy.' In constructing the Law of Peoples for a well-ordered society of peoples, which includes only reasonable liberal and decent peoples, Rawls affirms that 'Peoples are to observe a duty of non-intervention.' This duty is 'qualified in the general case of outlaw states and grave violations of human rights.'[52] The fulfillment of what Rawls calls 'human rights proper,' however, 'is sufficient to exclude justified and forceful intervention by other peoples, for example, by diplomatic and economic sanctions, or in grave cases by military forces.' According to Rawls, then, unsolicited intervention of any kind is unjustified against nonliberal decent societies. Although Rawls admits that such societies are not fully just or reasonable, by the standards of a liberal conception of justice, liberal societies must accept them as 'equal participating members in good standing' in the society of peoples, and thus observe the duty of nonintervention in their relations. He criticizes specifically the argument that 'nonliberal societies are always properly subject to some form of sanction – political, economic, or even military, depending on the case.'[53] Furthermore, Rawls argues that 'it is not reasonable for a liberal people to adopt as part of its own foreign policy the granting of subsidies to other peoples as incentives to become more liberal, although persons in civil society may raise private funds for that purpose.'[54]

Charles Beitz has been one of the most prominent critics of Rawls's conception of human rights and inter-societal justice. In his work, Beitz has consistently argued for a cosmopolitan liberal conception of international morality that is 'concerned with the moral relations of members of a universal community in which state boundaries have a merely derivative significance.'[55] He has subsequently clarified his position as a version of 'cosmopolitan liberalism,' an offspring of 'individualist moral egalitarianism,' that evaluates the morality of domestic and international institutions based on 'an impartial consideration of the claims of each person who would be affected.'[56] A cosmopolitan liberal theory of global justice thus begins with a conception of humanity as a common moral community of free and equal persons.

Such an approach to international ethics and morality entails positing a fundamental continuity and deep interconnection between international and domestic realms.[57] Indeed, one of the most significant aspects of Beitz's work is his continual questioning of the empirical and normative significance of the international/domestic distinction. Challenging this distinction not only has enabled Beitz to contest the separation of moral and political theory from International Relations; it is also integral to his critique of the priority for compatriots thesis in matters of global economic distribution, as well as his critique of the 'morality of states' view of state autonomy and nonintervention in international society.[58]

According to Beitz, the rise of human rights doctrine 'as an acceptable justification for various kinds of international intervention, ranging from diplomatic and economic sanctions to military action, in the domestic affairs of states,' indicates the ascendancy of a cosmopolitan view of global injustice that includes violations of common rights and duties owed to all human beings by virtue of their humanity, irrespective of whether these violations are committed by governments within or beyond the boundaries of a sovereign state. Beitz also notes that beyond justifying coercive measures against offending governments, human rights play an important 'public role...beyond the sphere of intergovernmental relations. Human rights have served as bases for standard setting, monitoring, reporting and advocacy by nongovernmental organizations at both the domestic and the international levels of world politics.'[59]

While Beitz and Rawls agree that any legitimate inter-societal order must honour human rights, they disagree over how expansively such rights ought to be conceived. By limiting his account of human rights to a special urgent class, Rawls is able to 'distinguish between minimal and full legitimacy, with human rights serving as necessary conditions of minimal legitimacy.'[60] Beitz argues, however, that there is no principled reason to distinguish between a 'restricted conception of human rights' and a 'liberal or full conception' of such rights. In consequence, he cannot see a principled reason to grant nonliberal (and not fully just) decent societies an entitlement to be 'members in good standing' in the society of peoples. He questions why 'decent but not just societies should be regarded as legitimate and, therefore, as qualified for treatment as "members in good standing" of the international order.'[61]

According to Beitz, if the role of ideal normative theory is to set a critical standard by which to evaluate actual social and political practices, 'why stop short of a full description of evaluative standards for social and political institutions?' There may be prudential or strategic reasons to describe conditions for minimal legitimacy, but why does the idea of minimal legitimacy, and the consequent acceptance of decent but not just societies as 'members in good standing' in the society of peoples, occur at the level of ideal theory?

What, indeed, can explain Rawls's assertion that decent societies deserve to be treated as 'members in good standing' of the society of peoples, despite his acknowledgement that they are not fully just by liberal standards? According to Rawls, nonintervention against the injustices permitted in decent societies is justified because of the moral imperative of preserving the conditions of mutual respect between peoples: 'lack of respect may wound the self-respect of decent nonliberal peoples as peoples, as well as their individual members, and may lead to great bitterness and resentment.... Most important is maintaining mutual respect among peoples. Lapsing into contempt on the one side, and bitterness and resentment on the other, can only cause damage.'[62] Mutual respect between peoples is an enabling condition for moral learning. Rawls is thus not as interested in securing peoples' compliance with the Law of Peoples as with securing their moral allegiance to it. For decent peoples to be persuaded of the rightness of liberal standards of justice, and for such people to come to affirm them of their own accord, 'Liberal peoples should not suppose that decent societies are unable to reform themselves in their own way. By recognizing these societies as *bona fide* members of the Society of Peoples, liberal peoples encourage this change. They do not in any case stifle such change, as withholding respect from decent peoples might well do.'[63]

Rawls's concern about interventionary practices by states or organized political communities lies in the coercive nature of such practices, rather than in their crossing a political boundary. Given the vast disparities in economic, social and political power that exist between states, interventions by states are likely to take on the 'appearance of being coercive.'[64] Because Rawls is concerned to establish the moral authority of the Law of Peoples, independent of its coercive capacity, he must construct his theory to provide moral space for the process of moral learning, whereby peoples come to affirm the Law of Peoples through reflective processes of deliberation rather than coercive pressures of socialization. The coercive nature of inter-governmental interventions thus makes them morally unsuited to the task of developing a well-ordered society of peoples.

Rawls asserts a different standard for evaluating the ethics of intervention by members of global civil society. The interpretation of the public/private distinction as a division between public coercive states and private voluntaristic (global) civil society seems to explain Rawls's disapproval of interventions by governments, and his endorsement of interventionary activities by agents of global civil society. Rawls assumes that the agents of global civil society possess few overtly coercive capacities. Indeed, organizations such as Amnesty International and Human Rights Watch cannot coerce compliance with human rights standards; they only have the power of their moral authority. When Rawls uses a distinction between public coercive states, and private voluntaristic civil society, however, he may be overlooking the enormous economic resources and coercive power of some private or nonstate global actors, such as multinational corporations. While Rawls seems to grant global civil society greater moral agency to act beyond borders, it is not clear how Rawls would propose to limit the potentially coercive agency of corporations that may, for example, offer incentives to burdened societies that are not conducive to establishing just domestic institutions.[65]

Ultimately, Rawls's argument for the toleration of decent peoples in the society of peoples is a product of the way he conceives of the task of political philosophy, which is to construct a 'realistic utopia.'[66] For Rawls, the task of ideal theory is to describe a target scenario to which people *who have not yet reached it* may nevertheless aspire. That is why ideal theory cannot be divorced from basic realities or social facts of the human world, such as that humans will be organized into distinct social groups of some kind. The acknowledgement and incorporation of such facts in the structure of an ideal theory helps to form a bridge between where we are now and where the ideal theory says we ought to go. As political theorists hope to offer not only aspirational, but also practical, normative guidance for their time, this 'bridgeability' is a constitutive feature of any ideal political theory. Thus, the task of ideal theory is not to construct a utopia; rather, it is to construct a 'realistic utopia.' In this vein, Rawls asserts that the 'Law of Peoples proceeds from the international political world as we see it.'[67] Ideal theory, conceived in 'realistic utopian' terms, is still distinct from nonideal theory, in that the latter's starting point not only includes basic social facts about the world – such as that people will be organized into social groups, and that human beings are capable of moral learning – but also explicitly addresses nonideal conditions – such as that some societies will not possess the means to maintain just domestic institutions, or that some states will act unjustly and violate reasonable terms of inter-societal cooperation for their own advantage. Beitz's account of the task of political philosophy is similar to that of Rawls; he also asserts that 'any reasonable theory must be constrained by what is possible,' and therefore that proponents of cosmopolitan morality should seek 'incremental or reformist goals.'[68] What counts as an enduring social fact, however, may be quite contentious, and it is a dispute over how to characterize the morally relevant social facts that I think lies at the source of the disagreements between Rawls and Beitz.

If one evaluates the real world according to Rawls's 'realistic utopia,' it should be clear that actually existing liberal democracies do not consistently fulfill Rawls's standards of liberal justice. Although his example of a decent society is nonliberal in its orientation, if we evaluated actually existing societies using his categories, there may be no fully liberal or reasonable peoples, but only decent near-liberal societies. As he states, 'one should allow...a space between the fully unreasonable and the fully reasonable.'[69] This point indicates that the typology of societies and regimes in Rawls's *Law of Peoples* cannot be used to categorize societies into those that are decent and those that are not. This is because the standard of decency operates more like a spectrum with many points between decency and indecency, rather than like a sword separating the just from the unjust. There are multiple aspects to Rawls's standard of decency, and societies can meet the standard in one respect but fail in another. Most societies are not wholly decent or indecent, but fall within that space between the 'fully unreasonable and the fully reasonable.' In allowing decent peoples to be 'members in good standing' in the society of peoples, Rawls is allowing actually existing liberal democracies, that are not fully unjust but also not fully or always just in a liberal sense, to participate in such a society, develop mutual respect and confidence and eventually, perhaps, progress towards a fully liberal ideal. The toleration of decent peoples, then, is one way to make his Law of Peoples a morally constructive and relevant standard of inter-societal justice, to which actually existing societies, including actually existing nonideal liberal societies, may aspire.

V Conclusion

From a liberal cosmopolitan perspective, the exercise of sovereign authority, to be legitimate, must respect the claims of common humanity. Both Rawls and Beitz agree that human rights 'state conditions for political and social institutions, the systematic violation of which may justify efforts to bring about reform by agents external to the society in which the violation occurs.'[70] But how should their disagreement about the definition of human rights be resolved? One way to answer this question is to note the evolutionary development of human rights norms. The fundamental idea behind the notion of human rights may be 'the dignity and worth inherent in the human person,'[71] but what that means specifically for the design of religious, social, economic and political practices and institutions ought to be the subject of considerable reflection, dialogue and debate.

At the global level, advocates of human rights in global civil society may forward various interpretations of human rights, some of which may challenge practices and policies of specific governments and social agents, or push the boundaries of the contemporary consensus regarding human rights among international institutions or the society of states.[72] From a cosmopolitan perspective, the aim of interventions by such global civil society actors should be to encourage domestic reform in the target society, and to prompt broader discussion, acknowledgement and vindication of the claims of common humanity in the design and operation of international social, economic and political institutions. It is, indeed, the active exchange between agents of global civil society and of international society that has historically shaped the development of human rights norms and standards. Acknowledging the mutual interplay between international and domestic, government and nongovernmental, international and transnational, public and private, agents and structures allows us to recognize that actors in these diverse realms have different kinds of moral space and agency with which to contribute to the evolution of norms of global governance.

In the society of states, despite the extensive codification of human rights norms in international law, there is still some debate about the appropriateness of any interventionary measures by member states in response to human rights violations within a sovereign state. The Chinese government, for example, has over the years consistently appealed to an interpretation of sovereignty as immunity from external interference or criticism in matters of domestic jurisdiction, including the treatment of a country's own citizens. It is not the substantive content of human rights so much as the assertion of its universal reach that creates problems for the Chinese government's insistence on retaining a traditional notion of 'sovereignty as privacy.' Rejecting the universality of any conception of human rights, however, carries great moral risks, for it entails a morally irreconcilable world of unlimited pluralism among peoples. It may ultimately be harder to live well in such a world, compared to one that recognizes the universal reach of a limited set of human rights with consequent specified restrictions of internal autonomy.

In rejecting an absolutist interpretation of 'sovereignty as privacy,' a cosmopolitan ethical perspective allows for and encourages open, continuous and potentially transformative dialogue between cultures and societies on the substance of the moral claims we can make of each other as human beings sharing a common world. Such an endeavour is incompatible with an absolutist conception of 'sovereignty as privacy' that tends to pre-empt any substantive debate about human rights norms. If we are concerned to establish the conditions for such an inter-societal dialogue, the virtue of Rawls's work is again apparent; for in his account, members in good standing of the society of peoples bear certain obligations, 'including the duty of civility requiring that they offer other peoples public reasons appropriate to the Society of Peoples for their actions.' In other words, while coercive forms of intervention are prohibited, members of a Rawlsian society of peoples are required to engage in processes of public (inter-societal) justification of their internal and external actions and policies. Through such open engagement, the society of peoples may realistically progress towards the adoption of more and more robust formulations of inter-societal justice that may even come to include duties of global distributive justice.

My argument in this chapter favouring the qualification and reconceptualization of the norms of state sovereignty and nonintervention should not be read as one that justifies military action in all cases of abusive or negligent sovereign power. Indeed, as I noted in Chapter 4, we should be careful not to conflate the problem of intervention with the problem of the use of force. When sovereigns fail to respect the claims of common humanity, even in the case of their own citizens, from cases affecting only one individual to those involving an entire social group, the relevant normative question for international and global societies is not whether or not to intervene, but *how*. This becomes a particularly vexing moral question in the face of politically induced humanitarian disaster.

7
Cosmopolitan Humanitarianism and the Use of Force

It has been quite rightly said that suffering, like light, knows no national boundaries.

Cornelio Sommargua,
Hard Choices: Moral Dilemmas in Humanitarian Intervention[1]

America believes that all people are entitled to hope and human rights, to the non-negotiable demands of human dignity. People everywhere prefer freedom to slavery, prosperity to squalor, self-government to the rule of terror and torture.

George W. Bush, *The New York Times*[2]

I Introduction

Our contemporary world presents us with a steady array of undeniable expressions of common *inhumanity*, confirming the notion of common humanity by negative example. Ironically, the conditions that most urgently lead to calls for international intervention expose the fragmented nature of human solidarity and the attendant frailty of notions of universal moral obligation based on the idea of common humanity. In the face of widespread human suffering caused by various kinds of intrastate violent conflict, state repression or political incompetence leading to state failure, who has a moral obligation to respond? And what do they have as an obligation to do? A cosmopolitan conception of 'sovereignty as responsibility' clearly obligates sovereigns to be agents of the domestic public good. When they fail to provide basic public goods such as security, subsistence and justice within their borders, and when domestic accountability systems are inadequate or incompetent, a cosmopolitan view of global order obligates the society

135

of states, as well as the larger global civil society, to call sovereign power to account, and to intervene to alleviate the human suffering caused by the neglect, breakdown or abuse of sovereign power. From a cosmopolitan moral view, then, it is not just domestic or international political leaders who have moral responsibilities to respond to situations of politically induced humanitarian disaster – we all do, in our various individual, collective and institutional capacities. A cosmopolitan conception of duties of humanity as global in scope thus grounds the justification for many contemporary practices of 'humanitarianism,' from the delivery of relief supplies and services to populations in crisis, to military actions by states against failed states and negligent or oppressive regimes.

Although a cosmopolitan ethical perspective provides clear justification for the abrogation of state sovereignty for humanitarian purposes, this chapter deals with the moral challenges faced by agents of global civil society, and agents of the society of states, when they attempt to respond to politically induced humanitarian disasters in current world political, social and economic conditions. In addition to facing many 'hard choices'[3] in such nonideal conditions, both sets of agents must also grapple with the issue of how they ought to relate to each other. What ought to be the relationship between human rights and humanitarian relief organizations, and states intervening for humanitarian purposes? Should nongovernmental humanitarian relief organizations, for example, publicly call for or endorse military intervention by states when there is a humanitarian crisis?[4] Should they or human rights advocacy groups have some role in determining the legitimacy of uses of force by states for humanitarian purposes? When agents of intervening states, international institutions and nongovernmental organizations are all in the field, how should their various tasks be coordinated? To whom should human rights advocacy groups and humanitarian relief organizations be accountable? Should accountability processes and mechanisms for such agents of global civil society be different from the models of accountability for agents of international society? Answering these questions involves some account of the public/private distinction, understood as a distinction between the (public or governmental) society of states and the (private or nongovernmental) global civil society. I will argue that a liberal cosmopolitan conception of this distinction is helpful for illuminating how their relationship ought to be organized, with attendant implications for the agency and accountability of these two sets of actors in situations of humanitarian crisis.

In Section III of this chapter, I will focus on the ethical challenges raised by these questions for practitioners of cosmopolitan humanitarianism from global civil society, such as nongovernmental human rights and humanitarian relief organizations. In Section IV, I examine legitimacy challenges to 'humanitarian intervention,' understood as the use of force by states for humanitarian purposes. It will become clear in both discussions that the moral legitimacy and efficacy of these diverse cosmopolitan interventionary practices are severely hampered by current world political, economic and social conditions, and not just by the specific nonideal contexts of humanitarian disaster.

II 'Humanitarian intervention': A caveat

Before embarking on the main themes of this chapter, I should note my ambivalence about the term 'humanitarian intervention' itself. To clarify the way in which I will use the term in the following discussion, I want to examine here how the term has been used in international political discourse, and how it has been conceptualized by some scholars of International Relations and ethics.

'Humanitarian intervention,' in International Relations discourse, typically refers to the use of military force by states against a sovereign authority for the purpose of human protection. Given that any use of force by states in world politics usually produces much immediate suffering, death and destruction, the adjective 'humanitarian' hardly seems appropriate as a descriptive label. In the post-Cold War era, some state leaders in the West became increasingly open to using the term, partly as a way to convey a break with the Cold War past; the term 'humanitarian' referred to their claim that the military action proposed was prompted by humanitarian concerns rather than geopolitical or self-aggrandizing aims. In addition to expressing intentions, however, the term also seemed at times to convey an entire evaluative judgement, so that labelling a proposed military action 'humanitarian intervention' amounted to declaring that it was morally legitimate or justified. 'Humanitarianism,' according to this usage, is a term of art that serves to demarcate one criterion for legitimate uses of force by states.

'Humanitarian intervention' may also be used to refer to activities such as the provision of food, water, shelter, clothing and medical assistance, all of which are aimed at bringing immediate relief to a population in distress. Although such measures are more substantively or descriptively humanitarian in their immediate impact, this use of 'humanitarian intervention' also tends to carry an automatic positive evaluative judgement because relief measures are typically thought to be incontrovertible from any ethical perspective.

Some scholars have also conceptualized the term 'humanitarian intervention' as an evaluative notion. They argue, however, that political agents have not identified all the relevant normative criteria for determining whether or not an action constitutes 'humanitarian intervention.' For example, it is not enough that an intervenor's declared purpose or motive is humanitarian. Thus, Oliver Ramsbotham and Tom Woodhouse have argued that for an action to be declared 'humanitarian,' it must be humanitarian in cause, end, approach, means and outcome.[5] They assert that if intervenors do not act in accordance with their framework principles that address all of these aspects of the action, 'they should not call their intervention "humanitarian".'[6]

There is clearly more at stake here than the applicability of a merely descriptive label – for an intervention that contravenes their framework principles not only loses an adjective, but also a judgement: if an intervention fails to qualify as 'humanitarian,' it also, in consequence, loses most if not all claims to moral rightness and legitimacy. The reconceptualization offered by Ramsbotham and Woodhouse is thus not merely a redefinition, but an evaluative argument, not so much about what constitutes 'humanitarian intervention' as about what constitutes *right* or *just intervention*. The framework principles they offer actually constitute evaluative criteria with which to assess an intervention's essential rightness, similar to the way that just war criteria allow us to assess the justness, legitimacy or moral rightness of specific wars. If we employ the term in this way, then debates about whether or not a specific action, such as the NATO military action in the Kosovo crisis, was a 'humanitarian intervention' are, in fact, debates about whether or not the abrogation of sovereignty and the use of force in that specific situation, in that specific manner and by those specific agents were morally and legally justified.

A significant problem of making 'humanitarian' coterminous with 'right' and 'just,' however, is the air of legitimacy it lends to all forms of humanitarian action, understood in the narrow descriptive sense. Yet even the provision of humanitarian relief may be conducted in ways that are unjust or illegitimate, even if not unhumanitarian.[7] Descriptively humanitarian practices, such as the distribution of medical aid and food supplies, cannot be judged morally appropriate in all circumstances. As participants in humanitarian relief organizations have noticed, enacting the duty of humanity understood as an obligation to relieve suffering as an end-in-itself can generate morally perverse consequences, such as prolonging or exacerbating violent conflict by indirectly providing militants with resources.[8] 'Humanitarian' therefore does not automatically equal 'ethical' or 'legitimate,' and the use of the term to imply or declare this evaluative conclusion should be discouraged in the scholarship and practice of International Relations.

Perhaps, to avoid the rhetorical dangers, it would be better to label interventions in terms of the substantive activities that define them: the NATO military action in the Kosovo crisis would thus be a 'military intervention,' albeit for declared humanitarian purposes; economic sanctions, boycotts and trade embargoes as well as positive trade incentives and foreign aid would constitute forms of 'economic intervention;' and the provision of relief supplies and services to populations in distress would be 'humanitarian intervention,' but only in a descriptive sense and without the automatic positive moral evaluation typically associated with the term.

In the following discussion, however, I will conform to international political discourse and use the term 'humanitarian intervention' mainly to refer to military actions by states for declared humanitarian purposes. According to this usage, the US-led invasion of Iraq in 2003 could be called a 'humanitarian intervention,' since the US administration cited the suffering of the Iraqi population under Saddam Hussein's repressive regime as a reason for the intervention. But since I do not conceive of the term itself as carrying any evaluative judgement, we are able to discuss whether this case constitutes a 'failed' or 'successful,' legitimate or illegitimate, justifiable or unjustifiable 'humanitarian intervention.' Instead of wrangling over the definition of 'humanitarian intervention,' then, we are able to engage more directly in a debate about the ethics of 'humanitarian intervention,' which mainly has to do with the ethics of the use of force to secure or promote humanitarian ends.

I will use the terms 'humanitarian action' and 'humanitarian assistance' to refer to relief measures for populations in distress, provided mainly by international or nongovernmental humanitarian organizations, and 'human rights advocacy' to describe the work of human rights organizations, which includes investigating, monitoring and reporting of human rights violations. In reality, all of these practices – military action against a sovereign state for humanitarian reasons, the delivery of humanitarian assistance to victims of intrastate violence and human rights advocacy – are forms of 'humanitarian intervention.' That is, they are all interventionary in the sense that they challenge, albeit using radically different means, the way that a domestic sovereign authority is treating people within its borders, and they all share a common justificatory framework for their actions that is located within a cosmopolitan moral orientation.

One morally positive consequence of using the term 'humanitarian intervention' to describe all of these activities, then, may be that it makes more explicit and present the evaluative standard by which the abrogation of sovereignty and the various means of intervention must be justified and measured. The contemporary focus on 'humanitarian interventions' thus illuminates changes in the moral foundations of international and global societies as they embrace a more explicitly cosmopolitan moral agenda. Although it is the moral claims of common humanity that provide the justification for all of these types of intervention, in practice they all face considerable normative challenges, given current world political, social and economic conditions. The public/private or international/domestic distinction is once again central to understanding how and why different types of agents face distinct but interrelated normative challenges for each type of interventionary practice.

III   Cosmopolitan humanitarianism: Problems of private agency and accountability

According to liberal theory, the preservation of human freedom requires a distinction between state and society. Liberalism developed historically against various forms of absolutism, political and theological, and the public/private distinction, understood as a separation of political and civil society, has been indispensable to a liberal conception of a free domestic political order.[9] In this context, the public/private distinction translates into a coercion/freedom distinction, where the (public) state is characterized as a regulatory and coercive realm, and the (private) civil society is depicted as a free and consensual or voluntaristic realm of sociability. Liberals thus view civil society as a source of protection against absolutist political power, and as a site of individual and social self-direction. Although the agents and institutions of civil society are distinct from the agents and institutions of the state, they are not entirely nonpolitical in the sense of being divorced from politics, since the establishment and maintenance of such a free civil society requires the political commitment of the citizenry and the state. Thus, according to Charles Taylor, drawing from Montesquieu, a free civil society is not a pre-political or nonpolitical sphere; rather it is a product of a liberal political order that seeks to avoid absolutism, and protect and promote human (moral and social) agency through fragmenting and multiplying centres of power.[10]

A liberal cosmopolitan conception of global order would also aim to prevent the rise of a global political despotism by sustaining a free global civil society that fragments and multiplies centres of power within the system of global governance. A liberal cosmopolitan world order thus makes a distinction between a society of states or representatives of organized political communities, and a global civil society that includes religious groups and institutions, social and professional associations, corporations, human rights and relief organizations, environmental groups, a plethora of other nongovernmental organizations, as well as individuals. How has such a free global civil society contributed to the evolution of a global order that is responsive to the claims of common humanity?

On the positive side, some agents of global civil society have supported and pushed the society of states towards building a more responsive and accountable international political order that provides the conditions for effective human social and moral agency. Activities that are not directly regulated by states or inter-governmental institutions at the international level have proved to be an important source of the moral renewal and transformation of international and global societies. This is because 'private' nongovernmental agents, free from the dominant norms of the international public order of states, have been able to subscribe to and act on different ethical standards, norms and perspectives. It is therefore a mistake to assume that such 'private' actors necessarily operate with no moral standards (or immoral ones) just because they are not directly accountable to public international law and political authority. The ethical diversity emanating from private agents of civil society can play a vital role in moral learning and transformation at all levels of human interaction.[11]

The emergence of international nongovernmental human rights and humanitarian organizations with self-declared mandates to vindicate the claims of common humanity and to protect vulnerable populations, for example, has contributed to the steady erosion of the instrumental pact between states to turn a blind eye to domestically abusive or neglectful sovereign power. The society of states has become more attentive to the claims of common humanity, in large part due to the efforts of individuals such as Henry Dunant, whose searing account of the Battle of Solferino in 1859 led eventually to the establishment of the Geneva Conventions and the International Committee for the Red

Cross (ICRC). These political, legal and institutional innovations injected basic humanitarian rules and practices into the conduct of war between sovereigns. More recently, in response to civilian suffering resulting from the US-led military interventions in Afghanistan and Iraq, a 28-year-old woman from California, Marla Ruzicka, formed the organization, Campaign for Innocent Victims in Conflict (CIVIC). Working with US politicians such as Senator Patrick J. Leahy, she was able to secure $2.5 million of US government assistance for civilian victims of US military actions in Afghanistan, and later $20 million for their Iraqi counterparts.[12] Such developments are often started by private individuals and groups of individuals, and enjoy increasing visibility, agency and legitimacy in the global order.[13] Their activities and concerns advance a cosmopolitan ethical perspective, unsettling the prevailing rules of international sociability and privacy hitherto set by states at the international level.

Mass media and communications technology has also allowed hardships and injustices suffered alone to become almost instantaneously shared by a global audience. The 'CNN effect' or 'phenomenon,' as it has been dubbed, describes the activities of the media who, in offering mass publics information on a wide range of external conditions and events not only contribute to global and international social awareness, but may also sometimes galvanize potential intervenors into action.[14] The media, however, are not omnipotent. For example, the continuing hostilities in Iraq receive much more coverage than the unmitigated misery of victims of the conflict in the Darfur region of Sudan, where an estimated 2.4 million people have been displaced, and 300,000 black African villagers killed by pro-government Arab militias.[15] Not only does contemporary media have limited vision, but they may also suffer from distorted vision. Mainstream, largely western, media, with increasing concentration of ownership, typically present information that is prejudiced, intentionally or unintentionally, by the agenda of powerful political, economic and social interests. The eye of the media has thus been an inconsistent and unreliable guardian of common humanity.

The potential for media bias illuminates the problem of accountability, not of public actors but of private agents in global civil society. Even humanitarian relief organizations can suffer from moral selectivity, and may serve other organizational interests than their professed humanitarian mandates. On the negative side, then, a global political order committed to respecting the relative independence of global civil society has afforded some individuals and groups agency across borders with unclear accountability processes or mechanisms. Global civil society includes not only morally and socially progressive organizations and groups, such as Greenpeace and Human Rights Watch; it also includes multinational corporations, extremist religious groups and various kinds of militant organizations, such as Al Qaeda. As global civil society continues to evolve, all the associations within it may enjoy greater agency at the global level, but their invisibility or exclusion from the political and often legal accountability structures of international society prompts the question of how they may be held accountable. Indeed, the conventional forceful but largely ineffectual (and some might say counterproductive) responses of the Bush administration to the 9/11 attacks, committed by a nongovernmental network of militants, Al Qaeda, reveal the difficulties of holding such groups accountable through existing international legal and political structures, mechanisms and practices.

The issue of accountability has gained visibility in the humanitarian relief community since the 1990s, when observers began to highlight some of the negative moral and political consequences of humanitarian assistance. Michael Ignatieff has noted, 'Outside humanitarian intervention may...be helping, not to contain war, but to keep it going.'[16] In the aftermath of the Rwandan genocide, for example, international and humanitarian organizations poured aid into the refugee camps in Zaire, where former *genocidaires* 'controlled the refugee population through misuse of the aid distribution system and violence.' International humanitarian aid nourished and refreshed the perpetrators of the genocide, allowing them to re-group and carry on destabilizing activities against the new Rwandan government, resulting in a situation of insecurity that still pervades all of Central Africa today.[17] Accountability became an issue in the 1990s also because of the considerable budgets available to humanitarian relief organizations.[18]

Hugo Slim notes that humanitarian agencies took up the accountability challenge, and created several mechanisms, including: a 'Code of Conduct; a Humanitarian Charter and a set of technical standards; a not-quite Ombudsman called the Humanitarian Accountability Project (HAP); a new emphasis on the quality and transparency of evaluations; an active learning network gathering and sharing the lessons learnt from humanitarian operations (ALNAP), together with initiatives to explore quality models and professional accreditation.'[19] A central question in thinking about the accountability of humanitarian agencies is, to whom ought they to be accountable?

Requiring such groups to be accountable to states or governments creates several problems. Humanitarian organizations have historically cherished their impartiality in aid distribution, neutrality with respect to the political conflict at hand and independence from the political agents involved. These principles have proven to be important practically for such organizations to secure access to vulnerable populations, and to operate in zones of violent political conflict. But what if intervening states are engaging in the use of force for declared humanitarian ends? Should human rights and humanitarian organizations remain neutral about the legitimacy of the intervention? Do humanitarian relief organizations need to maintain their independence from intervening states whose forces may not only be fighting, but also distributing aid supplies to affected populations?

A distinction should be made between 'human rights advocacy' groups such as Human Rights Watch, and 'humanitarian assistance' agencies and organizations such as ICRC and Oxfam. It is the job of human rights advocacy groups to investigate, monitor and report on human rights violations by political agents, whatever their declared intentions and objectives. It seems therefore unproblematic and indeed important for such groups to remain politically independent and critical voices in any conversation about the legitimacy of proposed military actions for humanitarian purposes. The ethical mandate of human rights advocacy groups is precisely to evaluate state practices according to human rights principles and, at times, to condemn their conduct publicly, including in cases of declared 'humanitarian interventions.'

For organizations involved in humanitarian assistance, however, their public condemnation or approval of any 'humanitarian intervention' by states is likely to prove counterproductive to their humanitarian mandate, undermining their own security in conflict zones and hampering their ability to gain access to and assist populations made vulnerable by the military action. Thus Cornelio Sommaruga, President of ICRC, argued in his address to the UN General Assembly in 1992:

> humanitarian endeavour and political action must go their separate ways if the neutrality and impartiality of humanitarian work is not to be jeopardised... it is dangerous to link humanitarian activities aimed at meeting the needs of victims of a conflict with political measures designed to bring about the settlement of the dispute between the parties.[20]

In extreme cases where the political agents involved in the conflict are able to thwart or corrupt entirely the impartial or effective delivery of humanitarian assistance, such humanitarian organizations may express their disapproval of the political actors involved by withdrawing from the field.[21] Cosmopolitan humanitarianism, as practised by humanitarian relief organizations, however, must avoid seeking to be a perfectionist humanitarianism. As Judith Shklar noted, 'Nothing but cruelty comes from those who seek perfection and forget the little good that lies directly within their powers.'[22] In the normal, highly nonideal conditions that characterize situations of politically induced humanitarian disaster, then, such organizations inevitably must make many hard choices, and engage in moral compromises with the controlling political powers in order to provide some relief among the vulnerable populations.

Indeed, states have attempted to instrumentalize and regulate how and where humanitarian nongovernmental organizations (NGOs) operate in a variety of ways.[23] Intervening states, for example, have attempted to boost their own legitimacy by requiring overt support from humanitarian organizations. In the US-led invasion and occupation of Iraq, for example, the US government made its funding of humanitarian agencies conditional on their agreement to display the American flag.[24] States have also attempted to gain legitimacy for their interventionary actions by playing a role in coordinating and delivering humanitarian assistance. Coordination to standardize and make more efficient the delivery of humanitarian assistance is certainly a collective action problem in need of resolution, given the plethora of humanitarian actors that are typically involved in any case of large-scale humanitarian disaster.[25] In Somalia, Kosovo and Afghanistan, however, intervening states sought to control humanitarian relief efforts under the guise of resolving coordination issues, and to have their troops engaged in delivering humanitarian assistance as a way to legitimate their military actions. Furthermore, by earmarking funds for specific cases as well, states have been able to direct where humanitarian assistance goes. While this may serve to ensure some NGO accountability, it is clear that states may also use such techniques to control the direction of humanitarian aid towards areas and issues of interest to them, rather than to areas that are in most need of such assistance. Thus since 9/11, Afghanistan and Iraq have received far more funding from humanitarian agencies relying on donor governments, while places suffering from comparatively worse humanitarian crises, such as Sudan and Congo, have received comparatively much less humanitarian assistance.[26]

These issues raised by the interaction between states and nongovernmental humanitarian organizations reveal the extent to which a free or politically independent global civil society depends on the commitment of agents from both the society of states and global civil society. When US government officials consider nongovernmental humanitarian organizations to be 'an arm of the U.S. government,'[27] they implicitly reject a liberal cosmopolitan conception of the international society/global civil society distinction that enables the maintenance of a free global civil society.

A liberal cosmopolitan commitment to a free global civil society should lead us to reject the idea that human rights and humanitarian organizations should be accountable to individual states, because too often in practice, such accountability translates into the loss of their political independence and the instrumentalization of their work by powerful states. Ultimately, human rights and humanitarian relief organizations ought to be accountable to the populations they aim to help. Helping, under a cosmopolitan view, means providing the people affected with the means to exercise their own moral and social agency. Often, this depends on the construction of responsible domestic political authority structures and the development of an active domestic civil society, tasks that are beyond the mandate or powers of any humanitarian relief organization. Humanitarian relief organizations, however, have to be careful in their work to support rather than undermine these developments. The focus on restoring people's agency should remind such organizations that their job is, in essence, to put themselves out of a job, sooner rather than later.

The problem of vast resource disparities between global and local humanitarian and human rights organizations, however, means that the conduct of external global civil society organizations may also threaten to undermine the moral and social agency of vulnerable populations. As Slim notes, 'some voiceless-ness [of vulnerable populations] may be the result of NGO oppression as well as government or other violent oppression. The problem of northern NGOs "capturing" the agenda and taking over the voice of southern NGOs is well known.'[28] If cosmopolitan humanitarianism is to avoid the charge of imperialism, it must avoid becoming a naïve or arrogant humanitarianism, 'unshaken by skepticism and unmindful of its own limitations.'[29]

IV The use of force: Legitimacy challenges for international law and community[30]

A global order that affirms 'our common humanity' must construct state sovereignty as the authority and responsibility of political agents and structures to protect the humanitarian interests of their members.

An international society within such a global order acquires an obligation to confront and discipline irresponsible sovereigns that, through abuse or neglect, undermine the very conditions for human (social and moral) agency and responsibility. In some situations of extreme humanitarian catastrophe, the society of states confronts the question of whether the use of force would be an appropriate means of intervention.

Indeed, much of the debate about the legitimacy of 'humanitarian intervention' has nothing to do with the abrogation of sovereignty *per se*, but with the use of force by states in an international context as a means to protect or promote humanitarian interests. Scepticism abounds from the apparent contradictions between humanitarian aims and the immediate outcomes of uses of military force. Indeed, the devastation wrought by the two World Wars made the scourge of war the greatest threat to the claims of common humanity. As Jutta Brunnée and Stephen Toope have argued, 'One can read the history of twentieth-century international law primarily as an attempt to reduce the evil of war by codifying a restrictive doctrine of "just war" that limits justifications for recourse to the use of force in international relations.'[31] The UN Charter prohibits forcible military interventions under Article 2(4); exceptions to this prohibition are permitted only when the UN Security Council authorizes the use of force for the sake of international peace and security under Chapter VII, Article 42, or if a state or collective of states can claim reasons of self-defence under Article 51.

Thomas Franck shows that the legitimacy of 'humanitarian intervention' cannot be determined simply by reference to the text of the UN Charter. This is because the text itself admits various interpretations, and any application of the Charter inevitably involves interpretation in a broader normative, ideological and political context. Against positivist accounts of law that seek to isolate it from morality, Franck asserts the interconnectedness of law with both morality and politics.[32] As he has argued, law among mortals is 'a system of norms constantly engaged in a process of challenge, adaptation, and reformulation.'[33] The content and function of law are thus inextricably wedded to issues of power and ideas about justice in any society, whether domestic, international or global.

Franck argues that the debate between states about the legitimacy of 'humanitarian intervention' is not necessarily over the moral cogency of humanitarian claims or even over the moral necessity of overriding sovereign rights to avert humanitarian disaster. Rather, disputes about the legitimacy of 'humanitarian intervention' reside in arguments over the process by which state actions, especially the use of force, come to be legitimized. Even if a law of 'humanitarian intervention' were to enjoy widespread moral endorsement, the validation of specific interventions that claim to be applications of that law would depend on the development of a credible jury that 'makes the definitive decision as to how the law – or the exception – is to be applied in specific instances.' Jurors are 'those to whom is to be entrusted the crucial work of finding the facts, applying the law to them situationally, and, in doing so, narrowing, when necessary, the gaps between law's legality and legitimacy.'[34]

In 'anarchical' international society, the idea of judgment by a jury of peers has more obvious resonance than the more typical legal image of judgment dispensed by an overarching supreme judge. Some might dispute the use of domestic law as an analogy for international law as a misleadingly optimistic exercise, but this would only be true if one held an excessively idealized view of the operation of domestic law. I think the analogy is appropriate and especially useful in highlighting the potential problems that attend attempts, at either the domestic or the international levels, to establish a credible jurying process in a pluralistic, unequal and divided society. The acknowledgement of these problems does not constitute a rejection of the idea that an authoritative jurying process is necessary for legitimizing 'humanitarian intervention,' but it does reveal defects, deficiencies and limitations in current international conditions that need to be addressed for any jurying process to achieve widespread authoritativeness.

The problem of the legitimacy of the jurying process through which the rightness of any military intervention for humanitarian purposes would be evaluated involves two related questions: who can be part of the jury, and to whom must a jurying process be credible? The idea of trial by jury involves the idea of judgment by one's peers. Jury members are typically disinterested or not personally involved with the victim or defendant, but they are not entirely uninvolved, since to be a peer is to be connected especially to the defendant either through common membership in a community or through equal status. This is to ensure that judgments of the defendant's conduct or the complainant's claim occur with 'a degree of contextual reasonableness.'[35]

The question of who can be a juror is determined by one's view of the relevant community that can claim the right to judge the parties. International law has conceived the international community as a society of states because that law is made by states. In that society, as Franck suggests, it is states, in their capacity as members of regional and interstate organizations such as the UN Security Council and the General

Assembly, that decide when a situation has become a humanitarian crisis, 'whether the crisis is truly one of extreme necessity,' 'whether the force deployed is appropriate and commensurate with the necessity' and 'whether the motive of the intervener is humanitarian, as distinct from self-aggrandizing.'[36] States are peers through their common membership in the society of states, and since states are the self-professed agents of military force in world politics, it would seem logical to conclude that the people who can determine the legitimacy of military action by a state or collectivity of states must be the representatives of states themselves. From this perspective, just as most national militaries have special courts, distinct from their civilian counterparts, to judge professional transgressions by military personnel, the society of states can claim a distinct and exclusive authority to judge the conduct of its members.

Even within this restrictive view of international community, however, there are significant issues that affect the establishment of a credible jurying process. These problems – power asymmetries, gross economic inequality and ideological divides – point to the enduring problem of community in all societies, including international society. Historically, the society of states, although legally governed by the principle of sovereign equality, has been hierarchically ordered. What will motivate the powerful to encourage the development of an egalitarian jurying process? While all states can claim common membership in the society of states, the power asymmetries between them foster the development of different peer groups within that society. Since the concept of a jurying process depends on the idea of a community of peers, the existence of superpowers and great powers inhibits the likelihood of establishing an egalitarian jurying process that could hold the most powerful actors accountable to the wider society of states. At best, perhaps, great powers will endorse a process that requires them to submit to the judgment of a jury of other great powers, which may explain the structure of the Security Council that grants privileged authority to the five victorious powers of the Second World War.

At this time, the United States is the sole global military superpower, and it prefers to be its own judge. The Bush administration's rejection of the ICC and other various forms of international cooperation, as well as its evasion of Security Council judgement in its war against Iraq in 2003, indicates that it views the United States as peerless, making the idea of a jury or judgment by one's peers inoperable. In this context, Michael Byers and Simon Chesterman worry that 'the legal principle of sovereign equality is now, quietly but resolutely, under attack.'[37] Power asymmetries present another kind of problem for a credible jurying process when the powerful *are* involved in its establishment. Robust legal regimes that exist in a social context of extreme power disparities, whether their basis is economic, political and/or social, often serve to perpetuate established tyrannies and servilities, and thus suffer from limited moral authoritativeness. This is because law depends on political will for effectiveness in any society, and it is an unfortunate fact that in contexts where power and justice pull in opposing directions, law gains power or efficacy only by compromising on justice or moral legitimacy. Law by itself is not going to be able to create greater substantive equality between states, but it can at least resist becoming a legitimizing tool for great power and superpower domination, by adhering to its moral function as a check on unaccountable and arbitrary exercises of power. In the case of the ICC, for example, this would involve resisting US demands for formal exemptions of US personnel from the jurisdiction of the Court.[38]

The establishment of a credible jurying process within the society of states is also complicated by the prevalence of the friend–enemy distinction as an organizing principle of international politics. Although the Cold War is over, the friend–enemy distinction underlying Cold War politics continues to animate other conflicts and divides in international society, especially the current 'war on terror.' Consider the decision of the United States, in the aftermath of 9/11, to justify its military intervention in Afghanistan by presenting its evidence of Taliban complicity with Al Qaeda to NATO. Franck argues that the 'underlying rationale appears to be that... if a plea of extreme necessity is accepted by a multiplicity of governments, it is more likely to be believed than when asserted unilaterally by the government directly at interest.'[39] The legitimacy obtained by demonstrating evidence only to one's friends or allies, however, is not likely to be authoritative with those who may have less reason or interest to grant one the benefit of the doubt. Being able to secure endorsements from a multiplicity of states may only show that one has more friends (or power), rather than that one's case is morally legitimate or credible.[40]

Even in the society of states, then, the authoritativeness of a jurying process for legitimizing 'humanitarian interventions' will be hotly contested, given the power asymmetries, economic disparities and ideological divides that mark the international arena. Law presupposes community, but as Judith Shklar has noted, 'Law does not by itself generate institutions, cause wars to end, or states to behave as they should. It does not create a community.'[41] Establishing a jurying process that would be credible to the wider society of states thus depends less on legal transformation than on significant political, social and economic transformations within international society.

Franck suggests that there are actually three arenas where jurying of 'humanitarian interventions' may occur: the International Court of Justice, international political forums such as the Security Council and General Assembly, and the court of public opinion.[42] His acknowledgement of the 'court of public opinion' as another jurying arena reveals the embeddedness of the society of states within a wider and more diverse global society encompassing all of humanity.

Indeed since the 1990s, one challenge to restrictive interpretations of international law that prohibit military interventions for humanitarian purposes has come from global civil society actors. As Adam Roberts has observed, the security problems encountered by nongovernmental humanitarian relief organizations attempting to deliver humanitarian assistance to populations in crisis have contributed to the development of a humanitarian rationale for military interventions.[43] In a recent initiative, students at Swarthmore, a liberal arts college in Pennsylvania, started the Genocide Intervention Fund (GIF) to raise money from private citizens to fund African Union peacekeeping troops in Darfur.[44] These developments show that although the basis of legality in world politics may be located in the society of states, since states alone are the lawmakers of international society, the basis of moral legitimacy in world politics ultimately lies beyond that society, and this larger society is one source that provides direction and substance to changes in the legality and legitimacy of various state and interstate norms and practices. Indeed, the student GIF initiative, in the end, may not be about the dollars, but about 'shaming governments to ante up.'[45]

Given the humanitarian justifications to be scrutinized, it would be reasonable to argue that it is not representatives of states but representatives of humanity that ought to form the jury. But where are these representatives? One might look for them in the emerging global nongovernmental organizations dedicated to the promotion of humanitarian and other aspects of a global 'public interest.'[46] There are, of course, significant moral, and not just political, difficulties in designating nongovernmental organizations as potential jurors, given the uncertain character of their 'public' status and authority. There is currently no institutional expression of global democracy that would support the idea of a global citizenry from which prospective nongovernmental jurors could be drawn.

Still, these problems are not insurmountable, nor are current institutional arrangements of global governance unalterable, and once one accepts the idea that states ought to answer not only to a select society of like units, but to a wider global community, it becomes less clear why the jury for determining the legitimacy of 'humanitarian interventions' must be restricted to current state representatives. The important point is that the jury, to be legally proper, must be legally defined, but like an ordinary jury in domestic trials, those who are legally appointed as jurors are drawn not from the ranks of government or the police, but from the citizenry. The conduct of police officials is judged not only by internal review boards or other police organizations or members, but also by civilian boards and courts, especially in circumstances involving the use of force. Police officers are not thought to be accountable only to other police officers; they are accountable to the wider society of citizens because it is on behalf of their moral interests and protection that police officers acquire the authority to use force. Similarly, states and their representatives are accountable to a wider community beyond the society of states because it is ultimately the moral interests and protection of the members of the wider community of humanity that ground the moral legitimacy of states' resort to force. If one accepts this interpretation of state accountability for the use of force, current jurying mechanisms that draw exclusively from the pool of current state representatives seem inherently biased.

The ICISS rigorously outlines key judgements that must be made in determining the legitimacy of any military action for humanitarian purposes. The jury must evaluate whether the 'just cause threshold' ('large scale loss of life' or 'ethnic cleansing') has been met; whether the intervenor has the right intention ('to halt or avert human suffering'); whether the use of military force constitutes the last resort; and whether it is proportional to the scale of humanitarian catastrophe and can enjoy 'a reasonable chance of success in halting or averting the suffering which has justified the intervention.'[47] There is no principled reason why these issues cannot be adjudicated by a mixed group of past and current state and nongovernmental organizational and individual representatives. This is especially true in the context of an imperfectly and incompletely democratized international order, in which states may either lack domestic mechanisms of democratic accountability or have defective ones. Just as arms control experts ought to be the recognized authorities on whether or not there are weapons of mass destruction in a given location, for example, a team of government and international organization representatives, along with experts on genocide and crimes against humanity, could comprise an authoritative adjudicative panel that determines whether a military intervention is necessary and justified in any particular case. Properly constituted, such an institutionalized mechanism of adjudicating international responses to humanitarian crises would make it less possible for states and international organizations to evade or distort their humanitarian responsibilities by obscuring or manipulating the facts of the case.

V Conclusion

In the post-Cold War era, military actions explicitly justified on humanitarian grounds gained legitimacy, but the mixed results of those interventions reveal the difficulty of matching consequences to agency in the complicated political environments that generate humanitarian crises. The threat and use of force between states are well-worn, if not clearly effectual, roads to effecting desired political transformations. Even if one endorses the claims of common humanity, embraces the interpretation of 'sovereignty as responsibility' to protect basic humanitarian interests, and deems authoritative current international mechanisms for adjudicating uses of force by states for humanitarian purposes, the question remains whether military force can ever be effectively employed in the name of common humanity. Pacifists are likely to answer in the negative, and it may be difficult to disagree with them when one views the inevitable record of sorrow, death and destruction wrought by contemporary human warfare. Military intervention may be effective at changing the political *status quo*, but violence is an unpredictable teacher, and the indeterminacy of the lessons people learn from its use makes it a particularly risky and unreliable means of *directing* political transformation towards humanitarian ends. Nicholas Wheeler has thus argued that the US and UN intervention in Somalia in the early 1990s raises 'the troubling question' of 'whether the threat or use of force can ever promote conflict resolution in situations where societies are plunged into lawlessness as a consequence of civil war and the disintegration of state structures.'[48]

The greatest challenge to the legitimacy of 'humanitarian intervention,' then, is a practical consideration. In the complicated and desperate political and social environments that culminate in humanitarian catastrophes, what are the prospects for a successful intervention? If success is measured in terms of stopping or averting the suffering that prompted the intervention, there are likely to be cases in which 'humanitarian intervention' has a reasonable prospect of success. Roméo

Dallaire, for example, has argued that a 'humanitarian intervention' in the first weeks of April 1994 could have stopped the ensuing slaughter of 800,000 Rwandans; world leaders have since considered themselves blameworthy for this 'failure of humanity in Rwanda.'[49] Such an intervention, even if it did occur, however, might not have been enough to guarantee Rwanda and neighbouring African states security from future atrocities.

This is because the success of any 'humanitarian intervention,' measured in terms of its broader consequences for the establishment of accountable social structures that affirm the claims of common humanity, depends on international society's further commitment to meet 'post-intervention obligations' to rebuild the affected societies.[50] Without this commitment, 'humanitarian interventions' are likely to become more necessary more often while being less and less effective in advancing humanitarian interests.[51] The deeply tragic situation in Iraq shows that while military intervention may be successful in toppling domestic tyrants such as Saddam Hussein, it alone is unlikely to guarantee any progress towards a more humane or accountable political order. 'Humanitarian interventions,' even against abusive regimes, suffer from a legitimacy deficit if they do not include a commitment of the required resources to meet post-intervention obligations to help the affected population establish a better political alternative.

Indeed, the 2003 intervention in Iraq involves several legitimacy deficits, revealing faults in both public and private, external and internal, international and domestic, agents and structures of the contemporary world order. On the one hand, cosmopolitan ethical commitments have found vindication in international human rights and humanitarian law, providing grounds for denying legitimacy and the attendant entitlements to sovereignty and nonintervention to abusive or incompetent governments. On the other hand, the lack of authoritative and effectual mechanisms for adjudicating and legitimizing interventions in contemporary world political conditions means that the legitimacy of intervenors is also problematic, even when they are acting against an illegitimate regime. If we are living in a 'cosmopolitan moment,' one might have to conclude that it is decidedly half-baked, and the unhappy moral consequence seems to be a plethora of accountability gaps. That is, at the same time that a domestic political agent may be found defective and therefore to deserve to lose its entitlement to the rights of sovereignty, including nonintervention, international or external political agents and structures are also defective and therefore intervenors may lack the legitimacy to abrogate sovereignty and intervene, especially with military force. Thus by human rights standards, Saddam Hussein's regime in Iraq could not claim to be a legitimate sovereign authority, but external intervenors such as the US-led coalition that overthrew his regime and now occupies Iraq also cannot claim to have mounted a legitimate military or 'humanitarian' intervention.

Some have criticized the focus on 'bad governments,' arguing that ameliorating global economic disparities and their attendant human misery is key to preventing the kinds of political, social and economic dysfunctions that degenerate into humanitarian crises. This line of argument understands the vindication of an agency-based view of common humanity to require the commitment of more attention and resources to preventive rather than ameliorative measures. As John Tirman has asked, 'If obligations exist to ameliorate calamities underway, are there obligations to prevent calamities?'[52] The ICISS argues that prevention 'is the single most important dimension of the responsibility to protect [and] more commitment and resources must be devoted to it.'[53]

Focusing on preventive as opposed to reactive humanitarian measures raises contentious and complicated questions about causal and moral responsibility for humanitarian catastrophes. If one locates the causes of humanitarian crises in the global order itself, 'humanitarian interventions' against irresponsible or negligent domestic tyrants can at best treat symptoms but not causes. At worst, a preoccupation with humanitarian crises and 'humanitarian intervention' is actually a way for the rich and the powerful to avoid their own culpability in constructing and maintaining a global order that consistently produces such tragedies. The focus on 'humanitarian intervention' under this view betrays a faulty moral and causal assumption that humanitarian catastrophes 'have everything to do with the dictator, the warlords, or the ethnic rivalries, and nothing to do with us in the Western democracies.'[54]

It has to be admitted that the causes of humanitarian catastrophes are multiple and multilayered; in other words, there is usually enough blame to go around. For example, while responsibility for the 1994 Rwandan genocide obviously lies with those individuals who planned, orchestrated and conducted the mass slaughter, it would be difficult to explain how the genocide could have occurred without an account of nineteenth-century European racial ideologies that informed Belgian colonial practices in Rwanda; the politics of resentment and exclusion following independence; the wedding of politics and violence in the post-Cold War democratization process; the context of civil war, started by exiled Tutsis of the Rwandan Patriotic Front in 1990, and the attendant social, political and economic problems; the lack of moderating influences from external influential powers, such as the French, that could check extremist elements of the Habyarimana government; the decline of coffee prices and the implementation of World Bank structural adjustment policies that further exhausted the economy; as well as the weakness of international institutions such as the United Nations and the indifference of capable international agents such as the United States.[55]

Clearly, failures of humanity of the proportion of the Rwandan genocide require multiple failures at all levels of governance in practically every sphere of human relations, public and private. Moral condemnation of the direct perpetrators is not enough and constitutes only the first step towards preventing such failures from recurring in the future. Effective prevention requires the institutionalization of a humane and accountable global order that is proactive rather than merely reactive in its vindication of the claims of common humanity. Meanwhile, in our nonideal world, reactive responses to unfolding humanitarian catastrophes are still necessary if largely inadequate; thus sadly, the legitimacy of various forms of 'humanitarian intervention' will likely remain a pertinent and important, if tortured, theme of normative inquiry in world politics.

8
Conclusion

> The public and the private worlds are inseparably connected... The tyrannies and servilities of the one are the tyrannies and servilities of the other.
>
> Virginia Woolf, *Three Guineas*[1]

I Public and private worlds

This study has revealed the centrality of public/private constructs in disciplining normative debates about intervention in world politics.

Excessive dichotomization of the public/private or international/domestic distinction severs the connection between agency and accountability, yielding absolutist conceptions of state sovereignty as privacy, and a concomitant vilification of interventionary practices. Ultimately, such an account of the international/domestic distinction, and of sovereignty as privacy, is theoretically incoherent and untenable. This is because any normative right to sovereignty that states may enjoy can only exist in the embrace of community norms, which presupposes a fundamental interconnection between domestic and international normative and political structures.

What ought to be the scope of sovereign responsibility, and to whom are sovereigns accountable for the exercise of their sovereign rights? Historically, the scope of sovereign responsibility and accountability has been restrictively interpreted; internally, states were responsible only to their own citizens, and externally they were accountable only to the member states of international society. A dichotomized conception of the international/domestic distinction, however, meant that member states of international society were not held accountable by that society for domestic failures of responsibility towards their own citizens. This construction of sovereign responsibility and accountability yielded a world of public states and private humanity; consequently, domestic tyrants could feel at home in the world.

The ascendancy of the idea of universal human rights following the Second World War has challenged such restrictive notions of national and international responsibility, and led to significant social, legal and political innovations in international law and world politics. The language of human rights is grounded in a cosmopolitan ethical perspective. Such an ethic entails the acknowledgement of some notion of common humanity that translates into an idea of shared or common moral duties towards others by virtue of this humanity. From a cosmopolitan view, sovereigns are responsible to their own citizens, but they also have certain responsibilities towards noncitizens. Furthermore, the development of international human rights law expresses a universal standard by which international society and an emergent global civil society may hold sovereigns accountable for the treatment of their own citizens within their own borders. Indeed, not only are states accountable to the member states of international society, but they increasingly must also justify themselves to various 'guardians of humanity' located in global civil society.

From a cosmopolitan perspective, intervention, or the abrogation of sovereignty, is not objectionable in principle against abusive, oppressive or neglectful sovereigns who fail to meet their humanitarian responsibilities towards their own or others' citizens. More accurately, perhaps, such regimes expose themselves to legitimate external scrutiny and intervention even if the number of adversely affected individuals is quite small. The public/private or international/domestic distinction therefore cannot be used to shield sovereigns from external accountability when the issue involves human rights, broadly construed. In the face of politically induced large-scale humanitarian catastrophes, international society and the various members of global civil society have an obligation to intervene, to call power to account, and to help bring about political, social and economic conditions that are morally responsive to the claims of common humanity. In contemporary world political conditions, however, the lack of authoritative and effectual institutions and mechanisms for adjudicating the illegitimacy of regimes and the legitimacy of various interventionary practices, especially the use of force, means that the legitimacy of external intervenors is equally problematic, even when they are acting against an illegitimate regime. Thus interventions by states, even when humanitarian issues are present and valid, generate endless and tortured normative controversy.

Most of the normative debates about intervention in world politics have focused on the ethics of intervention by states and, consequently, on the ethics of the use of force for purposes of human protection. When one looks at any empirical contemporary case of politically induced humanitarian catastrophe, however, it becomes clear that the subject of intervention does not pertain only to states and international institutions, but also to various sectors of global civil society such as human rights and humanitarian NGOs. The public/private construct is once again useful for interrogating the distinct ethical challenges faced by these diverse actors engaged in various interventionary practices.

Indeed, exploring the public/private construct at the global level reveals a far more diverse and complex set of normative, political and social relationships in world politics than traditional state-centric International Relations scholarship has allowed. An exclusive focus on states and interstate relations exposes students of world politics to only half a picture of the subject matter, and misses important sources of change in domestic, international and global relations. The public/private construct allows us not only to recognize actors – individual, collective and institutional – other than states, such as the diverse members of global civil society, but also to *differentiate* between various types of actors in world politics. To say that multinational corporations, nongovernmental humanitarian organizations, human rights advocacy groups, churches, states and international organizations are all actors in world politics, then, is not to say that they enjoy the same kinds of agency, or ought to be subject to the same mechanisms of accountability at the global level. At the same time that the public/private construct allows us to distinguish between various kinds of agents, it also helps us to model different kinds of relationships between them, and to investigate their interrelated forms of agency and accountability.

Indeed, while International Relations has focused on state-to-state relationships within the public realm of international society, it has neglected the dynamic interaction between public and private realms of global relations. That is, it has typically neglected the role of domestic or national politics, as well as of global civil society politics, in shaping and transforming the conduct of states and the prevailing norms and practices of public international society. The end of the Cold War and the collapse of the Soviet Union revealed the inadequacy of focusing only on interstate politics, at the exclusion of domestic intrastate politics, and the attacks of 9/11 exposed an inadequate acknowledgement of the increasing agency of global nonstate actors, on the part of practitioners and scholars of International Relations. At the same time, the shape of the agency and accountability of various global civil society actors is also significantly affected by the agendas of powerful states and international institutions. Out of this dynamic, mutual, though not necessarily symmetrical, interaction between public and private worlds, the stuff of human relations is made.

In the light of these developments the study of ethics beyond borders cannot be confined to the ethics of statecraft or interstate relations, but must engage new normative challenges arising from an increasing diversity of agents, and their cross-border and transboundary activities. The study of world normative order must go beyond the agents, principles and structures of the society of states, and include investigations of the appropriate ethical framework for organizing a diversity of agents and their relationships. The public/private construct helps us to make sense of the complex structure of global relations, and to expose normative contestations about this structure itself among the players in world politics. Different models of the public/private construct illuminate different visions of world order, with attendant implications for the identities, agency, interests and obligations of individual, collective and institutional agents at different levels of human interaction.

For example, a *laissez-faire* model of the global economic order would presuppose a fairly rigid public/private or international society/global civil society distinction, and categorize the global market as 'private,' a sphere of relations whose agents, mainly corporations, ought to be free to conduct their activities with as little regulation as possible by the society of states and international economic institutions. Alternatively, a reformed liberal model of global economic order would justify greater international regulation of the global market and its players for the purpose of establishing, maintaining or promoting the necessary background conditions for fair and free economic competition. Such a model of global economic order would presuppose a more interconnected relationship between public international society and private global market to ensure greater accountability of corporate agents.

Liberal theory has played prominently in my analysis of the public/private distinction in world politics because the construct is integral to liberalism's main moral/political commitment: human freedom. Liberal theory employs the public/private distinction to enable diverse agents – individual, collective and corporate – to interact while maintaining distinct identities, roles and values, and pursuing diverse ends and interests. A liberal conception of the public/private distinction at the global level justifies the maintenance of a relatively free global civil society as a way to fragment and multiply centres of power at the global level in order to avoid the ascendancy of varieties of global political despotism or totalitarianism. But under a liberal *cosmopolitan* world order, the public/private distinction, understood as an international society/global civil society distinction, cannot be used to exempt either political or global civil society agents from fulfilling their duties to humanity. This is because the moral function of the distinction in a liberal cosmopolitan order is to establish enabling conditions for human moral and social agency *for every individual* in their various spheres of social relationships. From a liberal cosmopolitan perspective, the interconnectedness of domestic, international and global political and social orders means that none can claim agency without some form of accountability, especially with respect to the claims of common humanity. The precise content of those claims would be generated and transformed from time to time by the dynamic contestations between various agents of international and global societies.

The development of such a liberal cosmopolitan world order depends on the construction of a public/private distinction that preserves the autonomy of the political and the social, ensuring the structural prerequisites for individuals to enjoy both social and political freedom. Whatever moral defects exhibited by our contemporary public and private worlds, a liberal cosmopolitan perspective must acknowledge that they cannot be resolved by eliminating the boundary between them. The one and many faces of humanity will always require some such boundary. The establishment and maintenance of a liberal cosmopolitan structure of relationships depends on the most powerful agents in both public international society and private global civil society. When powerful states attempt to control not only weaker states, but also critical agents in global civil society, for their own political advantage, and when powerful civil society actors such as multinational corporations gain undue political influence using their economic advantage, they undermine the public/private distinction that is a structural requirement for varieties of human freedom. In the contemporary world, the challenge for developing a liberal cosmopolitan world order is to forestall the ascendancy of the twin dangers of global public *and* private despotisms.

II 'Humanitarian intervention' and the faces of global justice

The practice of 'humanitarian intervention,' or the use of force by states for purposes of human protection, has arisen in a world that increasingly acknowledges the moral significance of claims of common humanity, but lacks institutionalized and authoritative mechanisms for dealing with violations of those claims. If the key to resolving humanitarian crises is to transform the contemporary global order towards a greater affirmation of our common humanity, however, 'humanitarian intervention' cannot be the primary means of promoting such transformation. This is not only because military action produces inevitable humanity-depriving consequences; it is also because the use of force is largely irrelevant or inappropriate as a means to addressing the greatest assault on common humanity in contemporary times. As Thomas Pogge has observed, 'Our present global economic order produces a stable pattern of widespread malnutrition and starvation among the poor, with some 18 million persons dying each year from poverty-related causes, and there are likely to be feasible alternative regimes that would not produce similarly severe deprivations.'[2] According to the World Bank, 1.2 billion people on earth live in absolute poverty.[3]

The suffering generated by global poverty may be less spectacular than that which emanates from scenes of genocide and armed conflict, but a cosmopolitan concern to protect and promote conditions for the effective exercise of human moral and social agency must be as concerned with the 'culture of neglect' that produces and condones such mass poverty and inequality as with the 'culture of impunity' that has shielded domestically abusive sovereigns from international accountability. Clearly, the magnitude of the failures of humanity in both cases of global poverty and armed conflict involves a multiplicity of defective agents and structures, public and private, in national, international and global societies. Not only may international institutions and national governments be incompetent, neglectful or oppressive, but there may also be a plethora of powerful, self-interested or opportunistic civil society actors, at global and local levels, with the inclination to oppress, exploit or abuse the vulnerable.

The gross inequities of the contemporary world render morally problematic all public and private interventionary practices. The public/private construct has helped us to make sense of contemporary practices of cosmopolitan humanitarianism, engaged in not only by public agents of international society, but also by various private agents of global civil society. At the same time, however, the inevitable ethical dilemmas that confront both sets of agents, whether they are engaged in 'human rights advocacy,' 'humanitarian assistance' or 'humanitarian intervention' reveal deeper defects in the wider 'global background context' in which they operate.[4]

Part of the global background context affecting the accountability of sovereign power has changed with the recent introduction of the ICC. According to Amnesty International, the 'struggle for international justice has taken a major stride forward' with the establishment of the ICC, a sentiment echoed by most human rights and humanitarian organizations, as well as by the UN Secretary General and numerous state leaders who endorsed the creation of the Court.[5] Such an institution aims to vindicate the claims of common humanity by affirming the significance of human rights and humanitarian law in domestic and international societies. Specifically it attacks the 'culture of impunity' by dealing retributive justice to culpable political and civil society agents.[6] Although such an institution may be an essential component of an accountable international political order, it should be clear that even if the ICC were to enjoy universal endorsement in the society of states, it alone would be insufficient to establish a legitimate international order.[7] Indeed, an international society that is quick to punish through the ICC, but slow to help empower the destitute and the marginalized, would constitute a perversion rather than a fulfillment of liberal cosmopolitan ideals.

These observations suggest that just as different faces of injustice, such as global poverty, armed conflict and mass atrocity, share strong family resemblances, so the various faces of justice – retributive, reparative and distributive – must also be interrelated and mutually reinforcing. This turn towards the concept of justice suggests the limited moral utility of focusing solely on cosmopolitan humanitarianism, or the ethics of 'humanitarian intervention,' even in its various forms. To grasp fully the demands of a cosmopolitan moral perspective, any discussion of cosmopolitan humanitarianism must evolve towards a more comprehensive debate about the requirements of justice in a cosmopolitan world order.[8]

In the absence of more equitable global background conditions, 'humanitarian intervention' as a concept and practice involves a cruel set of ironies. The subject of 'humanitarian intervention' enjoys moral salience only because the world in which we live is far removed from one that universally affirms the claims of common humanity. This is to say that 'humanitarian intervention' illuminates the profoundly tragic contours of political, social and moral agency in a nonideal world of domestic, international and global, social and political, agents and structures that are morally limited, defective and fallible. The effectiveness, and hence legitimacy, of 'humanitarian interventions,' however, depends on the extent to which the overall global order represents an accountable social structure that is morally responsive to the claims of common humanity. The conditions required to maximize the overall success and legitimacy of 'humanitarian interventions' are also the conditions that would render them less necessary or in need of legitimation. Ironically, an increase in the number of legitimate 'humanitarian interventions' therefore may not indicate progress towards a more humane and accountable world order founded on a respect for our common humanity; rather, it might actually signify moral regress and a decreasingly legitimate global order.

A world order founded upon a respect for our common humanity would be one in which agency-depriving conditions such as absolute poverty were not tolerated as an acceptable or inevitable outcome of domestic or global economic structures and forces. Commitment to our common humanity would require the world's politically and economically powerful to establish greater formal and substantive equality in the rules and institutions governing the society of states and the international economy, as well as to institutionalize a duty of assistance[9] to societies burdened by incompetent governance, toxic regimes or the legacies of historical injustice.

Some might argue that global poverty is a distinct problem from that of violently abusive domestic tyrants, the kind of cases which typically generate calls for 'humanitarian intervention.' The relation between these two faces of inhumanity, however, may be deep. Since both constitute affronts to our common humanity, it is likely that the 'change in moral consciousness'[10] required to mount legitimate 'humanitarian interventions' is the same attitudinal change required to implement effective solutions to global poverty. More practically, if wealthier states and publics cannot bring themselves to make the material sacrifices required by a more equitable global economic order, it is difficult to see how they could be made to accept the burden of more significant sacrifices in terms of lives that would be required by any 'humanitarian intervention.'[11] The ethical challenges confronting practitioners of 'humanitarian intervention' are thus inextricably linked to issues of global justice.

III   In the name of humanity, again

It should not be too controversial today to assert that every human being who is born ought to live in security and with dignity; to have adequate nourishment, clothing and shelter; affordable access to basic health care and medicines for curable diseases; the means and opportunity to learn, and to work for at least a 'living wage'; and to develop into a mature adult, capable of leading a meaningful and productive life in community with others. When those responsible for shaping political, social and economic orders – familial, local, national, international and global – do not take seriously the idea that all human individuals are entitled to these goods, means and opportunities, the least powerful among us will inevitably become vulnerable to a variety of public and private 'tyrannies and servilities.'

Thus, in our contemporary world, it is often children who must bear the terrible burdens of adult social, political and institutional failings. Almost 50 percent of children under age five in developing countries suffer from malnourishment.[12] The United Nations Children's Fund (UNICEF) estimates that 'child soldiers' are used in over thirty ongoing or recent armed conflicts around the world. In addition, millions of vulnerable children fall prey to child-traffickers and become abused and exploited through a combination of political incompetence, neglect or complicity with a variety of criminal and opportunistic civil society actors. According to the International Labour Organization (ILO), 1.8 million children are being exploited in the commercial sex industry. Contexts of political and social dysfunction, coupled with economic deprivation, afford such children few opportunities to escape lives filled with drudgery, cruelty and humiliation:

> Hidden from view and without legal protection, children in poor countries are often lured [away from their destitute families] by promises of a good education or a 'better job.' Far from home or in a foreign country, trafficked children – disoriented, without papers, and excluded from any form of protection – can be forced to endure prostitution, domestic servitude, early and involuntary marriage, or hazardous and punishing labour.[13]

For these children, the idea that they may be entitled to anything in this world must seem a fantastical notion.

Recognizing their suffering is uncontroversial. Assigning responsibility for alleviating such suffering or eliminating its sources, however, proves to be a more challenging task. The cosmopolitan ethical perspective that I have forwarded in this book does not allow us to see such suffering as mere personal misfortune, or as the inevitable consequences of structural forces (of politics, economics or culture) beyond human design and control. War, poverty and exploitation are all too human creations. Under a cosmopolitan view, the public/private distinction, whether in the form of an international/domestic distinction or an international society/global civil society distinction, also cannot function to help us to evade our common moral duties. The moral function of the distinction, in global as in domestic politics, is to promote varieties of human freedom – individual, social and political – not to enable agency-depriving practices or shield them from external scrutiny and intervention. Whatever boundaries we are apt to make between public and private, insiders and outsiders, citizens and noncitizens, international and domestic, international society and global civil society, no boundary can sever the moral bonds of common humanity. In the face of inhumanity, injustice and intolerance, intervention to alleviate suffering and to construct a more morally responsive and responsible world order becomes both a public and a private duty of us all.

Notes

1 Introduction

1. J.B. Bossuet, *Politique tirée des propres paroles de l'Ecriture sainte* [Politics Drawn from the Very Words of Holy Scripture, 1709] (Geneva: Droz, 1967), p. 92; quoted in D. Gordon, *Citizens without Sovereignty: Equality and Sociability in French Thought, 1670–1789* (Princeton: Princeton University Press, 1994), p. 9.
2. See United Nations Secretary General Kofi Annan, Address to the 54th session of the UN General Assembly, 1999; and his Millenium Report to the General Assembly, 2000. Quoted in International Commission on Intervention and State Sovereignty (ICISS), *The Responsibility to Protect: Report of the International Commission on Intervention and State Sovereignty* (Ottawa, Canada: International Development Research Centre, December 2001), p. 2.
3. R. Falk, 'The Complexities of Humanitarian Intervention: A New World Order Challenge,' *Michigan Journal of International Law*, 17 (1996) 491–513 at 513.
4. 'Transcript: Bush's Speech to U.N. on Iraq,' *The New York Times*, 12 September 2002.
5. 'Transcript: Bush's Speech on Iraq,' *The New York Times*, 18 March 2003.
6. In June 2005 there were approximately 135,000 US troops in Iraq. See B. Graham, 'Little Change in Troop Levels Expected Soon,' *The Washington Post*, 22 June 2005, A16.
7. See R. Dallaire, 'Looking at Darfur, Seeing Rwanda,' *The New York Times*, 4 October 2004.
8. H. Bull ed., *Intervention in World Politics* (Oxford: Clarendon Press, 1986), p. 1. More recently, Oliver Ramsbotham and Tom Woodhouse have characterized the classical view of intervention as 'the abrogation of sovereignty' or 'when one or more external powers exercise sovereign functions within the domestic jurisdiction of a state.' See Ramsbotham and Woodhouse, *Humanitarian Intervention in Contemporary Conflict: A Reconceptualization* (Oxford: Blackwell, 1996), p. 40.
9. C. Navari, 'Intervention, Non-Intervention and the Construction of the State,' in *Political Theory, International Relations and the Ethics of Intervention*, Ian Forbes and Mark Hoffman eds (New York: St. Martin's Press, 1993), pp. 43–60 at p. 43.
10. G. Allan and G. Crow, *Home and Family: Creating the Domestic Sphere* (London: MacMillan Press, 1989), p. 7.
11. K.J. Holsti, *The Dividing Discipline: Hegemony and Diversity in International Theory* (Boston: Unwin Hyman, 1985).
12. M. Wight, 'Why is there no International Theory?' in *Diplomatic Investigations: Essays in the Theory of International Politics*, H. Butterfield and M. Wight eds (Cambridge, MA: Harvard University Press, 1966), p. 18.
13. Wight, 'Why is there no International Theory?' p. 33. Kenneth Waltz has similarly argued, 'National politics is the realm of authority, of administration, and of law. International politics is the realm of power, of struggle, and of

accommodation.' See Waltz, *Theory of International Politics* (Toronto: McGraw-Hill, 1979), p. 113.

14. S. Hoffmann, *Duties Beyond Borders: On the Limits and Possibilities of Ethical International Politics* (Syracuse, NY: Syracuse University Press, 1981), p. 23.

15. See, for example, M. Wright, 'Central but Ambiguous: States and International Theory,' *Review of International Studies*, 10 (1984) 233–237.

16. S. Hoffmann, 'The Problem of Intervention,' in *Intervention in World Politics*, Bull ed., pp. 7–28 at p. 27.

17. R.J. Vincent, 'Grotius, Human Rights, and Intervention,' in *Hugo Grotius and International Relations*, H. Bull, B. Kingsbury and A. Roberts eds (Oxford: Clarendon Press, 1992), pp. 241–256 at p. 251.

18. Only a decade ago, Steve Smith discussed the normative silence of international theory in Smith, 'The Self-Images of a Discipline: A Genealogy of International Relations Theory,' in *International Relations Theory Today*, K. Booth and S. Smith eds (University Park, Pennsylvania: The Pennsylvania State University Press, 1995), pp. 1–37 at p. 3.

19. Moral questions are not limited to relations between human beings, but also pertain to human relations with the nonhuman world of living things.

2 Public and private: Towards conceptual clarification

1. J.N. Shklar, 'The Liberalism of Fear,' in *Liberalism and the Moral Life*, N. Rosenblum ed. (Cambridge: Harvard University Press, 1984), pp. 21–38 at p. 24.

2. N. Paton, 'Ukraine Crisis Threatens Rift between US and Russia,' *The Guardian*, November 24, 2004. http://www.guardian.co.uk/ukraine/story/0,15569, 1358199,00.html.

3. The European Court of Human Rights, with jurisdiction over 45 countries or over 800 million people, as well as the European Court of Justice and Court of First Instance, with jurisdiction over 400 million citizens of the 25 member nations of the European Union, constitute a significant albeit exceptional departure from this norm.

4. As S.I. Benn and G.F. Gaus have argued, 'because, in western culture at any rate, we apprehend a great deal of our social world by distinguishing things that are public and things that are private, how those concepts are structured necessarily informs not only what we ourselves say and do but also what responses to our actions we expect from others, how we assess their actions, and so on.' See their article, 'The Public and the Private: Concepts and Action,' in *Public and Private in Social Life*, S.I. Benn and G.F. Gaus eds (Canberra, Australia: Croom Helm, 1983), p. 6.

5. M. Walzer, *Just and Unjust Wars: A Moral Argument with Historical Illustrations*, 2nd edn (New York: Basic Books, 1992), pp. 51–73.

6. S.R. Ratner and J.S. Abrams, *Accountability for Human Rights Atrocities in International Law: Beyond the Nuremberg Legacy*, 2nd edn (Oxford: Oxford University Press, 2001), p. 225.

7. W.A. Schabas, *An Introduction to the International Criminal Court*, 2nd edn (Cambridge: Cambridge University Press, 2004).

8. See, for example, E. Eckholm, 'Russian Leader Complains of Lack of Respect from U.S.,' *New York Times*, 10 December 1999.

9. H. Charlesworth, 'Worlds Apart: Public/Private Distinctions in International Law,' in *Public and Private: Feminist Legal Debates*, Margaret Thornton ed. (Australia: Oxford University Press, 1995), pp. 243–260 at p. 246.

10. K. Walker, 'An Exploration of Article 2(7) of the United Nations Charter as an Embodiment of the Public/Private Distinction in International Law,' *International Law and Politics*, 26 (1994) 173–199, at 187.

11. Walker, 'An Exploration of Article 2(7),' 199.

12. C. Romany, 'Women as *Aliens*: A Feminist Critique of the Public/Private Distinction in International Human Rights Law,' *Harvard Human Rights Journal*, 6 (1993) 87–125 at 96.

13. Again, with the exception of European citizens, most people in the world do not yet have direct access to transnational legal institutions.

14. The literature in feminist political theory on the public/private distinction is extensive and varied. See J.B. Elshtain, *Public Man, Private Woman: Women in Social and Political Thought*, 2nd edn (Princeton, NJ: Princeton University Press, 1993); C.A. MacKinnon, *Toward a Feminist Theory of the State* (Cambridge: Harvard University Press, 1989); S.M. Okin, *Women in Western Political Thought* (Princeton: Princeton University Press, 1992); and C. Pateman, 'Feminist Critiques of the Public/Private Dichotomy,' in *The Disorder of Women: Democracy, Feminism and Political Theory* (Stanford: Stanford University Press, 1989). For a clear and insightful assessment of feminist critiques of the distinction, see R. Gavison, 'Feminism and the Public/Private Distinction,' *Stanford Law Review*, 45, 1 (1992) 1–45. For a critique of radical feminist interpretations of international law, with special focus on the public/private distinction, see F.R. Tesón, *A Philosophy of International Law* (Boulder, Colorado: Westview Press, 1998), pp. 157–187. On feminist critiques and reconceptualizations of privacy, see A.L. Allen, *Uneasy Access: Privacy for Women in a Free Society* (Totowa, New Jersey: Rowman & Littlefield Publishers, 1988); P. Boling, *Privacy and the Politics of Intimate Life* (Ithaca, NY: Cornell University Press, 1996); and J.W. DeCew, *In Pursuit of Privacy* (Ithaca, NY: Cornell University Press, 1997).

15. Okin, *Women in Western Political Thought*, pp. 313–314.

16. J.A. Weintraub, 'The Theory and Politics of the Public/Private Distinction,' in *Public and Private in Thought and Practice: Perspectives on a Grand Dichotomy*, J.A. Weintraub and K. Kumar eds (Chicago: University of Chicago Press, 1997), p. 12, footnote 24: 'Public law is that which regards the condition of the Roman commonwealth, private, that which pertains to the interests of single individuals.'

17. Benn and Gaus, 'The Public and the Private: Concepts and Action,' in *Public and Private in Social Life*, p. 5.

18. Benn and Gaus, 'The Public and the Private,' p. 5.

19. M. Krygier, 'Publicness, Privateness and "Primitive Law",' in *Public and Private in Social Life*, p. 337.

20. See H. Bull, *The Expansion of International Society* (Oxford: Clarendon Press, 1984). In International Relations discourse, it is typical to characterize twentieth-century international order based on equal legal sovereignty, nonaggression and nonintervention as 'Westphalian,' but this is somewhat misleading since at the time of Westphalia, the right of sovereign states to resort to the use of force was largely unrestricted, and equality of sovereignty

was denied to nonEuropean communities, which could be subjected to colonization. See J.L. Cohen, 'Whose Sovereignty? Empire Versus International Law,' *Ethics and International Affairs*, 18, 3 (2004) 1–24 at 12.

21. Weintraub, 'The Theory and Politics of the Public/Private Distinction,' p. 2.
22. For some controversy surrounding this depiction of international law, see M.W. Janis, *An Introduction to International Law*, 2nd edn (Toronto: Little, Brown and Company, 1993), p. 2.
23. H. Arendt, *The Human Condition* (Chicago: University of Chicago Press, 1958), p. 50.
24. As K.J. Holsti has noted, 'there was no question that the field of inquiry involved only the actions and interactions of *states*, no matter who their spokesmen. . . . States and the states system . . . remained the centerpieces of the study of international politics from the seventeenth century until the 1970s. See Holsti, *The Dividing Discipline: Hegemony and Diversity in International Theory* (Boston: Allen & Unwin, 1985), p. 23.
25. R. Jackson, *Quasi-States: Sovereignty, International Relations and the Third World* (Cambridge: Cambridge University Press, 1990), p. 114.
26. See D. Held, *Democracy and the Global Order: From the Modern State to Cosmopolitan Governance* (Stanford: Stanford University Press, 1995), for a cosmopolitan model of democracy.
27. Weintraub, 'The Theory and Politics of the Public/Private Distinctionp,' p. 5.
28. H. Spruyt, *The Sovereign State and Its Competitors: An Analysis of Systems Change* (Princeton: Princeton University Press, 1994), pp. 165–166: 'Through the subtle transition from royal domain, which was simply the personal holdings of the king, to the public realm, the quality and functions of the king had changed. The private domain became the public state. . . . Salisbury could, therefore, already plausibly argue in the twelfth century that the king 'is, and acts as, a persona publica. And in that capacity he is expected to consider all issues with regard to the well-being of the res publica, and not with regard to his privata voluntas.'
29. J.R. Lucas writes, 'States Without Justice are but Robber Bands Enlarged.' Lucas, *On Justice* (Oxford: Clarendon Press, 1980), p. 1.
30. Benn and Gaus, 'The Liberal Conception of the Public and the Private,' in *Public and Private in Social Life*, pp. 31–66.
31. The 'individualist' label is somewhat misleading since both models have a concern for the individual; they only differ in how they conceive of the individual in society. The 'individualist' label would also cause confusion when we explore how these models have guided normative International Relations theories, which tend to use the state rather than the individual as the basic unit of international social life.
32. J. Bentham, *Introduction to the Principles of Morals and Legislation*, J.H. Burns and H.L.A. Hart eds (London: Athlone Press, 1970), Chapter 1, Section 4.
33. Benn and Gaus, 'The Liberal Conception of the Public and the Private,' p. 49.
34. See J.J. Rousseau, *The Social Contract* in *The Social Contract and Discourses*, G.D.H. Cole trans. (London: J.M. Dent & Sons, 1988), Book II, Chapter 3, p. 203.
35. E.H. Carr, *The Twenty Years' Crisis 1919–1939: An Introduction to the Study of International Relations*, 2nd edn (New York: Harper & Row, 1946), p. 162.
36. W. Zhong, 'China's Human Rights Development in the 1990s,' *The Journal of Contemporary China*, 8 (1995) 79–97 at 85.

37. Arendt, *The Human Condition*, p. 31.
38. It is important to note that Hobbes did not consider liberty, so conceived, to be a moral entitlement or claim. The morally neutral definition of freedom as being able to do as one pleases without external restraint must be distinguished from the understanding of freedom, privacy or sovereignty as moral rights and claims. See T. Hobbes, *Leviathan* (Markham, Ontario: Penguin, 1986), Chapter 21, p. 271.
39. DeCew, *In Pursuit of Privacy*, p. 10.
40. Weintraub, 'The Theory and Politics of the Public/Private Distinction,' p. 11.
41. Shklar, 'The Liberalism of Fear,' p. 24.
42. Benn and Gaus, 'The Liberal Conception of the Public and the Private,' p. 31.
43. Ibid.
44. Weintraub, 'The Theory and Politics of the Public/Private Distinction,' p. 4.
45. See Elshtain, *Public Man, Private Woman*, pp. 14–16; and Pateman, 'Feminist Critiques of the Public/Private Dichotomy,' pp. 121–122.
46. Weintraub, 'The Theory and Politics of the Public/Private Distinction,' p. 31.
47. Ibid., p. 38.
48. M. Wight, 'Why is there no International Theory?' in *Diplomatic Investigations: Essays in the Theory of International Politics*, H. Butterfield and M. Wight eds (Cambridge, MA: Harvard University Press), p. 33.
49. H. Bull, *The Anarchical Society: A Study of Order in World Politics* (New York: Columbia University Press, 1977), p. 197.
50. N. Bobbio, *Democracy and Dictatorship: The Nature and Limits of State Power*, P. Kennealy trans. (Minneapolis: University of Minnesota Press, 1989), p. 10.
51. Weintraub, 'The Theory and Politics of the Public/Private Distinction,' p. 38.
52. Ibid., p. 36.
53. Hannah Arendt, for example, elevates the public at the expense of the private, and in doing so, misses the darker side of the public and the moral potential of the private. Arendt draws her views of public and private from her interpretation of Aristotle and the ancient Greek *polis*. For a compelling alternative account, see J.A. Swanson, *The Public and the Private in Aristotle's Political Philosophy* (Ithaca: Cornell University Press, 1992).
54. Gavison, 'Feminism and the Public/Private Distinction,' p. 4.
55. Benn and Gaus, 'The Public and the Private: Concepts and Action,' p. 12.
56. R.J. Vincent, *Nonintervention and International Order* (Princeton, New Jersey: Princeton University Press, 1974), pp. 11–12.
57. Allen, *Uneasy Access*, p. 3.
58. S. Hoffmann, 'The Problem of Intervention,' in *Intervention in World Politics*, H. Bull ed. (Oxford: Clarendon Press, 1986), p. 11.
59. See B. Crick, 'Sovereignty,' *International Encyclopedia of the Social Sciences*, 15 (1968), p. 77. Asserting that 'the state is sovereign . . . is usually a tautology, just as the expression "sovereign state" can be a neoplasm. For the concept of "the state" came into use at about the same time as the concept of sovereignty, and it served the same purpose and had substantially the same meaning.'
60. J. Feinberg, 'Autonomy, Sovereignty, and Privacy: Moral Ideals in the Constitution?' *The Notre Dame Law Review*, 58 (1983) 445–492 at 448.
61. Hoffmann, 'The Problem of Intervention,' p. 11.
62. Vincent, *Nonintervention and International Order*, p. 12.

63. C.R. Beitz, *Political Theory and International Relations*, 2nd edn (Princeton: Princeton University Press, 1999), p. 69.
64. Allen, *Uneasy Access*, pp. 35–53.
65. K. McShane, 'Why Environmental Ethics Shouldn't Give up on Intrinsic Value,' (paper presented at the Karbank Symposium in Environmental Philosophy, Boston University, 15 April 2005), p. 21.
66. McShane, 'Why Environmental Ethics Shouldn't Give up on Intrinsic Value,' pp. 8–9: 'intrinsic valuing attitudes [are] ways of valuing something for its own sake, or in its own right, while ... extrinsic valuing attitudes [are] ways of valuing something for the sake of some other valuable thing.'
67. Beitz thus argues that although a state's right of autonomy is 'derivative,' this 'is not to say that there are never cases in which a right of state autonomy ought to be respected.' See Beitz, *Political Theory and International Relations*, p. 69.

3   Realism and the tyranny of the private

1. K.N. Waltz, *Theory of International Politics* (Toronto, Ontario: McGraw-Hill Publishing Company, 1979), p. 107.
2. See J. Rosenthal, *Righteous Realists: Political Realism, Responsible Power, and American Culture in the Nuclear Age* (Baton Rouge: Louisiana State University, 1991); and M.W. Doyle, 'Thucydidean Realism,' *Review of International Studies*, 16 (1990) 223–237 at 224: 'If thinking like a Realist is thinking like Thucydides, which Realism can best sustain a claim to Thucydides? What sort of a Realist was Thucydides?' See also M. Doyle, *Ways of War and Peace: Realism, Liberalism and Socialism* (New York: W.W. Norton, 1997).
3. See B. Frankel ed. *The Roots of Realism* (Portland, Oregon: Frank Cass, 1996).
4. N. Machiavelli, *The Prince* in *The Prince and The Discourses* (New York: Random House, 1950), Chapter 15, p. 56.
5. R.C. Gilpin, 'The Richness of the Tradition of Political Realism,' in *Neorealism and Its Critics*, R.O. Keohane ed. (New York: Columbia University Press, 1986) p. 304.
6. See H.J. Morgenthau, *In Defense of the National Interest: A Critical Examination of American Foreign Policy* (Washington, DC: University Press of America, 1982).
7. Machiavelli, *The Prince*, Chapter 26, pp. 94–98. See also S. Wolin, *Politics and Vision: Continuity and Innovation in Western Political Thought* (Toronto: Little, Brown and Company, 1960).
8. D.A. Welch, 'Morality and "The National Interest,"' in *Ethics in International Affairs: Theory and Cases*, Andrew Valls ed. (Lanham, Md.: Rowman & Littlefield, 2000), pp. 7–8.
9. H. Kissinger, 'No U.S. Ground Forces for Kosovo: Leadership doesn't mean that we must do Everything Ourselves,' *The Washington Post*, 22 February 1999, A15.
10. See G.W. Bush, 'Transcript: Bush's Speech on Iraq,' *The New York Times*, 18 March 2003.
11. See *New York Times*, 26 September 2002. The signatories included Kenneth Waltz and John Mearsheimer.
12. S. Blumenthal, 'Utopian cul-de-sac,' *The Guardian*, 3 February 2005.
13. R. Dallaire, 'Looking at Darfur, Seeing Rwanda,' *The New York Times*, 4 October 2004.

14. On minimalist and maximalist conceptions of security, see P.J. Stoett, *Human and Global Security: An Exploration of Terms* (Toronto: University of Toronto Press, 1999), pp. 14–23.

15. T. Hobbes, *Leviathan* (Markham, Ontario: Penguin Books Canada Limited, 1986), Chapter 1.

16. Ibid., p. 185.

17. Ibid., Introduction, p. 81.

18. Waltz, *Theory of International Politics*, p. 117.

19. Welch, 'Morality and "The National Interest,"' p. 11.

20. Waltz, *Theory of International Politics*, p. 91.

21. J. Weintraub, 'The Theory and Politics of the Public/Private Distinction,' in *Public and Private in Thought and Practice: Perspectives on a Grand Dichotomy*, J.A. Weintraub and K. Kumar eds (Chicago: University of Chicago Press, 1997), p. 8.

22. A. Wendt, 'Anarchy is what States Make of it: The Social Construction of Power Politics,' *International Organization*, 46 (1992) 391–425; and Finnemore, *National Interests in International Society*.

23. Waltz, *Theory of International Politics*, p. 90.

24. Ibid., p. 112.

25. Ibid., p. 117, italics mine.

26. Ibid., p. 105.

27. S.I. Benn and G. Gaus, 'The Liberal Conception of the Public and the Private,' in *Public and Private in Social Life*, S.I. Benn and G.F. Gaus eds (Canberra, Australia: Croom Helm, 1983), p. 49.

28. L. McCarthy, 'International Anarchy, Realism and Non-Intervention,' in *Political Theory, International Relations, and the Ethics of Intervention*, Ian Forbes and Mark Hoffman eds (New York, NY: St. Martin's Press, 1993), p. 76.

29. In this light, it was really atomism rather than anarchy that Hedley Bull challenged in his classic work, *The Anarchical Society: A Study of Order in World Politics* (New York: Columbia University Press, 1977).

30. Waltz, *Theory of International Politics*, p. 96.

31. Ibid., pp. 111–112. Waltz's critique of world government is not that it would be universal, but that it, too, would be driven by its own particular or private organizational interests, which it would pursue at the expense of the interests and freedom of states.

32. Ibid., p. 112.

33. C. MacKinnon, *Towards a Feminist Theory of the State* (Harvard University Press, 1989), p. 190. MacKinnon claims to be critiquing the liberal *concept* of privacy, but her critique really pertains only to a certain atomistic *conception* of privacy, which many liberals would reject.

34. McCarthy, 'International Anarchy, Realism and Non-Intervention,' p. 76.

35. Hobbes, *Leviathan*, Chapter 13, p. 188.

36. McCarthy, 'International Anarchy, Realism and Non-Intervention,' p. 80. While this is an accurate depiction of the neorealist viewpoint, it is not necessarily Hobbes's viewpoint since his recognition of lawful leagues between nations makes it conceivable that norms of sovereignty and nonintervention, derived from the interests of member states, may become binding on them. See footnote 65.

37. H.J. Morgenthau, 'To Intervene or Not to Intervene,' *Foreign Affairs*, 45 (1967) 425–436 at 430.
38. Hobbes, *Leviathan*, Chapter 14, p. 190.
39. Ibid., p. 189.
40. Kissinger, 'No U.S. Ground Forces for Kosovo.'
41. R.C. Post, 'The Social Foundations of Privacy: Community and Self in the Common Law Tort,' *California Law Review*, 77, 5 (1989) 957–1010 at 959.
42. Post, 'The Social Foundations of Privacy,' p. 1010.
43. See Plato, *The Republic of Plato*, A. Bloom trans. 2nd edn (New York: Basic Books, 1991) for Thrasymachus's articulation of this view of justice, and Socrates's rebuttal.
44. See R.N. Lebow, *The Tragic Vision of Politics: Ethics, Interests, Orders* (Cambridge: Cambridge University Press, 2003), p. 392. Lebow charges contemporary realism with conceptual and moral poverty, making his case with some unlikely allies – Thucydides, Clausewitz and Morgenthau, the most prominent fathers of realism. His rich and meticulous study of these three classical realists – including an account of their historical context, intellectual setting, personal and professional lives and fortunes – reveals complex thinkers whose insights about the relationship between power, justice and interest have been tragically lost not only on contemporary foreign policymakers in the United States but also on the contemporary realist scholarly community that has dominated the study of International Relations since the Second World War.
45. Hobbes, *Leviathan*, Chapter 6, p. 120.
46. Ibid., Chapter 13, p. 188.
47. S. Forde, 'Classical Realism,' in *Traditions of International Ethics*, T. Nardin and D.R. Mapel eds (Cambridge: Cambridge University Press, 1993), p. 64.
48. Frankel, *Roots of Realism*, p. ix, italics mine.
49. H.J. Morgenthau, *Human Rights and Foreign Policy* (New York: Council on Religion and International Affairs, 1979), p. 11 (emphasis mine).
50. For a similar point, see Forde, 'Classical Realism,' p. 63.
51. This statistic was retrieved from a fund appeal letter by UNICEF Canada, December 1999.
52. B. Williams, *Shame and Necessity* (Berkeley, California: University of California Press, 1993), p. 128.
53. R. Joffé director, *The Mission*, R. Bolt screenplay (Warner Brothers, Goldcrest and Kingsmere, 1986).
54. See also Martha Finnemore's lucid constructivist account of the use of norms to understand international politics: 'a norms approach addresses an issue obscured by approaches that treat interest exogenously: It focuses attention on the ways in which interests change.' M. Finnemore, 'Constructing Norms of Humanitarian Intervention,' in *The Culture of National Security: Norms and Identity in World Politics*, P.J. Katzenstein ed. (New York: Columbia University Press, 1996), p. 157.
55. M. Finnemore, *National Interests in International Society* (Ithaca, NY: Cornell University Press, 1996), p. 2.
56. Finnemore, *National Interests in International Society*, p. 3.
57. Waltz, *Theory of International Politics*, p. 47. In his better work, *Man, the State and War: A Theoretical Analysis* (New York: Columbia University Press, 1959),

p. 123, Waltz explicitly makes this point, writing, 'the international political environment has much to do with the ways in which states behave.'

58. See H. Arendt, *The Human Condition* (Chicago: University of Chicago Press, 1958), pp. 50–67.
59. Arendt, *The Human Condition*, p. 35.
60. Ibid., p. 58, italics mine.
61. H.F. Pitkin, 'Justice: On Relating Private and Public,' *Political Theory*, 9, 3 (1981) 327–352 at 334.
62. Pitkin, 'Justice: On Relating Private and Public,' p. 344.
63. Ibid., p. 347.
64. Hobbes, *Leviathan*, Chapter 13, pp. 187–88.
65. Ibid., Chapter 22, p. 286.
66. Ibid., Chapter 13, p. 188.
67. Welch, 'Morality and "The National Interest," ' p. 8.
68. I will leave aside now the practical issues that might have prevented NATO's use of ground forces in Kosovo.
69. Welch similarly observes, 'The phrase "the national interest" masks exactly which values leaders are attempting to promote, and which they are willing to sacrifice.' 'Morality and "The National Interest," ' p. 9.
70. See for example, G.F. Kennan, 'Morality and Foreign Policy,' *Foreign Affairs*, 64 (1985) 205–218.
71. As Jeff Weintraub has noted, 'classical liberal economists held that in a properly structured market, the outcome of the pursuit by each private agent of his private interest would be to the public advantage, even though no individual in the market had either motive or duty to pursue it directly.' See Weintraub, 'The Theory and Politics of the Public/Private Distinction,' p. 10. Realists have consistently criticized liberal idealists for assuming such a harmony in domestic and international relations. As Waltz put it, 'Early liberals and utilitarians assumed an objective harmony of interests in society. The same assumption is applied to international relations,' mistakenly, in Waltz's view. See Waltz, *Man, the State and War*, p. 97.
72. E.H. Carr, *The Twenty Years' Crisis 1919–1939: An Introduction to the Study of International Relations*, 2nd edn (New York: Harper & Row, 1946), p. 45.
73. Carr, *The Twenty Years' Crisis*, p. 167.
74. Ibid.
75. See Waltz, *Man, the State and War*.
76. Waltz, *Theory of International Politics*, pp. 113–114.
77. Ibid., pp. 131–132.
78. As Waltz observes, 'That in war there is no victory but only varying degrees of defeat is a proposition that has gained increasing acceptance in the twentieth century.' See *Man, the State and War*, p. 1.
79. Cited in P. Hassner, 'From War and Peace to Violence and Intervention,' in *Hard Choices: Moral Dilemmas in Humanitarian Intervention*, Jonathan Moore ed. (New York: Rowman & Littlefield Publishers, 1998), p. 19.
80. G. Best, 'Justice, International Relations and Human Rights,' *International Affairs*, 71, 4 (1995) 775–799 at 778.
81. Kissinger, 'No U.S. Ground Forces for Kosovo.'
82. See R.A. Kaplan, 'Why the Balkans Demand Amorality,' *The Washington Post*, 28 February 1999, B2.

83. Morgenthau, 'To Intervene or Not to Intervene,' p. 430.
84. Welch, 'Morality and "The National Interest," ' pp. 8–9.
85. C.R. Beitz, 'Afterword,' in his *Political Theory and International Relations*, 2nd edn (Princeton, NJ: Princeton University Press, 1999), pp. 186–187:

> Skeptical and heuristic realism are easily conflated. The difference is this. Skeptical realism denies that moral considerations should have any weight in reasoning about international conduct, either because they have no meaning or because there is no reason to take an interest in them. Heuristic realism, while allowing in principle that moral considerations can have weight (and that we may have reason to take an interest in them), argues as a matter of historical fact that the attempt to apply these considerations in practical reasoning tends to produce undesirable outcomes or even to be self-defeating. To put the difference another way, skeptical realism is a philosophical doctrine, whereas heuristic realism is casuistical – that is, concerned with the application of principles to practice.

86. Kaplan, 'Why the Balkans Demand Amorality.'
87. Welch, 'Morality and "The National Interest," ' p. 7.

4   Sovereignty as privacy

1. M. Walzer, *Just and Unjust Wars: A Moral Argument with Historical illustrations*, 2nd edn (United States: Basic Books, 1992).
2. J.S. Mill, *Principles of Political Economy [and Chapters on Socialism]* (Oxford: Oxford University Press, 1994).
3. L.F. Damrosch, 'Politics Across Borders: Nonintervention and Nonforcible Influence over Domestic Affairs,' *The American Journal of International Law*, 83 (1989) 1–50 at 12.
4. H. Bull ed., *Intervention in World Politics* (Oxford: Clarendon Press, 1986), pp. 1–2.
5. Walzer, *Just and Unjust Wars*, p. 5.
6. S.D. Warren and L.D. Brandeis, 'The Right to Privacy' (1890), reprinted in *Philosophical Dimensions of Privacy: An Anthology*, F.D. Schoeman ed. (Cambridge, UK: Cambridge University Press, 1984), Chapter 4.
7. A. Allen, *Uneasy Access: Privacy for Women in a Free Society* (Totowa, New Jersey: Rowman & Littlefield Publishers, 1988).
8. G. Allan and G. Crow, *Home and Family: Creating the Domestic Sphere* (London: MacMillan, 1989), p. 4.
9. Allan and Crow, *Home and Family*, pp. 6 and 4.
10. Of course, exploring this analogy does not involve any attempt to equate or identify political relations with personal familial relations. G. Schochet help-fully reminds us of the difference between an identification and an analogous comparison:

> an identification requires a total transference of meaning from one entity to the institution for which it is being used as a symbol. A comparison or simile, on the other hand, leaves open the questions of the ways in which the two entities or institutions are alike and different. It allows, and even invites, debate about how well and how much a particular symbolic explanation fits.

See Schochet, *Patriarchalism in Political Thought: The Authoritarian Family and Political Speculation and Attitudes Especially in Seventeenth-Century England* (Oxford: Basil Blackwell, 1975), p. 146.

11. Quoted in H. Charlesworth, 'Worlds Apart: Public/Private Distinctions in International Law,' in *Public and Private: Feminist Legal Debates*, Margaret Thornton ed. (Australia: Oxford University Press, 1995), p. 244.
12. J. Bodin, *Six Books of the Commonwealth*, M.J. Tooley trans. (Oxford: Basil Blackwell, 1955), p. 6.
13. See Schochet, *Patriarchalism in Political Thought*.
14. R. Filmer, *Patriarcha: A Defence of the Natural Power of Kings against the Unnatural Liberty of the People* in *Patriarcha and other Political Works of Sir Robert Filmer*, P. Laslett ed. (Oxford: Basil Blackwell, 1949), p. 63.
15. Schochet, *Patriarchalism in Political Thought*, p. 6.
16. Filmer, *Patriarcha*, p. 96.
17. Bodin, *Six Books of the Commonwealth*, pp. 10 and 12. Bodin notes critically 'that the paternal power of life and death was gradually restricted by the ambition of the magistrates, who wished to extend their own jurisdiction over all such matters' (p. 13).
18. S.I. Benn and G.F. Gaus, 'The Liberal Conception of the Public and the Private,' in *Public and Private in Social Life* (London, Croom Helm, 1983), p. 54.
19. C. Lasch, *Haven in a Heartless World: The Family Besieged* (New York: Basic Books, Inc., 1977).
20. E. Pleck, *Domestic Tyranny: The Making of Social Policy Against Family Violence from Colonial Times to the Present* (New York: Oxford University Press, 1987), p. 8.
21. Bodin, *Six Books of the Commonwealth*, p. 14.
22. K. Kumar, 'Home: The Promise and Predicament of Private Life at the End of the Twentieth Century,' in *Public and Private in Thought and Practice: Perspectives on a Grand Dichotomy*, J.A. Weintraub and K. Kumar eds (Chicago: University of Chicago Press, 1997), p. 208.
23. H. Pilkington, 'Going Home? The Implications of Forced Migration for National Identity Formation in post-Soviet Russia,' in *The New Migration in Europe: Social Constructions and Social Realities*, K. Koser and H. Lutz eds (New York: St. Martin's Press, 1997), p. 88. See also S. Grosby, 'Territoriality: The Transcendental, Primordial Feature of Modern Societies,' *Nations and Nationalism*, 1, 2 (1995): 143–162.
24. Pilkington, 'Going Home,' p. 97.
25. See L. Barrington, 'The Domestic and International Consequences of Citizenship in the Soviet Successor States,' *Europe Asia Studies*, 47, 5 (1995): 731–763. Barrington examines the political implications of citizenship policies in the successor states. For example,

> In Estonia and Latvia, citizenship has been very difficult for the majority of Russian-speakers to receive. The Russian citizenship policy, however, is very inclusive, allowing permanent residents of the former Soviet Union to become Russian citizens with little effort. Thus, the policies have increased the 'Russianness' of ethnic Russians in Estonia and Latvia (p. 731).

26. Pilkington, 'Going Home,' pp. 95 and 102.
27. Y. Tamir, *Liberal Nationalism* (Princeton: Princeton University Press, 1993), p. 65.

28. B. Anderson, *Imagined Communities: Reflections on the Origin and Spread of Nationalism*, revised ed. (London: Verso, 1991).
29. See, for example, M. Sandel, *Liberalism and the Limits of Justice* (Cambridge: Cambridge University Press, 1982). He also uses the family as an ideal model of community to which political communities should aspire:

    In a more or less ideal family situation, where relations are governed in large part by spontaneous affection . . . individual rights and fair decision procedures are seldom invoked, not because injustice is rampant but because their appeal is pre-empted by a spirit of generosity in which I am rarely inclined to claim my fair share (p. 33).

    For a summary and critique of communitarian objections to individual privacy rights, see J.L. Cohen, 'Rethinking Privacy: Autonomy, Identity, and the Abortion Controversy,' in Weintraub and Kumar, *Public And Private In Thought And Practice*, pp. 146–150. See also T. Erskine, 'Citizen of Nowhere' or 'The Point Where Circles Intersect'? Impartialist and Embedded Cosmopolitanisms,' *Review of International Studies*, 28 (2002), 457–478.
30. M. Walzer, however, is ambivalent on this point. When discussing the value of community, he writes, 'I don't want to say that the whole is greater than the sum of its parts, for I don't know how to sum the parts or set a value on the whole.' See M. Walzer, *Arguing About War* (New Haven: Yale University Press, 2004) p. 42.
31. A. MacIntyre, 'Is Patriotism a Virtue?' in *Theorizing Citizenship*, R. Beiner ed. (Albany, New York: State University of New York, 1995), pp. 209–228 at p. 225.
32. Tamir, *Liberal Nationalism*, pp. 48–53, and p. 98.
33. See S. Caney, 'Individuals, Nations and Obligations,' in *National Rights, International Obligations*, S. Caney, D. George, and P. Jones eds (Boulder, Colorado: Westview Press, 1996), pp. 119–138, for a perceptive analysis and critique of intrinsic defences of special obligations towards one's fellow nationals.
34. J.N. Shklar, 'Obligation, Loyalty, Exile,' *Political Theory*, 21, 2 (1993) 181–197 at 185.
35. Even more problematic, individuals may feel positively fulfilled through such memberships, yet their sense of fulfillment may have no moral value. See Caney, 'Individuals, Nations and Obligations.'
36. Tamir, *Liberal Nationalism*, pp. 73 and 159.
37. Pilkington, 'Going Home,' p. 102.
38. J.N. Shklar, 'The Work of Michael Walzer,' in *Political Thought and Political Thinkers*, S. Hoffmann ed. (Chicago: University of Chicago Press, 1998), p. 384.
39. J. Weintraub, 'The Theory and Politics of the Public/Private Distinction,' in Weintraub and Kumar, *Public and Private in Thought and Practice*, p. 7.
40. Weintraub, 'The Theory and Politics of the Public/Private Distinction,' pp. 17–18.
41. Article 18 of the Charter of the Organization of American States reads as follows:

    No State or group of States has the right to intervene, directly or indirectly, for any reason whatever, in the internal or external affairs of any other State. The foregoing principle prohibits not only armed force but also any other form of interference or attempted threat against the personality of the State or against its political, economic and cultural elements.

Similar articles can be found in the Charters of the League of Arab States, and the Organization of African Unity. In contrast, states involved in the Conference on Security and Co-operation in Europe 'have "categorically and irrevocably" declared that human rights questions are matters of direct and legitimate concern to all participating states and do not belong to the internal affairs of the state concerned.' See M.T. Kamminga, *Inter-State Accountability for Violations of Human Rights* (Philadelphia: University of Pennsylvania Press, 1992), p. 78 and pp. 193–194.

42. R. Frost, 'Mending Wall,' in *The Poetry of Robert Frost*, E.C. Lathem ed. (New York: Holt, Rinehart and Winston, 1969). Frost's poem recounts a time every spring when he and a neighbour go to work together repairing a stone wall that separates their property. The neighbour states this proverb to account for their good relations, but the poem intends us to understand this advice in an ironical sense, since Frost leads us to believe that they are good neighbours not because the fence is maintained but because they share an activity together in maintaining it.

43. Walzer, *Arguing about War*, pp. 172 and 176.

44. Allan and Crow, *Home and Family: Creating the Domestic Sphere*, p. 5.

45. Quoted in *Family Violence in a Patriarchal Culture: A Challenge to Our Way of Living* (Ottawa: Church Council on Justice and Corrections, Canadian Council on Social Development, 1988), p. 9.

46. Weintraub, 'The Theory and Politics of the Public/Private Distinction,' p. 29.

47. J.W. DeCew, *In Pursuit of Privacy: Law, Ethics, and the Rise of Technology* (Ithaca, N.Y.: Cornell University Press, 1997), p. 177.

48. See, for example, C. Pateman, 'Feminist Critiques of the Public/Private Dichotomy,' in *The Disorder of Women* (Stanford, CA: Stanford University Press, 1989), pp. 118–140.

49. Pleck, *Domestic Tyranny*, p. 7.

50. R.L. Snow, *Family Abuse: Tough Solutions to Stop the Violence* (New York: Plenum Trade, 1997), p. 283.

51. Pleck, *Domestic Tyranny*, p. 79.

52. C. Calhoun, 'Nationalism and the Public Sphere,' in Weintraub and Kumar, *Public and Private in Thought and Practice*, p. 99.

53. Ontario Medical Association, *Reports on Wife Assault* (Ottawa: National Clearinghouse on Family Violence, 1991), p. 1.

54. Plato, *The Republic of Plato*, A. Bloom trans. (New York: Basic Books, 1991, second edition), pp. 37–38 (II, 359c–360d).

55. P.P. Hallie, *The Paradox of Cruelty* (Middletown, Connecticut: Wesleyan University Press, 1969), p. 108.

56. The usual cases cited include India's intervention in Pakistan in 1971 that led to the creation of Bangladesh; Vietnam's intervention in Cambodia in 1979 that overthrew the genocidal Pol Pot regime; and Tanzania's intervention in Uganda in 1979 that ousted the dictator Idi Amin. See Wheeler, *Saving Strangers*; and M. Akehurst, 'Humanitarian Intervention,' in *Intervention in World Politics*, H. Bull ed. (Oxford: Clarendon Press, 1986), pp. 95–99.

57. Akehurst, 'Humanitarian Intervention,' pp. 95–99. Akehurst notes, for example, that India initially justified its military intervention in Pakistan in 1971 on humanitarian grounds, but subsequently changed its explanation in the Official Records of the United Nations Security Council (p. 96).

58. See, for example, J.L. Brierly, 'Matters of Domestic Jurisdiction,' *British Yearbook of International Law*, 6 (1925) 8–19.
59. O. Ramsbotham and T. Woodhouse, *Humanitarian Intervention in Contemporary Conflict: A Reconceptualization* (Oxford: Blackwell, 1996), p. 56.
60. R. Dallaire with B. Beardsley, *Shake Hands With the Devil: The Failure of Humanity in Rwanda* (Toronto: Random House Canada, 2003), 375. Italics mine.
61. R.J. Vincent, *Human Rights and International Relations* (Cambridge: Cambridge University Press, 1986), p. 113. S. Hoffmann also writes, 'International society, for some centuries now, has been founded on the principle of sovereignty; in other words, the state is supposed to be the master of what goes on inside its territory, and international relations are relations between sovereign states, each one of which has certain rights and obligations derived from the very fact of statehood. If one accepts the principle of sovereignty as the corner-stone of international society, this means...that intervention, defined as an act aimed at influencing the domestic affairs of a state, is quite clearly illegitimate.' See Hoffmann, 'The Problem of Intervention,' in Bull, *Intervention in World Politics*, p. 11.
62. H. Bull, *The Anarchical Society: A Study of Order in World Politics* (New York: Columbia University Press, 1977), p. 8, italics mine.
63. See M. Walzer, *Arguing about War*, p. xiii.
64. Ibid., pp. 46 and 43.
65. Walzer, 'The Moral Standing of States,' p. 214.
66. See Walzer, 'Response to Veit Bader,' *Political Theory*, 23, 2 (1995) 247–249.
67. Walzer, *Just and Unjust Wars*, chapter 6.
68. Ibid., p. 101.
69. Ibid., p. 87.
70. M. Walzer, 'The Moral Standing of States: A Response to Four Critics,' *Philosophy and Public Affairs*, 9, 3 (1980) 209–229 at 211.
71. On the sovereign individual, see J.S. Mill, *On Liberty*, in *On Liberty with the Subjection of Women and Chapters on Socialism* (Cambridge: Cambridge University Press, 1989), pp. 1–116.
72. Walzer, *Just and Unjust Wars*, p. 87.
73. See J.J. Rousseau, *Project of Perpetual Peace*, E.M. Nuttall trans. (London: Richard Cobden-Sanderson, 1927).
74. M. Sandel, 'The Procedural Republic and the Unencumbered Self,' *Political Theory*, 12 (1984) 81–96 at p. 87.
75. MacIntyre, 'Is Patriotism a Virtue?' p. 215.
76. See, for example, M.J. Sandel, 'Moral Argument and Liberal Toleration: Abortion and Homosexuality,' *California Law Review*, 77, 3 (1989) 521–538.
77. Walzer, *Just and Unjust Wars*, pp. 94 and 87.
78. This is not to say that any claims individuals make can or must always override those of the collective, yet even when a collective's interests take moral precedence, it in no way demonstrates a moral primacy of the collective over the individual. As Simone Weil puts it,

> it may happen that the obligation towards a collectivity which is in danger reaches the point of entailing a total sacrifice. But it does not follow from this that collectivities are superior to human beings. It sometimes happens, too, that the obligation to go to the help of a human being in distress makes a total sacrifice necessary, without that implying any superiority on the part of the individual so helped.

See Weil, *The Need for Roots: Prelude to a Declaration of Duties toward Mankind* (New York: Routledge & Kegan Paul Ltd, 1987), p. 8.

79. Walzer, *Just and Unjust Wars*, pp. 104 and 90.
80. Ibid., pp. 89 and 93.
81. Another reason is that Walzer equates intervention with the use of military force, a conflation I criticize below.
82. Walzer, *Just and Unjust Wars*, p. 101.
83. Ibid., p. 87. Of course, intervenors would still have to justify their chosen means of intervention.
84. Ibid., pp. 96 and 97.
85. Snow, *Family Abuse*, p. 283.
86. Walzer, *Arguing about War*, p. xiii.
87. Ibid., p. 188.
88. R. Jackson, *The Global Covenant: Human Conduct in a World of States* (Oxford: Oxford University Press, 2000), p. 43.
89. In a later work, Walzer indeed draws on the family/state analogy to support the right of members of one state to divorce. He writes,

> The argument [against legitimizing the break-up of states] is very much like that of a Puritan minister in the 1640s, defending the union of husband and wife against the new doctrine of divorce...The problem, then as now, is that justice, whatever it requires, doesn't seem to permit the kinds of coercion that would be necessary to 'hold their noses together.' So we have to think about divorce, despite its difficulties.

See M. Walzer, *Thick and Thin: Moral Argument at Home and Abroad* (Notre Dame, Indiana: University of Notre Dame Press, 1994), p. 67.

90. J.S. Mill, *Principles of Political Economy*. Mill actually justifies foreign rule as a form of tutelage for 'barbarians,' although 'the universal rules of morality between man and man' must apply to civilized and barbarous peoples alike. See Mill, 'A Few Words on Non-Intervention,' in *Essays on Equality, Law, and Education* (Toronto: University of Toronto Press and Routledge Kegan Paul, 1984), p. 119. We can be rid of nineteenth-century civilizational prejudices and discard the categorization of whole societies as 'barbarian,' but Mill's justification for intervention against barbarism can surely be applied to scenes of inhumanity within the contemporary 'civilized' world.
91. Walzer, *Just and Unjust Wars*, p. 86.
92. Ibid., pp. 90 and 101.
93. Walzer, 'The Moral Standing of States,' p. 223, footnote 26.
94. Walzer, *Just and Unjust Wars*, pp. 101–108. As Charles Beitz has noted of Walzer's argument, 'it is the military character rather than intervention itself that is problematic' and 'the argument against military force has nothing to do with communal integrity.' C.R. Beitz, 'Nonintervention and Communal Integrity,' *Philosophy and Public Affairs*, 9, 4 (1980) 385–391 at 389.
95. M. Walzer, 'The Politics of Rescue,' *Dissent* (1995): 35–41 at p. 35.
96. For example, Hedley Bull includes coercion into his definition of intervention. See Bull, *Intervention in World Politics*, p. 3. Adam Roberts also defines humanitarian intervention as 'military intervention in a state, without the approval of its authorities, and with the purpose of preventing widespread suffering or death among the inhabitants.' See Roberts,

'Humanitarian War: Military Intervention and Human Rights,' *International Affairs*, 69, 3 (1993): 429.

97. P.W. Davis, 'Stranger Intervention into Child Punishment in Public Places,' *Social Problems*, 38, 2 (1991) 227–246.
98. Bull, *Intervention in World Politics*, p. 193.
99. Davis, 'Stranger Intervention into Child Punishment in Public Places,' pp. 227–246.
100. W. Rybczynski, *Home: A Short History of an Idea* (Toronto: Penguin Books), pp. 26–28.
101. Rybczynski, *Home*, p. 35.
102. B. Moore, *Privacy: Studies in Social and Cultural History* (London: M.E. Sharpe, 1984), p. 13.
103. Bodin, *Six Books of the Commonwealth*, pp. 25 and 28. Later, when discussing property rights, Bodin asserts that princes who take the property of others err, for doing so is 'the law of the jungle, an act of force and violence. For as we have shown above, absolute power only implies freedom in relation to positive laws, and not in relation to the law of God' (p. 35).
104. A. Hurrell, 'Vattel: Pluralism and Its Limits,' in *Classical Theories of International Relations*, I. Clark and I. Neumann eds (New York, St. Martin's Press, 1996), p. 244.
105. Hurrell, 'Vattel: Pluralism and Its Limits.'
106. According to Wheeler, a solidarist, as opposed to pluralist, conception of

> international society recognizes that individuals have rights and duties in international law, but it also acknowledges that individuals can have these rights enforced only by states. Consequently, the defining character of a solidarist society of states is one in which states accept not only a moral responsibility to protect the security of their own citizens, but also the wider one

to enforce minimum standards of humanity everywhere. See N.J. Wheeler, *Saving Strangers: Humanitarian Intervention in International Society* (Oxford: Oxford University Press, 2002), pp. 11–12.

5   The one and many faces of cosmopolitanism

1. A slightly different version of this chapter first appeared as the following: C. Lu, 'The One and Many Faces of Cosmopolitanism,' *The Journal of Political Philosophy*, 8, 2 (2000) 244–267.
2. W. Shakespeare, *The Tragedy of Hamlet* (Scarborough, Ontario: The New American Library, 1963), 2.2.312–317.
3. See D. Heater, *World Citizenship and Government: Cosmopolitan Ideas in the History of Western Political Thought* (New York: St. Martin's Press, 1996) for a comprehensive historical account of political cosmopolitanism, which advocates a global system of government entailing individual world citizenship. For a more contemporary analysis, see A. Carter, *The Political Theory of Global Citizenship* (New Jersey: Routledge, 2001).
4. For a popular example, see M. Nussbaum, 'Patriotism and Cosmopolitanism,' *The Boston Review*, 19, 5 (1994), pp. 3–9. Reprinted in Nussbaum, *For*

Love of Country: Debating the Limits of Patriotism, Joshua Cohen ed. (Boston: Beacon Press, 1996).

5. For a Rawlsian (but not Rawls's own) view of international distributive justice, see C.R. Beitz, *Political Theory and International Relations,* 2nd edn (Princeton: Princeton University Press, 1999), pp. 125–176; for a rights-based view, see H. Shue, *Basic Rights: Subsistence, Affluence, and U.S. Foreign Policy,* 2nd edn (Princeton: Princeton University Press, 1996). In contradiction or confusion, economic cosmopolitanism is sometimes considered synonymous with economic globalization and a neo-liberal economic agenda.

6. This definition comes from the *Oxford English Dictionary.*

7. While I will be focusing on the western tradition of cosmopolitan thought, cosmopolitan themes may also be found in the philosophic and moral lives of other civilizations. For a discussion of the concept of humanity in pre-Confucian as well as Confucian philosophy, see W.T. Chan (translator and compiler), *A Source Book in Chinese Philosophy* (Princeton: Princeton University Press, 1973), pp. 3–48. For a vivid picture of cosmopolitanism with a Chinese face, see Y.F. Tuan, *Cosmos and Hearth: A Cosmopolite's Viewpoint* (Minneapolis: University of Minnesota press, 1996), pp. 15–71.

8. H.C. Baldry, *The Unity of Mankind in Greek Thought* (Cambridge: Cambridge University Press, 1965), p. 122.

9. Nussbaum, 'Patriotism and Cosmopolitanism,' *The Boston Review,* p. 3.

10. See T. Pogge, 'Cosmopolitanism and Sovereignty,' *Ethics,* 103 (1992) 48–75.

11. Nussbaum, 'Patriotism and Cosmopolitanism,' p. 3.

12. E.H. Carr, *The Twenty Years' Crisis 1919–1939: An Introduction to the Study of International Relations,* 2nd edn (New York: Harper & Row, 1946).

13. R.C. Gilpin, 'The Richness of the Tradition of Political Realism,' in *Neorealism and Its Critics,* R.O. Keohane ed. (New York: Columbia University Press, 1986), p. 304.

14. M. Wight, *International Theory: The Three Traditions,* Gabriele Wight and Brian Porter eds (London: Leicester University Press, 1996), p. 45.

15. Gilpin, 'The Richness of the Tradition of Political Realism,' p. 305.

16. Ibid., p. 319.

17. H. Bull, 'Martin Wight and the Theory of International Relations,' *British Journal of International Studies,* 2 (1976) 101–116 at 105 and 109.

18. See T.J. Schlereth, *The Cosmopolitan Ideal in Enlightenment Thought: Its Form and Function in the Ideas of Franklin, Hume and Voltaire (1694–1790)* (Notre Dame: University of Notre Dame Press, 1977); and D. Gordon, 'The Origins of a Polarity: Cosmopolitanism versus Citizenship in Early Modern Europe,' unpublished paper delivered at the annual meeting of the Conference for the Study of Political Thought, Madison, Wisconsin, November 1998.

19. E. Cassirer, *The Philosophy of the Enlightenment,* F.C.A. Koelln and J.P. Pettegrove trans. (Princeton: Princeton University Press, 1979), p. 6.

20. P. Hazard, *The European Mind [1680–1715]* (Cleveland, Ohio: The World Publishing Company, 1963), p. 119.

21. Carr, *The Twenty Years' Crisis,* p. 26.

22. Schlereth, *The Cosmopolitan Ideal,* p. 14.

23. Ibid., p. 57.

24. S. Hackney, 'Pluralism in One Country,' *Boston Review,* 19, 5 (1994) 32.

25. Nussbaum, 'Patriotism and Cosmopolitanism,' p. 6.

26. See M. Sandel, 'The Procedural Republic and the Unencumbered Self,' *Political Theory* 12 (1984) 81–96.
27. M. Walzer, *Thick and Thin: Moral Argument at Home and Abroad* (Notre Dame, Indiana: University of Notre Dame Press, 1994), p. 83.
28. M. Lerner, 'Empires of Reason,' *Boston Review*, 19, 5 (1994) 22.
29. A. Schlesinger Jr., 'Our Country, Right or Wrong,' *Boston Review*, 19, 5 (1994) 21.
30. Gilpin, 'The Richness of the Tradition of Political Realism,' p. 305.
31. A. MacIntyre, 'Is Patriotism a Virtue?' in *Theorizing Citizenship*, R. Beiner ed. (Albany, New York: State University of New York, 1995), pp. 209–228 at p. 218. Similarly, '*I* find *my* justification for allegiance to these rules of morality in *my* particular community: deprived of the life of that community, *I* would have no reason to be moral' (p. 217).
32. M. Boehm, 'Cosmopolitanism,' *Encyclopedia of the Social Sciences*, 4 (New York: Macmillan, 1932), pp. 457–461 at p. 458, italics mine.
33. Wight, *International Theory*, p. 45, italics mine.
34. Baldry, *The Unity of Mankind*, p. 108.
35. A. Anderson, 'Cosmopolitanism, Universalism, and the Divided Legacies of Modernity,' in *Cosmopolitics: Thinking and Feeling beyond the Nation*, P. Cheah and B. Robbins eds (Minneapolis: University of Minnesota Press, 1998), pp. 265–289 at p. 266.
36. See J. Waldron, 'Minority Cultures and the Cosmopolitan Alternative,' *University of Michigan Journal of Law Reform*, 25, 3/4 (1992) 751–793. For example, in defence of the cosmopolitan self, Waldron argues that '*being without roots* in a particular community is not necessarily the same as being isolated or friendless' (p. 768; emphasis mine). He revised his views somewhat in 'What is Cosmopolitan?' *Journal of Political Philosophy*, 8, 2 (2000) 220–243.
37. Günter Grass tells us that the political right used this term in the 1930s 'to stigmatize German leftist intellectuals, many of whom were Jewish.' See his 'Short Speech by a Rootless Cosmopolitan' *Dissent* (1990), p. 458. Ironically, Voltaire criticized Jews for seeming 'to remain singularly *un*cosmopolitan in their relations with other peoples' (Schlereth, *The Cosmopolitan Ideal*, p. 82; emphasis mine).
38. J. Bryant,'"Nowhere a Stranger": Melville and Cosmopolitanism,' *Nineteenth-Century Fiction*, 39, 3 (1984) 275–291 at 278 and 280.
39. Boehm, 'Cosmopolitanism,' p. 458.
40. L. Rudolph, 'The Occidental Tagore,' *Boston Review*, 19, 5 (1994) 21.
41. Hazard, *The European Mind*, p. 120.
42. M. Wight, 'An Anatomy of International Thought,' *Review of International Studies*, 13 (1987) 226.
43. R. Beiner, '1989: Nationalism, Internationalism, and the Nairn-Hobsbawm Debate,' *Archives européennes de sociologie*, 40, 1 (1999) 171–184 at 178.
44. Quoted in Carr, *The Twenty Years' Crisis*, p. 85. Yi-Fu Tuan tells us that the Chinese have historically 'equated their own culture with universal culture (civilization).' See Tuan, *Cosmos and Hearth*, p. 64.
45. Carr, *The Twenty Years' Crisis*, p. 87.
46. I. Wallerstein, 'Neither Patriotism, Nor Cosmopolitanism,' *Boston Review*, 19, 5 (1994) 15.
47. M. Walzer, 'Spheres of Affection,' *Boston Review*, 19, 5 (1994) 29.

48. See I. Berlin, *Four Essays on Liberty* (Oxford: Oxford University Press, 1989).
49. L. Tolstoy, *Anna Karenina*, Louise and Aylmer Maude trans. (New York: Knopf, 1992), p. 1.
50. Baldry, *The Unity of Mankind*, p. 12.
51. Shakespeare, *Hamlet*, 2.2.312–317.
52. Thucydides, *History of the Peloponnesian War*, R. Warner trans. (Markham, Ontario: Penguin, 1954), pp. 151–156.
53. A. Camus, *The Plague*, S. Gilbert trans. (Markham, Ontario: Penguin, 1986). It is a fate, of course, that is not distinctly human, for our vulnerability to decay and death connects us with all living things. Remembering that a *cosmopolite* in classic times was a 'citizen of the *universe*' reminds us that cosmopolitanism as an ethical perspective likely entails moral obligations towards all living things, including animals and the natural environment.
54. Although Shklar does not call herself a cosmopolitan theorist, her sympathy for a cosmopolitan ethical perspective is apparent in her works, and is especially evident in her telling characterization of her disagreements with Michael Walzer as 'a dialogue between an exile and a citizen.' See J.N. Shklar, 'The Work of Michael Walzer,' in *Political Thought and Political Thinkers*, S. Hoffmann ed. (Chicago: The University of Chicago Press, 1998), p. 377. In her critique of an interpretivist approach to social criticism, Shklar writes, 'Surely "we" . . . want not only to say that Shakespeare and Kant wrote a great text, but we also want to say, as ordinary men and women, "this is unjust" and this is "fair," not just for you and me but for all humanity' (p. 379).
55. J.N. Shklar, *Ordinary Vices* (Cambridge, Mass.: Harvard University Press, 1984), p. 5.
56. Shklar, *Ordinary Vices*, p. 4, italics mine.
57. Ibid., p. 2.
58. J. Kekes, 'Cruelty and Liberalism,' *Ethics* 106 (1996) 834–844.
59. Shklar, 'Putting Cruelty First,' in *Ordinary Vices*, p. 8.
60. Ibid., p. 13.
61. The principle of humanity, so described, is found in *The Fundamental Principles of the International Red Cross and Red Crescent Movement* (proclaimed by the XXth International Conference of the Red Cross, Geneva, 1965).
62. W.H. Auden, 'Musée des Beaux Arts,' in *Selected Poems* (New York: Vintage International, 1989), p. 79.
63. See J.N. Shklar, *The Faces of Injustice* (New Haven: Yale University Press, 1990).
64. Shklar, *The Faces of Injustice*, p. 126.
65. Shklar, 'Putting Cruelty First,' p. 8.
66. Shklar, *Ordinary Vices*, p. 5.
67. Baldry, *The Unity of Mankind*, p. 15.
68. E. Scarry, *The Body in Pain: The Making and Unmaking of the World* (Oxford: Oxford University Press, 1985), p. 19.
69. See S.V. LaSelva, 'The One and the Many: Pluralism, Expressivism, and the Canadian Political Nationality,' in *The Moral Foundations of Canadian Federalism: Paradoxes, Achievements, and Tragedies of Nationhood* (Montreal & Kingston: McGill-Queen's University Press, 1996), pp. 155–170.
70. Simone Weil argued that each human being not only needs to be rooted, but 'needs to have multiple roots.' See Weil, *The Need for Roots: Prelude to*

a Declaration of Duties towards Mankind (London: Routledge & Kegan Paul, 1987), p. 41.

71. Shklar, 'The Ambiguities of Betrayal,' in *Ordinary Vices*, pp. 138–191.
72. See K.R. Monroe, 'Review Essay: The Psychology of Genocide,' *Ethics & International Affairs*, 9 (1995) 215–239, for a view of the crucial part played by dehumanization in genocide. Indeed, while some genocides occur in a context of 'ethnic' conflict, identifying others by their ethnicity still places them in the realm of *human* identities and relationships. Genocidal killing seems to involve even discarding this identification, and is made easier when victims are likened to nonhuman objects, like bushes that have to be cleared, or bad weeds that need uprooting, as happened in the Rwandan genocide of 1994. See G. Prunier, *The Rwanda Crisis: History of a Genocide* (New York: Columbia University Press, 1995), pp. 137–142.
73. J.N. Shklar, 'Obligation, Loyalty, Exile,' *Political Theory*, 21, 2 (1993) 181–197 at 184.
74. See W. Gamson, 'Hiroshima, the Holocaust and the Politics of Exclusion,' *American Sociological Review*, 60 (1995) 1–20.
75. R. Rorty, 'Justice as a Larger Loyalty,' in *Cosmopolitics: Thinking and Feeling beyond the Nation, Cosmopolitics: Thinking and Feeling beyond the Nation*, P. Cheah and B. Robbins eds (Minneapolis: University of Minnesota Press, 1998), pp. 47–57 at p. 47.
76. In a particularly poignant passage, Kent declares his reason for disobeying his master: 'My life I never held but as a pawn/To wage against thine enemies; nor fear to lose it,/Thy safety being motive.' W. Shakespeare, *The Tragedy of King Lear* (Ontario: The New American Library of Canada, 1987), 1.1.157–159.
77. MacIntyre, 'Is Patriotism a Virtue?' p. 210.
78. G. Orwell, 'Notes on Nationalism,' in *Decline of the English Murder and Other Essays* (Markham, Ontario: Penguin, 1988), pp. 155–179 at p. 156.
79. Of course, Rorty's misguided understanding of cosmopolitan justice as loyalty to a larger group reveals the problematic nature of characterizing cosmopolitanism as a moral allegiance to 'the human race' as 'the community that is, most fundamentally, the source of our moral obligations.' See Nussbaum, 'Patriotism and Cosmopolitanism,' p. 4.
80. This is not to suggest that such conflicts are completely unproblematic, since they involve considerable emotional and psychological turmoil.
81. K. Rostrup, director, *Memories of a Marriage* (Nordisk Film, The Danish Film Institute, 1989), based on a novel by Martha Christensen.
82. Monroe, *The Heart of Altruism*, pp. 91–120. See also P.P. Hallie, *Lest Innocent Blood be Shed: The Story of the Village of Chambon and how Goodness Happened there* (New York: HarperPerennial, 1994).
83. Quoted in Monroe, *The Heart of Altruism*, p. 156.
84. Indeed, in contexts of extreme injustice, rights as choices may have little moral meaning. Consider the choice a Nazi officer gives a Polish Jewish mother to save either her son or daughter, in *Sophie's Choice*. Sophie has a right to choose, but the moral perversity of this choice is apparent given that no choice she makes can be right. See A.J. Pakula, director, *Sophie's Choice* (ITC Entertainment, 1982), based on a novel of the same name by William Styron.

85. Weil, *The Need for Roots*, pp. 9–10.
86. This is a paraphrase of Mary Wollstonecraft, who wrote, 'It is justice, not charity, that is wanting in the world.' See Wollstonecraft, *A Vindication of the Rights of Women* (New York: Norton, 1967, originally published in 1792).
87. This definition can be found in the *Oxford English Dictionary*.
88. Tuan, *Cosmos and Hearth*, p. 31.
89. J. Locke, *A Letter Concerning Toleration* in *The Second Treatise of Civil Government and A Letter Concerning Toleration* (Oxford: Basil Blackwell, 1946), p. 163.
90. S.V. LaSelva, 'Traditions of Tolerance: Relativism, Coercion, and Truth in the political philosophy of W.J. Stankiewicz,' in *Holding One's Time in Thought: The Political Philosophy of W.J. Stankiewicz*, B. Czaykowski and S.V. LaSelva eds (Vancouver, Canada: Ronsdale Press, 1997), pp. 133 and 134.
91. LaSelva, 'Traditions of Tolerance,' p. 135.
92. Shklar, *The Faces of Injustice*, pp. 5 and 70.
93. Shklar, 'Obligation, Loyalty, Exile,' p. 191. For example, many children of abusive parents nevertheless still feel an overwhelming sense of loyalty towards them. We are more inclined to suffer internal rather than external injustice, perhaps not because the injustice committed against us by our own is less morally blameworthy, but because acknowledging the injustice entails a greater psychological and emotional cost.
94. See Waldron, 'Minority Cultures and the Cosmopolitan Alternative.'
95. Shklar, *The Faces of Injustice*, p. 30.
96. As Chris Brown has put it, 'something further is needed if an essentially *empirical* account of an increasingly unified world is to be accompanied by an essentially *normative* account of the emergence of a world community.' See Brown, 'International Political Theory and the Idea of World Community,' in *International Relations Theory Today*, K. Booth and S. Smith eds (University Park, Pennsylvania: Pennsylvania State University Press), pp. 93–94.
97. Cosmopolitanism is also typically understood to entail global distributive justice. Unfortunately, I cannot pursue this theme here, although I would like to note that it is most clear in the economic realm that a cosmopolitan normative orientation does not automatically accompany the globalization of economic processes and institutions. This means that a cosmopolitan ethical perspective, rather than being a handmaiden to globalization processes, may in fact be harnessed to critique them. For recent cosmopolitan arguments for global redistribution, see M. Nussbaum, 'Duties of Justice, Duties of Material Aid: Cicero's Problematic Legacy,' *The Journal of Political Philosophy* 8, 2 (June 2000); C.R. Beitz, 'International Liberalism and Distributive Justice: A Survey of Recent Thought,' *World Politics*, 51, 2 (1999): 269–296; T. Pogge, *World Poverty and Human Rights* (Cambridge, UK: Polity Press, 2002); and K.C. Tan, *Justice Without Borders: Cosmopolitanism, Nationalism and Patriotism* (Cambridge, UK: Cambridge University Press, 2004).
98. Baldry, *The Unity of Mankind*, p. 186.
99. Ibid., p. 47. Thucydides clearly perceived the cleavages of his day as social constructions and *not* as 'part of the nature of things,' in his recognition that early Greeks were like barbarians in his time.
100. Anderson, 'Cosmopolitanism, Universalism, and the Divided Legacies of Modernity,' p. 267.

101. Boehm, 'Cosmopolitanism,' p. 458.
102. Baldry, *The Unity of Mankind*, pp. 203 and 39.

6 Cosmopolitanism, liberalism and intervention

1. Reuters, 'Annan Wants Big Reforms on Force, Poverty, Rights,' *The New York Times*, 20 March 2005.
2. L. Tamahori, director, *Once Were Warriors*, R. Brown, screenplay (Communicado with the New Zealand Film Commission, 1994) based on a novel of the same name by Alan Duff.
3. J.N. Pieterse, 'Sociology of Humanitarian Intervention: Bosnia, Rwanda and Somalia Compared,' *International Political Science Review*, 18, 1 (1997) 71–93 at 81.
4. O. Ramsbotham and T. Woodhouse, *Humanitarian Intervention in Contemporary Conflict: A Reconceptualization* (Cambridge: Polity Press, 1996), p. 87.
5. G. Prunier, *The Rwanda Crisis: History of a Genocide* (New York: Columbia University Press, 1997), pp. 99–108.
6. This is a paraphrase of S.M. Okin, *Justice, Gender and the Family* (New York: Basic Books, 1989), who, in arguing that the state already does influence the structure of the family, wrote, 'The issue is not whether, but how the state intervenes' (p. 131). Ramsbotham and Woodhouse reach a similar conclusion; see *Humanitarian Intervention in Contemporary Conflict*, p. 137.
7. This section comes from my article, 'Whose Principles? Whose Institutions? Legitimacy Challenges for Humanitarian Intervention,' in *Humanitarian Intervention, Nomos XLVII*, T. Nardin and M.S. Williams eds (New York: New York University Press, 2005), pp. 188–216.
8. M. Finnemore, 'Constructing Norms of Humanitarian Intervention,' in *The Culture of National Security: Norms and Identity in World Politics*, P.J. Katzenstein ed. (New York: Columbia University Press, 1996), pp. 153–185 at p. 163.
9. See Prunier, *The Rwanda Crisis*, pp. 234–236.
10. See C. Taylor, 'Conditions of an Unforced Consensus on Human Rights,' in *The East Asian Challenge for Human Rights*, J.R. Bauer and D.A. Bell eds (Cambridge: Cambridge University Press, 1999), pp. 124–144.
11. Quoted in N.J. Wheeler, *Saving Strangers: Humanitarian Intervention in International Society* (Oxford: Oxford University Press, 2000), p. 196.
12. 'As flies to wanton boys, are we to th' gods, / They kill us for their sport.' W. Shakespeare, *The Tragedy of King Lear* (Scarborough, Ontario: New American Library of Canada, 1987), 4.1.36–37.
13. Elaine Scarry has argued that torture, or a wilful attack on bodily integrity and decisional agency, unmakes the individual self as well as the social world of which the individual was a part. Scarry, *The Body in Pain: The Making and Unmaking of the World* (Oxford: Oxford University Press, 1985). On the agency-denying effects of totalitarian systems, see P. Levi, *The Drowned and the Saved*, R. Rosenthal trans. (New York: Vintage International, 1989). On humans as self-interpreting agents, see C. Taylor, 'What is human agency?' and 'Self-interpreting animals,' in *Human Agency and Language: Philosophical Papers I* (Cambridge: Cambridge University Press, 1999), pp. 15–76.

14. J.N. Shklar, 'The Liberalism of Fear,' in *Liberalism and the Moral Life*, Nancy Rosenblum ed. (Cambridge: Harvard University Press, 1989), pp. 21–38 at p. 21.
15. J.N. Shklar, *Ordinary Vices* (Cambridge: Harvard University Press, 1984), p. 5.
16. T. Hobbes, *Leviathan* (Markham: Penguin, 1986), Part I, Chapter 14, p. 192.
17. Shklar, 'The Liberalism of Fear,' pp. 28–31.
18. Shakespeare, *King Lear*, 3.4.107–108.
19. Ramsbotham and Woodhouse, *Humanitarian Intervention in Contemporary Conflict*, pp. 9–10.
20. The mere existence of such rules reveals war to be an activity conducted by human agents with the capacity for moral agency and, therefore, for incurring moral responsibility.
21. *The Fundamental Principles of the International Red Cross and Red Crescent Movement* (proclaimed by the XXth International Conference of the Red Cross, Geneva, 1965). See Ramsbotham and Woodhouse, *Humanitarian Intervention in Contemporary Conflict*, 14–16.
22. In addition to the 1945 UN Charter and 1948 Universal Declaration of Human Rights, we can include: the 1926 Covenant to Suppress the Slave Trade and Slavery; the 1948 Convention on the Prevention and Punishment of the Crime of Genocide; the 1966 International Convention on the Elimination of All Forms of Racial Discrimination; and the 1984 UN Convention against Torture and Other Cruel, Inhuman or Degrading Treatment.
23. See John Locke, *Second Treatise of Government*, in *The Second Treatise of Civil Government and A Letter Concerning Toleration* (Oxford: Basil Blackwell, 1946).
24. A.L. Allen, *Uneasy Access: Privacy for Women in a Free Society* (Totowa, New Jersey: Rowman & Littlefield Publishers, 1988), pp. 116–117.
25. Annabelle Lever observes that

    feminist criticisms of the public/private distinction are as much directed at republican or participatory democrats, who celebrate political engagement and participation, and who exhort us to focus on the common good, as they are at liberals and democrats whose predominant concern is with the evils of government, or with the need to preserve the family as 'a haven in a heartless world'.

    See Lever, 'Feminism, Democracy and the Public/Private Distinction: An Effort to Untie Some Knots,' paper prepared for the Atlanta, Georgia, American Political Science Association Meetings, 1999, pp. 10–11.
26. See, for example, P. Boling, *Privacy and the Politics of Intimate Life* (Ithaca, NY: Cornell University Press, 1996).
27. See C.A. MacKinnon, *Toward a Feminist Theory of the State* (Cambridge: Harvard University Press, 1989).
28. See F.E. Olsen, 'The Myth of State Intervention in the Family,' *Journal of Law Reform*, 18, 4 (1985) 835–864.
29. Lever, 'Feminism, Democracy and the Public/Private Distinction.'
30. R. Gavison, 'Feminism and the Public/Private Distinction,' *Stanford Law Review*, 45, 1 (1992) 1–45 at 36.
31. See T.J. Biersteker and C. Weber editors, *State Sovereignty as Social Construct* (Cambridge: Cambridge University Press, 1996).

32. Jean L. Cohen, 'Whose Sovereignty? Empire Versus International Law,' *Ethics and International Affairs*, 18, 3 (2004) 18. The 'theorists of cosmopolitan law and justice' she criticizes include Allen Buchanan, *Justice, Legitimacy, and Self-Determination: Moral foundations for International Law* (New York: Oxford University Press, 2004); and Anne-Marie Slaughter, *A New World Order* (Princeton: Princeton University Press, 2004).
33. R.H. Jackson, 'The Political Theory of International Society,' in *International Relations Theory Today*, K. Booth and S. Smith eds (University Park, Pennsylvania: Pennsylvania University Press, 1995), pp. 110–111.
34. Bentham's conception of international law, introduced in 1789, was restricted in its subject to the rights and obligations of states *inter se*, whereas Blackstone's older conception of the law of nations embraced all nonmunicipal sources of law that related to various subjects, including states and individuals. 'A source-based definition of "international law"...might admit a rule relating to a government's mistreatment of its own citizens into the ambit of the discipline, but a subject-based...definition might deny such coverage.' In contemporary developments, we see a waning of the positivist legal subject-based interpretation of international law, and a return to a source-based interpretation.' See M. Janis, *An Introduction to International Law*, 2nd edn (Toronto: Little, Brown and Company, 1993), pp. 234 and 245.
35. M.T. Kamminga, *Inter-State Accountability for Violations of Human Rights* (Philadelphia: University of Pennsylvania Press, 1992), pp. 67–68.
36. Janis, *An Introduction to International Law*, p. 233.
37. International Commission on Intervention and State Sovereignty (ICISS), *The Responsibility to Protect: Report of the International Commission on Intervention and State Sovereignty* (Ottawa, Canada: International Development Research Centre, 2001) p. xi. Italics mine.
38. Quoted in K.W. Abbott, 'International Relations Theory, International Law, and the Regime Governing Atrocities in Internal Conflicts,' *The American Journal of International Law*, 93 (1999) 361–379 at 363, footnote 13.
39. The most contentious category is the crime of 'aggression.' States have not yet come to an agreement on how to define the term and the conditions for its application.
40. See W.A. Schabas, *An Introduction to the International Criminal Court* (Cambridge: Cambridge University Press, 2001), pp. 1–8 and p. 19.
41. In his dissenting opinion, Justice Scalia condemns the majority's decision, writing, 'the basic premise of the Court's argument – that American law should conform to the laws of the rest of the world – ought to be rejected out of hand.' See Supreme Court of the United States, *Donald P. Roper v. Christopher Simmons* (2005 US Lexis 2200), 1 March 2005, pp. 43 and 127.
42. The lack of sovereign consent may certainly present problems of practicality and efficiency, which are no doubt greater for intervenors entering a hostile environment.
43. Cohen, 'Rethinking Privacy,' p. 160.
44. See Jane Mayer, 'Annals of Justice: Outsourcing Torture,' *The New Yorker*, 14/21 February 2005, pp. 106–123.
45. I thank Simon Keller for bringing out this argument.
46. T. Pogge, *World Poverty and Human Rights* (Cambridge, UK: Polity Press, 2002), p. 169.

47. According to Rawls, a well-ordered society of peoples would endorse the following eight principles: the freedom and equality of peoples (Principles 1 and 3); the keeping of treaties (2); the rule of nonintervention (4); the right of self-defence (5); the observance of human rights (6); 'jus in bello' (7); and a 'duty of assistance' (8). See J. Rawls, *The Law of Peoples* (Cambridge: Harvard University Press, 1999), p. 37.
48. Rawls, *Law of Peoples*, p. 27.
49. Ibid., pp. 68, 80, 67, 59 (italics mine), and 121.
50. According to Rawls, 'Human rights set a necessary, though not sufficient, standard for the decency of domestic political and social institutions.' See Rawls, *Law of Peoples*, p. 80.
51. Rawls, *Law of Peoples*, pp. 65, 79, 68, 65 and 81.
52. Ibid., p. 37.
53. Ibid., p. 60.
54. Ibid., p. 85.
55. C.R. Beitz, *Political Theory and International Relations*, 2nd edn (Princeton: Princeton University Press, 1999), pp. 181–182.
56. See C.R. Beitz, 'International Liberalism and Distributive Justice: A Survey of Recent Thought,' *World Politics*, 51, 2 (1999) 269–296 at 287.
57. This follows Kant who argued that 'The problem of solving a perfect civil constitution is subordinate to the problem of a law-governed external relationship with other states, and cannot be solved unless the latter is also solved.' See Kant, 'Idea for a University History with a Cosmopolitan Purpose' (1784) in *Political Writings*, trans. H.B. Nisbet, ed. Hans Reiss, 2nd edn (New York: Cambridge University Press, 1991), p. 187.
58. See C. Lu, 'Cosmopolitan Liberalism and the Faces of Injustice in International Relations,' *Review of International Studies*, 31 (2005) 401–408.
59. C.R. Beitz, 'Human Rights as a Common Concern,' *American Political Science Review*, 95, 2 (June 2001) 269–282 at 269.
60. Beitz, 'Human Rights as a Common Concern,' p. 274.
61. Ibid., p. 275.
62. Rawls, *Law of Peoples*, pp. 61–62.
63. Ibid., p. 61. Rawls notes,

> when the Law of Peoples is honoured by peoples over a certain period of time, with the evident intention to comply, and these intentions are mutually recognized, these peoples tend to develop mutual trust and confidence in one another. Moreover, peoples see those norms as advantageous for themselves and for those they care for, and therefore as time goes on they tend to accept that law as an ideal of conduct. Without such a psychological process, which I shall call moral learning, the idea of realistic utopia for the Law of Peoples lacks an essential element (p. 44).

64. Ibid., p. 85.
65. Perhaps he is assuming the operation of a fair global economic order that regulates their agency and accountability. I will discuss in more detail the problems of private agency and accountability at the global level in the next chapter.
66. Rawls, *Law of Peoples*, p. 15.
67. Ibid., p. 83.

68. Beitz, 'International Liberalism and Distributive Justice,' p. 390. See also C.R. Beitz, 'Reflections,' *Review of International Studies*, 31 (2005) 409–423 at 421–422.
69. Rawls, *Law of Peoples*, p. 74.
70. Beitz, 'Human Rights as a Common Concern,' p. 280.
71. From the Preamble of the Vienna Declaration; quoted in Beitz, 'Human Rights as a Common Concern,' p. 280.
72. See M. Frost, *Constituting Human Rights: Global Civil Society and the Society of Democratic States* (London: Routledge, 2002).

7   Cosmopolitan humanitarianism and the use of force

1. C. Sommaruga, 'Foreword,' in *Hard Choices: Moral Dilemmas in Humanitarian Intervention*, J. Moore ed. (New York: Rowman & Littlefield, 1998), p. ix. Sommaruga was President of the International Committee of the Red Cross.
2. 'Transcript: President Bush's Speech on the Use of Force,' *The New York Times*, 8 October 2002.
3. See Moore, *Hard Choices*.
4. See M. Blake, 'Collateral Benefit,' (paper presented in 'The Intervention Seminar,' Kennedy School of Government, Harvard University, 14 March 2005).
5. O. Ramsbotham and T. Woodhouse, *Humanitarian Intervention in Contemporary Conflict: A Reconceptualization* (Cambridge: Polity Press, 1996), p. 226. See also L. Minear and T. Weiss, *Humanitarian Action in Times of War* (Boulder, Colorado: Lynne Rienner, 1993).
6. Ramsbotham and Woodhouse, *Humanitarian Intervention in Contemporary Conflict*, p. 231.
7. For some of the morally problematic consequences of humanitarian action in internal conflicts, see A. Roberts, *Humanitarian Action in War: Aid, Protection and Impartiality in a Policy Vacuum* (Oxford: Oxford University Press for The International Institute for Strategic Studies, 1996), pp. 33–34.
8. See F. Terry, *Condemned to Repeat?: The Paradox of Humanitarian Action* (Ithaca: Cornell University Press, 2002).
9. See A. Ryan, 'Liberalism,' in *A Companion to Contemporary Political Philosophy*, R.E. Goodin and P. Pettit eds (UK: Blackwell, 2001), pp. 291–311.
10. C. Taylor, 'The Idea of Civil Society,' in Goodin and Pettit, *A Companion to Contemporary Political Philosophy*.
11. This argument follows Judith A. Swanson's interpretation of Aristotle's understanding of the ethical value of the private: 'insofar as [Aristotle] suggests that private activity in the form of, say, friendship or philosophy can transform common opinion into right opinion, he believes that the private serves the public. His account suggests, moreover, that human beings carry virtue earned in private into the public, whereas the human propensity to cherish what is one's own and desirable protects the private from being corrupted by opinions learned in public.' Swanson, *The Public and the Private in Aristotle's Political Philosophy* (Ithaca: Cornell University Press, 1992), p. 3.
12. Sadly, Ruzicka as well as an Iraqi working for CIVIC were killed by a suicide bomber attack near their vehicle on the airport road in Baghdad, on 15 April

2005. See Robert F. Worth, 'An American Aid Worker Is Killed in Her Line of Duty,' *The New York Times*, 18 April 2005. For information on CIVIC, see www.civicworldwide.org.

13. See Ramsbotham and Woodhouse, *Humanitarian Intervention in Contemporary Conflict*, p. 118–119. Médecins Sans Frontières, for example, was created in 1971 from the experience of doctors providing medical relief in Biafra during the 1967–1970 war. The organization won the Nobel Peace Prize in 1999.

14. R.A. Dallaire, 'The Changing Role of UN Peacekeeping Forces: The Relationship between UN Peacekeepers and NGOs in Rwanda,' in *After Rwanda: The Coordination of United Nations Humanitarian Assistance*, J. Whitman and D. Popock eds (New York: St. Martin's Press, 1996), p. 207.

15. See W. Hoge, '10,000 Peacekeepers to be Sent to Sudan, U.N. Council Decides,' *The New York Times*, 25 March 2005.

16. M. Ignatieff, *The Warrior's Honor: Ethnic War and the Modern Conscience* (Viking Press, 1997), p. 158. Of course, the morality of humanitarian action and its consequences may change according to context. Thus, while the consequence of prolonging contemporary intrastate wars has been viewed as a negative moral side effect of humanitarian action, there are cases in which this consequence might be considered morally positive. Outside intervention that kept the war going against Nazi Germany, for example, is less morally controversial than that which perpetuates a senseless, aggressive or unjust war. Moral judgements about the political consequences of humanitarian assistance are thus intricately connected with the perceived legitimacy of the wars being fought.

17. See Terry, *Condemned to Repeat?*, pp. 6 and 10.

18. For some budget figures in that time period, see Roberts, *Humanitarian Action in War*, pp. 17–18; on accountability frameworks, see pp. 60–61.

19. H. Slim, 'By What Authority? The Legitimacy and Accountability of Non-governmental Organisations,' *Journal of Humanitarian Assistance*, March 2002. [http://www.jha.ac/articles/a082.htm]. See The Code of Conduct for the International Red Cross and Red Crescent Movement and NGOs in Disaster Relief (Adopted at the 26th International Conference of the Red Cross and Red Crescent, Geneva, Switzerland, December 3–7, 1995), which was later broadened to include relief operations in conflict zones; SPHERE, *Humanitarian Charter and Minimum Standards in Disaster Response* (Oxfam, 2000), detailing minimal standards of humanitarian action in providing water, sanitation, nutrition, shelter and health; ALNAP, *Humanitarian Action: Learning from Evaluation* (London, 2001); and HAP Project, *Humanitarian Accountability: Key Elements and Operational Framework* (Geneva, 2001).

20. Quoted in Roberts, *Humanitarian Action in War*, p. 55.

21. The French section of Médecins Sans Frontières and the International Rescue Committee (IRC) did withdraw from the Rwandan refugee camps in protest, but only after 'the critical needs of the populations were met.' See Terry, *Condemned to Repeat?*, p. 10.

22. J.N. Shklar, *Ordinary Vices* (Cambridge, Mass.: Harvard University Press, 1984), p. 39.

23. See M. Barnett, 'Humanitarianism Transformed,' *Perspectives on Politics* (forthcoming).

24. A. Niatsos, 'NGOs Must Show Results; Promote US or We Will "Find New Partners,"' [www.interaction.org/forum2003/panels.html#Natsios]. Niatsos is a US Agency for International Development (USAID) administrator.
25. Dallaire, 'The Changing Role of UN Peacekeeping Forces,' p. 207.
26. This selectivity according to donor governments' interests rather than according to comparative need assessments of vulnerable populations was also apparent before 9/11. See J. Randel and T. German, 'Trends in the Financing of Humanitarian Assistance,' in *The New Humanitarianism: A Review of Trends in Global Humanitarian Action*, Joanne McRae ed. (London: Overseas Development Institute, 2002), pp. 12–28.
27. Niatsos, 'NGOs Must Show Results,' [www.interaction.org/forum2003/panels.html#Natsios].
28. Slim, 'By What Authority?' [http://www.jha.ac/articles/a082.htm].
29. Shklar, *Ordinary Vices*, p. 37.
30. The following discussion comes from my article, 'Whose Principles? Whose Institutions? Legitimacy Challenges for Humanitarian Intervention,' in *Humanitarian Intervention, Nomos XLVII*, T. Nardin and M.S. Williams eds (New York: New York University Press, 2005), pp. 188–216.
31. See J. Brunnée and S. Toope, 'Slouching Towards New "Just" Wars: The Hegemon After September 11th,' *International Relations*, 18, 4 (2004) 406.
32. For a thorough critique of positivist and realist accounts of law, see J.N. Shklar, *Legalism: Law, Morals and Political Trials*, 2nd edn (Cambridge: Harvard University Press, 1986).
33. See T. Franck, 'Interpretation and Change in the Law of Humanitarian Intervention,' in *Humanitarian Intervention: Ethical, Legal, and Political Dilemmas*, ed. J.L. Holzgrefe and R.O. Keohane eds (Cambridge, UK: Cambridge University Press, 2003), pp. 204–231 at p. 204.
34. T. Franck, 'Legality and Legitimacy in Humanitarian Intervention,' in *Nomos: Humanitarian Intervention*, T. Nardin and M. Williams eds (New York: New York University Press, 2005).
35. Franck, 'Interpretation and Change in the Law of Humanitarian Intervention,' p. 205.
36. Franck, 'Legality and Legitimacy in Humanitarian Intervention.'
37. M. Byers and S. Chesterman, 'Changing the Rules about Rules? Unilateral Humanitarian Intervention and the Future of International Law,' in *Humanitarian Intervention: Ethical, Legal, and Political Dilemmas*, pp. 177–203 at p. 193.
38. Byers and Chesterman argue that

   providing a formal exception for a powerful state (or states) to violate rules that continue to apply to all other actors severely undermines respect for a particular rule and for international law more generally. It would probably also encourage violations of the law – at least insofar as the capacity to violate the law and get away with it was the benchmark of being a 'leading state.'

   Byers and Chesterman, 'Changing the Rules about the Rules?,' 197. In a recent UN Security Council resolution to send war crimes suspects from the conflict in the Darfur region of Sudan to the ICC, the United States abstained and did not veto the resolution, only after a clause was included giving 'exclusive jurisdiction to troop-contributing states over any of their citizens arrested abroad,' which basically exempted Americans from the ICC's jurisdiction. See W. Hoge, 'U.N. Votes to Send Any Sudan War Crime Suspects to World Court,' *The New York Times*, 1 April 2005.

39. Franck, 'Legality and Legitimacy in Humanitarian Intervention.'
40. As Byers and Chesterman have noted, to secure enhanced legitimacy for Operation Desert Storm to repel Iraq's invasion of Kuwait, 'the United States made various promises to resume normal trade relations, provide aid, support World Bank loans, and exclude certain states from international conferences in order to secure the adoption of Security Council Resolution 678 in November 1990 ... It is [also] well known that Yemen lost US $70 million in annual aid from the United States because of its vote against Resolution 678.' See Byers and Chesterman, 'Changing the Rules about Rules?,' p. 192.
41. Shklar, *Legalism*, p. 131.
42. Franck, 'Interpretation and Change in the Law of Humanitarian Intervention,' p. 228.
43. A. Roberts, 'Humanitarian Issues and Agencies as Triggers for International Military Action,' in *Civilians in War*, S. Chesterman ed. (Boulder, Colorado: Lynne Rienner, 2001), pp. 177–196.
44. See N. Thompson, 'Adopt-a-Peacekeeper,' *The Boston Globe*, 6 March 2005. I thank Dominic Tierney for bringing this development to my attention.
45. Thompson, 'Adopt-a-Peacekeeper.'
46. It is not that in a state-centric jury model, nongovernmental organizations would have no role, since their representatives could be (and have been) called as expert witnesses. Decisional agency, however, is denied to them.
47. International Commission on Intervention and State Sovereignty (ICISS), *The Responsibility to Protect: Report of the International Commission on Intervention and State Sovereignty* (Ottawa, Canada: International Development Research Centre, 2001), p. xii.
48. N.J. Wheeler, *Saving Strangers: Humanitarian Intervention in International Society* (Oxford: Oxford University Press, 2000), p. 206.
49. R. Dallaire with B. Beardsley, *Shake Hands with the Devil: The Failure of Humanity in Rwanda* (Toronto: Random House Canada, 2003), pp. 515–516. In a visit to Rwanda four years after the genocide, US President Bill Clinton expressed his regret for the unresponsiveness of the international community. See Wheeler, *Saving Strangers*, p. 240.
50. See ICISS, *Responsibility to Protect*, pp. 39–46.
51. Similarly, familial domestic violence cannot be resolved by repeated police interventions alone; changing the dynamics of such families requires a much wider social effort, including the assistance of teachers, doctors, social workers and children's aid societies, and the support of friends, employers and neighbourhood associations.
52. J. Tirman, 'The New Humanitarianism: How Military Intervention became the Norm,' *Boston Review*, 28, 6 (December 2003/January 2004). http://bostonreview.net/BR28.6/tirman.html.
53. ICISS, *Responsibility to Protect*, p. xi.
54. Tirman, 'The New Humanitarianism.' As he puts this argument, 'humanitarianism itself is seen then as the superficial if pervasive policing (i.e., intervention) of the complex and often deteriorating situations that liberal

economic and political governance (i.e., globalization) has been so intimately involved in creating.'

55. See Prunier, *The Rwanda Crisis*; Dallaire, *Shake Hands With the Devil*; M. Mamdani, *When Victims Become Killers: Colonialism, Nativism, and the Genocide in Rwanda* (Princeton: Princeton University Press, 2001); and M. Barnett, *Eyewitness to a Genocide: The United Nations and Rwanda* (Ithaca: Cornell University Press, 2002).

8 Conclusion

1. V. Woolf, *Three Guineas*, in *A Room of One's Own [1929] and Three Guineas [1938]* (Toronto: Penguin, 2000).
2. See T. Pogge, *World Poverty and Human Rights* (Cambridge, UK: Polity Press, 2002), p. 176.
3. Those living on less than US $1 a day are considered to be living in absolute poverty. See World Bank, *World Development Report 2000/1* (Oxford: Oxford University Press, 2000).
4. This follows Kok-chor Tan, who has argued with respect to the problems of global poverty and inequality that 'we need to address the global background context within which countries interact, and not simply take this context as a given.' See Tan, *Justice Without Borders: Cosmopolitanism, Nationalism and Patriotism* (Cambridge: Cambridge University Press, 2004), p. 25.
5. *The International Criminal Court*, online: Amnesty International [http://www.web.amnesty.org/web/web.nsf/pages/ICChome].
6. The ICC also attempts to address the needs of victims by providing reparations to victims and their families for restitutive, compensatory and rehabilitative purposes. For a more elaborate discussion of the ICC, see my forthcoming book, *Great Transformations: The Idea of Moral Regeneration in World Politics*.
7. India and China have neither signed nor ratified the ICC Statute. Russia has signed but not yet ratified. The United States renounced or 'unsigned' the treaty in 2002.
8. See also Tan, *Justice Without Borders*, pp. 19–39.
9. See J. Rawls, *The Law of Peoples* (Cambridge: Harvard University Press, 1999).
10. N.J. Wheeler, *Saving Strangers: Humanitarian Intervention in International Society* (Oxford: Oxford University Press, 2000), p. 310.
11. On the limits of sacrifice, see Wheeler, *Saving Strangers*, pp. 299–310.
12. See the annual *Human Development Reports* by the United Nations Development Program (UNDP) (New York: Oxford University Press).
13. UNICEF press release, 'Bellamy urges legislators to use their power to protect children from exploitation,' 4 April 2005. [http://www.unicef.org/media/media_25845.html].

Bibliography

Abbott, K.W. 'International Relations Theory, International Law, and the Regime Governing Atrocities in Internal Conflicts,' *The American Journal of International Law*, 93 (1999) 361–379.

Akehurst, M. 'Humanitarian Intervention.' In *Intervention in World Politics*, H. Bull ed.

Allan, G. and G. Crow. *Home and Family: Creating the Domestic Sphere* (London: MacMillan, 1989).

Allen, A. *Uneasy Access: Privacy for Women in a Free Society* (Totowa, New Jersey: Rowman & Littlefield, 1988).

Anderson, A. 'Cosmopolitanism, Universalism, and the Divided Legacies of Modernity.' In *Cosmopolitics: Thinking and Feeling Beyond the Nation*, P. Cheah and B. Robbins eds.

Anderson, B. *Imagined Communities: Reflections on the Origin and Spread of Nationalism*, Revised ed. (New York: Verso, 1991).

Arendt, H. *The Human Condition* (Chicago: University of Chicago Press, 1958).

Baldry, H.C. *The Unity of Mankind in Greek Thought* (Cambridge, UK: Cambridge University Press, 1965).

Barnett, M. 'Humanitarianism Transformed,' *Perspectives on Politics* (forthcoming, 2005).

—— *Eyewitness to a Genocide: The United Nations and Rwanda* (Ithaca: Cornell University Press, 2002).

Barrington, L. 'The Domestic and International Consequences of Citizenship in the Soviet Successor States,' *Europe Asia Studies*, 47, 5 (1995) 731–763.

Bauer, J.R. and D.A. Bell eds, *The East Asian Challenge for Human Rights* (Cambridge: Cambridge University Press, 1999).

Beiner, R. '1989: Nationalism, Internationalism, and the Nairn-Hobsbawm Debate,' *Archives européennes de sociologie*, 40, 1 (1999) 171–184.

—— *Theorizing Citizenship*, R. Beiner ed. (Albany, New York: State University of New York, 1995).

Beitz, C.R. 'Human Rights as a Common Concern,' *American Political Science Review*, 95, 2 (2002) 269–282.

—— *Political Theory and International Relations*, 2nd edn (Princeton, NJ: Princeton University Press, 1999).

—— 'International Liberalism and Distributive Justice: A Survey of Recent Thought,' *World Politics*, 51, 2 (1999) 269–296.

—— 'Nonintervention and Communal Integrity,' *Philosophy and Public Affairs*, 9, 4 (1980) 385–391.

Benn, S.I. and G.F. Gaus eds, *Public and Private in Social Life* (Canberra, Australia: Croom Helm, 1983).

Bentham, J. *Introduction to the Principles of Morals and Legislation*, J.H. Burns and H.L.A. Hart eds (London: Athlone Press, 1970).

Berlin, I. *Four Essays on Liberty* (Oxford: Oxford University Press, 1989).

Best, G. 'Justice, International Relations and Human Rights,' *International Affairs*, 71, 4 (1995) 775–799.

Biersteker, T.J. and C. Weber eds, *State Sovereignty as Social Construct* (Cambridge: Cambridge University Press, 1996).

Blake, M. 'Collateral Benefit,' paper presented in 'The Intervention Seminar,' Kennedy School of Government, Harvard University, 14 March 2005.

Bobbio, N. *Democracy and Dictatorship: The Nature and Limits of State Power*, P. Kennealy trans. (Minneapolis: University of Minnesota Press, 1989).

Bodin, J. *Six Books of the Commonwealth*, M.J. Tooley trans. (Oxford: Basil Blackwell, 1955).

Boehm, M. 'Cosmopolitanism,' *Encyclopedia of the Social Sciences*, 4 (New York: Macmillan, 1932) 457–461.

Boling, P. *Privacy and the Politics of Intimate Life* (Ithaca, NY: Cornell University Press, 1996).

Bolt, R. screenplay. *The Mission* (New York: Berkeley Publication Group, 1986).

Booth, K. and S. Smith eds, *International Relations Theory Today* (University Park, Pennsylvania: Pennsylvania State University Press, 1995).

Brierly, J.L. 'Matters of Domestic Jurisdiction,' *British Yearbook of International Law*, 6 (1925) 8–19.

Brown, C. 'International Political Theory and the Idea of World Community.' In *International Relations Theory Today*, K. Booth and S. Smith eds.

Brunnée, J. and S. Toope. 'Slouching Towards New "Just" Wars: The Hegemon After September 11th,' *International Relations*, 18, 4 (2004) 405–424.

Bryant, J. ' "Nowhere a Stranger": Melville and Cosmopolitanism,' *Nineteenth-Century Fiction*, 39, 3 (1984) 275–291.

Buchanan, A. *Justice, Legitimacy, and Self-Determination: Moral Foundations for International Law* (New York: Oxford University Press, 2004).

Bull, H. ed. *Intervention in World Politics* (Oxford: Clarendon Press, 1986).

—— *Justice in International Relations* (Waterloo, Ontario: University of Waterloo Press, 1984).

—— *The Expansion of International Society* (Oxford: Clarendon Press, 1984).

—— *The Anarchical Society: A Study of Order in World Politics* (New York: Columbia University Press, 1977).

—— 'Martin Wight and the Theory of International Relations,' *British Journal of International Studies*, 2 (1976) 101–116.

Butterfield, H. and M. Wight eds, *Diplomatic Investigations: Essays in the Theory of International Politics* (Cambridge, Mass.: Harvard University Press, 1966).

Byers, M. and S. Chesterman. 'Changing the Rules about Rules? Unilateral Humanitarian Intervention and the Future of International Law.' In *Humanitarian Intervention: Ethical, Legal, and Political Dilemmas*, J.L. Holzgrefe and R.O. Keohane eds.

Calhoun, C. 'Nationalism and the Public Sphere.' In *Public and Private in Thought and Practice*, J.A. Weintraub and K. Kumar eds (1997).

Camus, A. *The Plague*. S. Gilbert trans. (Markham, Ontario: Penguin, 1986).

Caney, S., D. George, and P. Jones eds, *National Rights, International Obligations* (Boulder, Colorado: Westview Press, 1996).

Caney, S. 'Individuals, Nations and Obligations.' In *National Rights, International Obligations*, Caney, George and Jones eds.

Carr, E.H. *The Twenty Years' Crisis 1919–1939: An Introduction to the Study of International Relations*, 2nd edn (New York: Harper & Row, 1946).

Carter, A. *The Political Theory of Global Citizenship* (New Jersey: Routledge, 2001).

Cassirer, E. *The Philosophy of the Enlightenment*, F.C.A. Koelln and J.P. Pettegrove trans. (Princeton: Princeton University Press, 1979).

Chan, W.T., trans. and compiler. *A Source Book in Chinese Philosophy* (Princeton: Princeton University Press, 1973).

Charlesworth, H. 'Worlds Apart: Public/Private Distinctions in International Law.' In *Public and Private: Feminist Legal Debates*, M. Thornton ed. (Australia: Oxford University Press, 1995).

Cheah, P. and B. Robbins eds, *Cosmopolitics: Thinking and Feeling Beyond the Nation* (Minneapolis: University of Minnesota Press, 1998).

Chesterman, S. ed. *Civilians in War* (Boulder, Colorado: Lynne Rienner, 2001).

Church Council on Justice and Corrections. *Family Violence in a Patriarchal Culture: A Challenge to Our Way of Living* (Ottawa: Canadian Council on Social Development,1988).

Cohen, J.L. 'Whose Sovereignty? Empire Versus International Law,' *Ethics and International Affairs*, 18, 3 (2004) 1–24.

—— 'Rethinking Privacy: Autonomy, Identity, and the Abortion Controversy.' In *Public and Private in Thought and Practice*, Weintraub and Kumar eds.

Crick, B. 'Sovereignty,' *International Encyclopedia of the Social Sciences*, 15 (1968).

Dallaire, R. with B. Beardsley. *Shake Hands With the Devil: The Failure of Humanity in Rwanda* (Toronto: Random House Canada, 2003).

Dallaire, R. 'The Changing Role of UN Peacekeeping Forces: The Relationship between UN Peacekeepers and NGOs in Rwanda.' In *After Rwanda: The Coordination of United Nations Humanitarian Assistance*, J. Whitman and D. Popock eds (New York: St. Martin's Press, 1996).

Damrosch, L.F. 'Politics Across Borders: Nonintervention and Nonforcible Influence over Domestic Affairs,' *The American Journal of International Law*, 83 (1989) 1–50.

Davis, P.W. 'Stranger Intervention into Child Punishment in Public Places,' *Social Problems*, 38, 2 (1991) 227–246.

DeCew, J.W. *In Pursuit of Privacy: Law, Ethics, and the Rise of Technology* (Ithaca, NY: Cornell University Press, 1997).

Donnelly, J. *Universal Human Rights in Theory and Practice* (New York: Cornell University Press, 1989).

Doyle, M.W. *Ways of War and Peace: Realism, Liberalism and Socialism* (New York: W.W. Norton, 1997).

—— 'Thucydidean Realism,' *Review of International Studies*, 16 (1990) 223–237.

Elshtain, J.B. *Public Man, Private Woman: Women in Social and Political Thought*, 2nd edn (Princeton, New Jersey: Princeton University Press, 1993).

Erskine, T. 'Citizen of Nowhere' or 'The Point Where Circles Intersect'? Impartialist and Embedded Cosmopolitanisms,' *Review of International Studies*, 28 (2002) 457–478.

Feinberg, J. 'Autonomy, Sovereignty, and Privacy: Moral Ideals in the Constitution?' *The Notre Dame Law Review*, 58 (1983) 445–492.

Filmer, R. *Patriarcha: A Defence of the Natural Power of Kings against the Unnatural Liberty of the People.* In *Patriarcha and Other Political Works of Sir Robert Filmer*, P. Laslett ed. (Oxford: Basil Blackwell, 1949).

Finnemore, M. 'Constructing Norms of Humanitarian Intervention.' In *The Culture of National Security: Norms and Identity in World Politics*, P.J. Katzenstein ed. (New York: Columbia University Press, 1996).

—— *National Interests in International Society* (Ithaca, NY: Cornell University Press, 1996).

Forbes, I. and M. Hoffman eds, *Political Theory, International Relations, and the Ethics of Intervention* (New York: St. Martin's Press, 1993).

Forde, S. 'Classical Realism.' In *Traditions of International Ethics*, T. Nardin and D.R. Mapel eds (Cambridge: Cambridge University Press, 1993).

Franck, T. 'Legality and Legitimacy in Humanitarian Intervention.' In *Humanitarian Intervention, Nomos XLVII* (Yearbook of the American Society for Political and Legal Philosophy), T. Nardin and M.S. Williams eds (NY: New York University Press, 2005).

—— 'Interpretation and Change in the Law of Humanitarian Intervention.' In *Humanitarian Intervention: Ethical, Legal, and Political Dilemmas*, J.L. Holzgrefe and R.O. Keohane eds (Cambridge, UK: Cambridge University Press, 2003).

Frankel, B. ed. *The Roots of Realism* (Portland, Oregon: Frank Cass, 1996).

Frost, M. *Constituting Human Rights: Global Civil Society and the Society of Democratic States* (London: Routledge, 2002).

Gamson, W. 'Hiroshima, the Holocaust, and the Politics of Exclusion: 1994 Presidential Address,' *American Sociological Review*, 60 (1995) 1–20.

Gavison, R. 'Feminism and the Public/Private Distinction,' *Stanford Law Review*, 45, 1 (1992) 1–45.

Gilpin, R.C. 'The Richness of the Tradition of Political Realism.' In *Neorealism and Its Critics*, R.O. Keohane ed. (New York: Columbia University Press, 1986).

Goffmann, E. *Relations in Public* (New York: Harper, 1971).

Goodin, R.E. and P. Pettit eds, *A Companion to Contemporary Political Philosophy* (UK: Blackwell, 2001).

Gordon, D. *Citizens Without Sovereignty: Equality and Sociability in French Thought, 1670–1789* (Princeton: Princeton University Press, 1994).

Grass, G. 'Short Speech by a Rootless Cosmopolitan,' *Dissent* (1990) 458–460.

Grosby, S. 'Territoriality: The Transcendental, Primordial Feature of Modern Societies,' *Nations and Nationalism*, 1, 2 (1995) 143–162.

Hackney, S. 'Pluralism in One Country,' *The Boston Review*, 19, 5 (1994) 32.

Hallie, P.P. *Lest Innocent Blood Be Shed: The Story of the Village of Chambon and how Goodness Happened there* (New York: HarperPerennial, 1994).

—— *The Paradox of Cruelty* (Middletown, Connecticut: Wesleyan University Press, 1969).

Hassner, P. 'From War and Peace to Violence and Intervention.' In *Hard Choices: Moral Dilemmas in Humanitarian Intervention*, Moore ed.

Hazard, P. *The European Mind [1680–1715]* (Cleveland, Ohio: The World Publishing Company, 1963).

Heater, D. *World Citizenship and Government: Cosmopolitan Ideas in the History of Western Political Thought* (New York: St. Martin's Press, 1996).

Held, D. *Democracy and the Global Order: From the Modern State to Cosmopolitan Governance* (Stanford: Stanford University Press, 1995).

Hobbes, T. *Leviathan* (Markham, Ontario: Penguin, 1986).

Hoffmann, S. 'The Problem of Intervention.' In *Intervention in World Politics*, H. Bull ed.

—— *Duties Beyond Borders: On the Limits and Possibilities of Ethical International Politics* (Syracuse, NY: Syracuse University Press, 1981).

Holzgrefe, J.L. and R.O. Keohane eds, *Humanitarian Intervention: Ethical, Legal, and Political Dilemmas* (Cambridge, UK: Cambridge University Press, 2003).

Holsti, K.J. *The Dividing Discipline: Hegemony and Diversity in International Theory* (Boston: Unwin Hyman, 1985).

Hurrell, A. 'Vattel: Pluralism and Its Limits.' In *Classical Theories of International Relations*, I. Clark and I. Neumann eds (New York: St. Martin's Press, 1996).

Ignatieff, M. *The Warrior's Honor: Ethnic War and the Modern Conscience* (Toronto: Viking Press, 1998).

International Commission on Intervention and State Sovereignty (ICISS). *The Responsibility to Protect: Report of the International Commission on Intervention and State Sovereignty* (Ottawa, Canada: International Development Research Centre, 2001).

Jackson, R. *The Global Covenant: Human Conduct in a World of States* (Oxford: Oxford University Press, 2000).

—— 'The Political Theory of International Society.' In *International Relations Theory Today*, S. Smith and K. Booth eds.

—— *Quasi-States: Sovereignty, International Relations and the Third World* (Cambridge: Cambridge University Press, 1990).

Janis, M.W. *An Introduction to International Law*, 2nd edn (Toronto: Little, Brown and Company, 1993).

Joffé, R., director. *The Mission*, R. Bolt, screenplay. (Warner Brothers, Goldcrest and Kingsmere, 1986).

Kamminga, M.T. *Inter-State Accountability for Violations of Human Rights* (Philadelphia: University of Pennsylvania Press, 1992).

Kant, I. *Kant: Political Writings*, H. Reiss ed. and H.B. Nisbet trans. (Cambridge, UK: Cambridge University Press, 1991).

Kekes, J. 'Cruelty and Liberalism,' *Ethics*, 106 (1996) 834–844.

Kennan, G.F. 'Morality and Foreign Policy,' *Foreign Affairs*, 64 (1985) 205–218.

Knutsen, T.L. 'The Westphalian Moment: The Classical Situation in International Relations Analysis,' unpublished manuscript.

Krygier, M. 1983. 'Publicness, Privateness and "Primitive Law".' In *Public and Private in Social Life*, Benn and Gaus eds.

Kumar, K. 'Home: The Promise and Predicament of Private Life at the End of the Twentieth Century.' In *Public and Private in Thought and Practice: Perspectives on a Grand Dichotomy*, Weintraub and Kumar eds.

Lasch, C. *Haven in a Heartless World: The Family Besieged* (New York: Basic Books, 1977).

LaSelva, S.V. 'Traditions of Tolerance: Relativism, Coercion, and Truth in the Political Philosophy of W.J. Stankiewicz.' In *Holding One's Time in Thought: The Political Philosophy of W.J. Stankiewicz*, B. Czaykowski and S.V. LaSelva eds (Vancouver, Canada: Ronsdale Press, 1997).

—— *The Moral Foundations of Canadian Federalism: Paradoxes, Achievements, and Tragedies of Nationhood* (Montreal/Kingston: McGill-Queen's University Press, 1996).

Lebow, R.N. *The Tragic Vision of Politics: Ethics, Interests, Orders* (Cambridge: Cambridge University Press, 2003).

Lerner, M. 'Empires of Reason,' *The Boston Review*, 19, 5 (1994) 22.

Lever, A. 'Feminism, Democracy and the Public/Private Distinction: An Effort to Untie Some Knots.' Paper prepared for American Political Science Association Meetings, Atlanta, Georgia, 1999.

Levi, P. *The Drowned and the Saved*, Raymond Rosenthal trans. (New York: Vintage International, 1989).

Lewis, A. 'War Crimes.' In *The Black Book of Bosnia: The Consequences of Appeasement*, N. Mousavizadeh ed. (New York: Basic Books, 1996).

Locke, J. *A Letter Concerning Toleration*. In *The Second Treatise of Civil Government and A Letter Concerning Toleration* (Oxford: Basil Blackwell, 1946).

Lu, C. *Great Transformations: The Idea of Moral Regeneration in World Politics* (forthcoming).

—— 'Whose Principles? Whose Institutions? Legitimacy Challenges for Humanitarian Intervention.' In *Humanitarian Intervention, Nomos XLVII*, T. Nardin and M.S. Williams eds, 188–216.

—— 'Cosmopolitan Liberalism and the Faces of Injustice in International Relations,' *Review of International Studies*, 31 (2005) 401–408.

—— 'The One and Many Faces of Cosmopolitanism,' *The Journal of Political Philosophy*, 8, 2 (2000) 244–267.

—— 'Images of Justice: Justice as a Bond, a Boundary and a Balance,' *The Journal of Political Philosophy*, 6, 1 (1998) 1–26.

Lucas, J.R. *On Justice* (Oxford: Clarendon Press, 1980).

Machiavelli, N. 'The Prince.' In *The Prince and The Discourses* (New York: Random House, 1950).

MacIntyre, A. 'Is Patriotism a Virtue?' In *Theorizing Citizenship*, R. Beiner ed.

MacKinnon, C.A. *Toward a Feminist Theory of the State* (Cambridge: Harvard University Press, 1989).

Mamdani, M. *When Victims Become Killers: Colonialism, Nativism, and the Genocide in Rwanda* (Princeton: Princeton University Press, 2001).

Mayall, J. ed. *The Community of States* (London: Allen & Unwin, 1982).

Mayer, J. 'Annals of Justice: Outsourcing Torture,' *The New Yorker*, 14/21 February 2005, 106–123.

McCarthy, L. 'International Anarchy, Realism and Non-Intervention.' In *Political Theory, International Relations, and the Ethics of Intervention*, Forbes and Hoffman eds.

McRae, J. ed. *The New Humanitarianism: A Review of Trends in Global Humanitarian Action* (London: Overseas Development Institute, 2002).

McShane, K. 'Why Environmental Ethics Shouldn't Give up on Intrinsic Value,' paper presented at the Karbank Symposium in Environmental Philosophy, Boston University, 15 April 2005.

Mill, J.S. *Principles of Political Economy [and Chapters on Socialism]* (Oxford: Oxford University Press, 1994).

—— *On Liberty*. In *On Liberty with The Subjection of Women and Chapters on Socialism* (Cambridge: Cambridge University Press, 1989).

Minear, L. and T. Weiss. *Humanitarian Action in Times of War* (Boulder, Colorado: Lynne Rienner, 1993).

Monroe, K.R. *The Heart of Altruism: Perceptions of a Common Humanity* (Princeton: Princeton University Press, 1996).

Moore, B. *Privacy: Studies in Social and Cultural History* (London: M.E. Sharpe, 1984).

Moore, J. ed. *Hard Choices: Moral Dilemmas in Humanitarian Intervention* (New York: Rowman & Littlefield, 1998).

Morgenthau, H.J. *In Defense of the National Interest: A Critical Examination of American Foreign Policy* (Washington, DC: University Press of America, 1982).

—— *Human Rights and Foreign Policy* (New York: Council on Religion and International Affairs, 1979).

—— 'To Intervene or Not to Intervene,' *Foreign Affairs*, 45 (1967) 425–436.

Nardin, T. and D.R. Mapel eds, *Traditions of International Ethics* (Cambridge, UK: Cambridge University Press, 1992).

Nardin, T. and M.S. Williams eds, *Humanitarian Intervention, Nomos XLVII* (New York: New York University Press, 2005).

Navari, C. 'Intervention, Non-intervention and the Construction of the State.' In *Political Theory, International Relations and the Ethics of Intervention*, Ian Forbes and Mark Hoffmann eds.

Niatsos, A. 'NGOs Must Show Results; Promote US or We Will "Find New Partners," 2003 [www.interaction.org/forum2003/panels.html#Natsios].

Nussbaum, M. 'Duties of Justice, Duties of Material Aid: Cicero's Problematic Legacy,' *The Journal of Political Philosophy*, 8, 2 (2000).

—— 'Patriotism and Cosmopolitanism,' *The Boston Review*, 19, 5 (1994) 3–9. Reprinted in *For Love of Country: Debating the Limits of Patriotism*, J. Cohen ed. (Boston: Beacon Press, 1996).

Okin, S.M. *Women in Western Political Thought* (Princeton: Princeton University Press, 1992).

—— *Justice, Gender and the Family* (New York: Basic Books, 1989).

Olsen, F.E. 'The Myth of State Intervention in the Family,' *Journal of Law Reform*, 18, 4 (1985) 835–864.

Ontario Medical Association. *Reports on Wife Assault* (Ottawa: National Clearinghouse on Family Violence, 1991).

Orwell, G. 'Notes on Nationalism.' In *Decline of the English Murder and Other Essays* (Markham, Ontario: Penguin, 1988).

Pakula, A.J., director. *Sophie's Choice* (ITC Entertainment, 1982). Based on a novel of the same name by William Styron.

Parekh, B. 'Rethinking Humanitarian Intervention,' *International Political Science Review*, 18, 1 (1997) 49–69.

Pateman, C. 'Feminist Critiques of the Public/Private Dichotomy.' In *The Disorder of Women* (Stanford: Stanford University Press, 1989).

Pieterse, J.N. 'Sociology of Humanitarian Intervention: Bosnia, Rwanda and Somalia Compared,' *International Political Science Review*, 18, 1 (1997) 71–93.

Pilkington, H. 'Going Home? The Implications of Forced Migration for National Identity Formation in post-Soviet Russia.' In *The New Migration in Europe: Social Constructions and Social Realities*, K. Koser and H. Lutz eds (New York: St. Martin's Press, 1997).

Pitkin, H.F. 'Justice: On Relating Private and Public,' *Political Theory*, 9, 3 (1981) 327–352.

Plato. *The Republic of Plato*, A. Bloom trans., 2nd edn (New York: Basic Books, 1991).

Pleck, E. *Domestic Tyranny: The Making of Social Policy Against Family Violence from Colonial Times to the Present* (New York: Oxford University Press, 1987).

Pogge, T.W. *World Poverty and Human Rights* (Cambridge, UK: Polity Press, 2002).

—— 'Cosmopolitanism and Sovereignty,' *Ethics*, 103 (1992) 48–75.

Post, R.C. 'The Social Foundations of Privacy: Community and Self in the Common Law Tort,' *California Law Review*, 77, 5 (1989) 957–1010.

Prunier, G. *The Rwanda Crisis: History of a Genocide* (New York: Columbia University Press, 1995).

Ramsbotham, O. and T. Woodhouse. *Humanitarian Intervention in Contemporary Conflict: A Reconceptualization* (Oxford: Blackwell, 1996).

Randel, J. and T. German. 'Trends in the Financing of Humanitarian Assistance.' In *The New Humanitarianism: A Review of Trends in Global Humanitarian Action*, Joanne McRae, ed.

Ratner, S.R. and J.S. Abrams. *Accountability for Human Rights Atrocities in International Law: Beyond the Nuremberg Legacy*, 2nd edn (Oxford: Oxford University Press, 2001).

Rawls, J. *The Law of Peoples* (Cambridge: Harvard University Press, 1999).

—— *A Theory of Justice* (Cambridge: Harvard University Press, 1971).

Roberts, A. 'Humanitarian Issues and Agencies as Triggers for International Military Action.' In *Civilians in War*, Simon Chesterman ed.

—— *Humanitarian Action in War: Aid, Protection and Impartiality in a Policy Vacuum* (London: International Institute for Strategic Studies, 1996).

—— 'Humanitarian War: Military Intervention and Human Rights,' *International Affairs*, 69, 3 (1993) 429–449.

Romany, C. 'Women as *Aliens*: A Feminist Critique of the Public/Private Distinction in International Human Rights Law,' *Harvard Human Rights Journal*, 6 (1993) 87–125.

Rorty, R. 'Justice as a Larger Loyalty.' In *Cosmopolitics: Thinking and Feeling Beyond the Nation*, P. Cheah and B. Robbins eds.

Rosenblum, N. ed. *Liberalism and the Moral Life* (Cambridge: Harvard University Press, 1989).

Rosenthal, J. *Righteous Realists: Political Realism, Responsible Power, and American Culture in the Nuclear Age* (Baton Rouge: Louisiana State University, 1991).

Rostrup, K., director. *Memories of a Marriage* (Nordisk Film, The Danish Film Institute, 1989). Based on a novel by Martha Christensen.

Rousseau, J.J. *The Social Contract*. In *The Social Contract and Discourses*, G.D.H. Cole trans. (London: J.M. Dent & Sons, 1988).

Rousseau, J.J. *Project of Perpetual Peace*, E.M. Nuttall trans. (London: Richard Cobden-Sanderson, 1927).

Rudolph, L. 'The Occidental Tagore,' *The Boston Review*, 19, 5 (1994) 21.

Russell, F.H. *The Just War in the Middle Ages* (Cambridge: Cambridge University Press, 1975).

Ryan, A. 'Liberalism.' In *A Companion to Contemporary Political Philosophy*, R.E. Goodin and P. Pettit eds.

Rybczynski, W. *Home: A Short History of an Idea* (Toronto: Penguin, 1986).

Sandel, M.J. 'Moral Argument and Liberal Toleration: Abortion and Homosexuality,' *California Law Review*, 77, 3 (1989) 521–538.

—— 'The Procedural Republic and the Unencumbered Self,' *Political Theory*, 12 (1984) 81–96.

—— *Liberalism and the Limits of Justice* (Cambridge: Cambridge University Press, 1982).

Scarry, E. *The Body in Pain: The Making and Unmaking of the World* (Oxford: Oxford University Press, 1985).

Schabas, W.A. *An Introduction to the International Criminal Court*, 2nd edn (Cambridge: Cambridge University Press, 2004).

Schlereth, T.J. *The Cosmopolitan Ideal in Enlightenment Thought: Its Form and Function in the Ideas of Franklin, Hume and Voltaire (1694–1790)* (Notre Dame: University of Notre Dame Press, 1977).

Schlesinger, A. 'Our Country, Right or Wrong,' *Boston Review*, 19, 5 (1994) 21.

Schochet, G.J. *Patriarchalism in Political Thought: The Authoritarian Family and Political Speculation and Attitudes Especially in Seventeenth-Century England* (Oxford: Basil Blackwell, 1975).

Schoeman, F.D. *Philosophical Dimensions of Privacy: An Anthology* (Cambridge, UK: Cambridge University Press, 1984).

Shakespeare, W. *The Tragedy of King Lear* (Ontario: The New American Library of Canada, 1987).

—— *The Tragedy of Hamlet* (Scarborough, Ontario: The New American Library, 1963).

Shklar, J.N. 'The Work of Michael Walzer.' In *Political Thought and Political Thinkers*, S. Hoffmann ed. (Chicago: University of Chicago Press, 1998).

—— 'Obligation, Loyalty, Exile,' *Political Theory*, 21, 2 (1993) 181–197.

—— *The Faces of Injustice* (New Haven: Yale University Press, 1990).

—— *Legalism: Law, Morals and Political Trials*, 2nd edn (Cambridge: Harvard University Press, 1986).

—— 'The Liberalism of Fear.' In *Liberalism and the Moral Life*, Nancy Rosenblum ed. (Cambridge: Harvard University Press, 1984).

—— *Ordinary Vices* (Cambridge: Harvard University Press, 1984).

Shue, H. *Basic Rights: Subsistence, Affluence, and U.S. Foreign Policy*, 2nd edn (Princeton: Princeton University Press, 1996).

Slaughter, A.M. *A New World Order* (Princeton: Princeton University Press, 2004).

Slim, H. 'By What Authority? The Legitimacy and Accountability of Non-governmental Organisations,' *Journal of Humanitarian Assistance* (2002). [http://www.jha.ac/articles/a082.htm].

Smith, S. 1995. 'The Self-Images of a Discipline: A Genealogy of International Relations Theory.' In *International Relations Theory Today*, K. Booth and S. Smith eds.

Snow, R.L. *Family Abuse: Tough Solutions to Stop the Violence* (New York: Plenum Trade, 1997).

Spruyt, H. *The Sovereign State and Its Competitors: An Analysis of Systems Change* (Princeton: Princeton University Press, 1994).

Stoett, P.J. *Human and Global Security: An Exploration of Terms* (Toronto: University of Toronto Press, 1999).

Supreme Court of the United States. *Donald P. Roper v. Christopher Simmons* (2005 US Lexis 2200) 1 March 2005.

Swanson, J.A. *The Public and the Private in Aristotle's Political Philosophy* (Ithaca: Cornell University Press, 1992).

Tamahori, L., director. *Once Were Warriors*, R. Brown, screenplay (Communicado with the New Zealand Film Commission, 1994). Based on a novel of the same name by Alan Duff.

Tamir, Y. *Liberal Nationalism* (Princeton: Princeton University Press, 1993).

Tan, K.C. *Justice Without Borders: Cosmopolitanism, Nationalism and Patriotism* (Cambridge: Cambridge University Press, 2004).

Taylor, C. 'The Idea of Civil Society.' In *A Companion to Contemporary Political Philosophy*, Goodin and Pettit eds.

—— 'Conditions of an Unforced Consensus on Human Rights.' In *The East Asian Challenge for Human Rights*, Bauer and Bell eds.

—— *Human Agency and Language: Philosophical Papers I* (Cambridge: Cambridge University Press, 1999).

Terry, F. *Condemned to Repeat? The Paradox of Humanitarian Action* (Ithaca: Cornell University Press, 2002).

Tesón, F.R. *A Philosophy of International Law* (Boulder, Colorado: Westview Press, 1998).

Thucydides. *History of the Peloponnesian War*, R. Warner trans. (Markham, Ontario: Penguin, 1954)

Tirman, J. 'The New Humanitarianism: How Military Intervention became the Norm,' *Boston Review*, 28, 6 (2003/2004).

Tuan, Y.F. *Cosmos and Hearth: A Cosmopolite's Viewpoint* (Minneapolis: University of Minnesota Press, 1996).

Valls, A. ed. *Ethics in International Affairs: Theory and Cases* (Lanham, Md.: Rowman & Littlefield, 2000).

Vincent, R.J. *Human Rights and International Relations* (Cambridge: Cambridge University Press, 1986).

—— *Nonintervention and International Order* (Princeton: Princeton University Press, 1974).

Waldron, J. 'What is Cosmopolitan?' *The Journal of Political Philosophy*, 8, 2 (2000) 227–243.

—— 'Minority Cultures and the Cosmopolitan Alternative,' *University of Michigan Journal of Law Reform*, 25, 3/4 (1992) 751–793.

Walker, K. 'An Exploration of Article 2(7) of the United Nations Charter as an Embodiment of the Public/Private Distinction in International Law,' *International Law and Politics*, 26 (1994) 173–199.

Wallerstein, I. 'Neither Patriotism, Nor Cosmopolitanism,' *The Boston Review*, 19, 5 (1994) 15.

Waltz, K.N. *Theory of International Politics* (Toronto, Ontario: McGraw-Hill, 1979).

—— *Man, the State and War: A Theoretical Analysis* (New York: Columbia University Press, 1959).

Walzer, M. *Arguing about War* (New Haven: Yale University Press, 2004).

—— 'The Politics of Rescue,' *Dissent* (1995) 35–41.

—— *Thick and Thin: Moral Argument at Home and Abroad* (Notre Dame, Indiana: Notre Dame Press, 1994).

—— 'Spheres of Affection,' *The Boston Review*, 19, 5 (1994) 29.

—— *Just and Unjust Wars: A Moral Argument with Historical Illustrations*, 2nd edn (New York: Basic Books, 1992).

—— 'The Moral Standing of States: A Response to Four Critics,' *Philosophy and Public Affairs*, 9, 3 (1980) 209–229.

Warren, S.D. and L.D. Brandeis. 'The Right to Privacy [1890].' In *Philosophical Dimensions of Privacy: An Anthology*, F.D. Schoeman ed.

Weil, S. *The Need for Roots: Prelude to a Declaration of Duties toward Mankind* (New York: Routledge & Kegan Paul, 1987).

Weintraub, J.A. and K. Kumar eds, *Public and Private in Thought and Practice: Perspectives on a Grand Dichotomy* (Chicago: University of Chicago Press, 1997).

Welch, D.A. 'Morality and "The National Interest".' In *Ethics in International Affairs: Theory and Cases*, A. Valls ed.

—— *Justice and the Genesis of War* (Cambridge: Cambridge University Press, 1993).

Wendt, A. 'Anarchy is what States Make of it: The Social Construction of Power Politics,' *International Organization*, 46, 2 (1992) 391–425.

Wheeler, N.J. *Saving Strangers: Humanitarian Intervention in International Society* (Oxford: Oxford University Press, 2000).

Wight, M. *International Theory: The Three Traditions*, G. Wight and B. Porter eds (London: Leicester University Press, 1996).

—— 'An Anatomy of International Thought,' *Review of International Studies*, 13 (1987) 221–227.

—— 'Why is there no International Theory?' In *Diplomatic Investigations: Essays in the Theory of International Politics*, H. Butterfield and M. Wight eds.

Williams, B. *Shame and Necessity* (Berkeley, California: University of California Press, 1993).

Wolin, S. *Politics and Vision: Continuity and Innovation in Western Political Thought* (Toronto: Little, Brown and Company, 1960).

Wollstonecraft, M. *A Vindication of the Rights of Women [1792]* (New York: Norton, 1967).

Woolf, V. *Three Guineas*, in *A Room of One's Own [1929] and Three Guineas [1938]* (Toronto: Penguin, 2000).

World Bank. *World Development Report 2000/1* (Oxford: Oxford University Press, 2000).

Wright, M. 'Central but Ambiguous: States and International Theory,' *Review of International Studies*, 10 (1984) 233–237.

Zhong, W. 'China's Human Rights Development in the 1990s,' *The Journal of Contemporary China*, 8 (1995) 79–97.

Index

Abbott, K.W., 190n38
Abrams, J.S., 168n6
accountability, 140–6
  global civil society, 141–3, 145–6
  individual, 13–14
  international society, 3, 13, 136
  state, 13, 152
Afghanistan, 2, 142, 150
Akehurst, M., 179n56–7
Allan, G., 167n10, 176n8, 179n44
Allen, A.L., 31, 33, 58, 118, 169n14,
  171n57, 176n7, 189n24, 190n32
Amnesty International (AI), 125,
  131, 163
anarchy, international, 52–3, 89
Anderson, A., 91, 108, 184n35,
  187n100
Anderson, B., 178n28
Arar, M., 125
Arendt, H., 25, 47–8, 171

Baldry, H.C., 87, 95, 109
Barnett, M., 193n23, 196n55
Barrington, L., 177n25
Beardsley, B., 180n60, 195n49
Beiner, R., 92, 178n31, 184nn31, 43
Beitz, C.R.
  on human rights, 113, 126–32
  skeptical and heuristic realism,
    55, 176n85
  social and cosmopolitan liberalism,
    126–32
Benn, S.I., 16, 22, 26, 30, 168n4,
  169n17–18, 170nn30, 33,
  171nn42–3, 55, 173n27, 177n18
Bentham, J., 22, 120, 170n32, 190n34
Berlin, I., 185n48
Best, G., 54, 175n80
Biersteker, T.J., 189n31
Blake, M., 192n4
Bobbio, N., 29, 171n50
Bodin, J., 60, 61

Boehm, M., 91, 92, 106, 184nn32,
  39, 188n101
Boling, P., 169n14, 189n26
Bolt, R., 174n53
Bosnian war, 54
Bossuet, J.B., 1, 167n1
Brandeis, L.D., 58, 176n6
Brierly, J.L., 180n58
Brown, C., 187n96
Brunnée, J., 147, 194n31
Bryant, J., 184n38
Buchanan, A., 190n32
Bull, H., 183n17
Bush, G.W., 2, 37, 135, 143, 149,
  167n4–5, 172n10, 186n72, 192n2
Byers, M., 149–50, 194n37–8, 195n40

Calhoun, C., 69, 179n52
Campaign for Innocent Victims in
  Conflict (CIVIC), 142, 192n12
Camus, A., 53, 95
Canada
  and Quebec secession, 67, 79
Caney, S., 178nn33, 35
Carr, E.H., 23, 52, 88, 89, 93, 170n35,
  175n72–3, 183nn12, 21,
  184n44–5
Carter, A., 182n3
Cassirer, E., 183n19
Chan, W.T., 183n7
Charlesworth, H., 14, 60, 169n9,
  177n11
Chesterman, S., 149–50, 194n37–8,
  195n90
China, People's Republic of
  and Taiwan, 14
Clinton, W., 37, 195
Cohen, J.L., 119, 169n20, 178n29,
  190n32
communitarianism
  and collective self-determination,
    65, 66, 74

208